YOU WILL MAKE MONEY IN YOUR SLEEP

The Story of
DANA GIACCHETTO,
Financial Adviser to the Stars

Emily White

SCRIBNER

New York   London   Toronto   Sydney

SCRIBNER
1230 Avenue of the Americas
New York, NY 10020

SCRIBNER and design are trademarks of
Macmillan Library Reference USA, Inc., used under license
by Simon & Schuster, the publisher of this work.

For information about special discounts for bulk purchases,
please contact Simon & Schuster Special Sales:
1-800-456-6798 or business@simonandschuster.com

Certain names and identifying characterstics of people
referenced in this book have been changed.

Designed by Kyoko Watanabe
Text set in Sabon

Manufactured in the United States of America

1   3   5   7   9   10   8   6   4   2

Library of Congress Control Number: 2006037885

ISBN-13: 978-0-7432-5996-5
ISBN-10: 0-7432-5996-3

The author gratefully acknowledges permission to use lines from Lisa Robertson's
"The Men" from *The Men: A Lyric Book,* reprinted with permission.

Inside the men are people. They have a small dreamy heart. Sometimes I am immobilized by sadness as the night enters their window.

Both things perceive: the men and inside them the people. Nothing originates that does not come through their window.

—LISA ROBERTSON, *The Men*

**YOU WILL
MAKE MONEY
IN YOUR SLEEP**

INTRODUCTION

IN THE SPRING AND SUMMER OF THE YEAR 2000, DANA Giacchetto became infamous as the Scammer to the Stars. According to the *Post,* he was the "baby-faced broker" who'd fleeced the most bankable celebrities of the day. Anybody reading *Vanity Fair* or watching the E channel would eventually encounter his name; the story of his disgrace was being consumed, it was something the gossips were chewing on. At the height of his infamy he was arrested at Newark airport with a pile of cash and an expired passport—he'd been out on bail, and it looked like he was trying to flee the country. He was escorted to jail, and the paparazzi waited along the red carpet of the perp walk. Did he really think he could get away? the entertainment reporters asked. "GROUNDED" read the *Newsday* cover headline. In the photograph he looked sad and undone, his striped tie clashing with his wrinkled plaid shirt.

For Hollywood-watchers he became the evil character in a good and evil story, a reprehensible con man—slick, shining, someone no one should've believed, a snake in the garden of Hollywood. In the wake of the scandal, Hollywood shut him out and pretended to forget about him. He had been so close to Leo DiCaprio they once told reporters, We are like brothers. Michael Ovitz called him his life adviser. But after the scandal, the celebrities acted like he'd never existed. He pled guilty to fraud and was sent to federal prison for fifty-seven months. He was banned from working in the financial sector for life and fined more than $14 million in civil and criminal penalties.

For the eight years prior to his fall Dana had been a close friend to me and my husband. If he was a con man, I was one of his most ardent believers. I was enthralled with him. "You must meet him, he is inspired," I told a successful friend. "Oh, if you have any money you should invest it with him." Now this friend says to me, "Emily, I'm glad I didn't listen to you."

I knew Dana before the time of the celebrities and I watched as the celebrities transformed his life. I knew him before the nineties boom really took hold, a boom he would ride almost all the way to its implosion. He was my husband's investment adviser; after an unexpected windfall, Rich gave him $100,000 to put into a "safe bond." Rich was one in a herd of investors who left as the nineties ended and Dana seemed to be flaming out. Rich ended up losing $80,000 of the investment, but that was later, after the scandal had faded into the background and Dana had become just another felon.

Because of my entanglement with Dana, this is not an objective book about his life; and although he initially cooperated with it, it could hardly be called an authorized biography. He agreed to a rule of "no editorial control"—that the story I wrote would be the one I remembered and uncovered. Yet as the story unfolded for me, he became furious that he couldn't control it. We parted ways before I finished the manuscript.

INTRODUCTION

Throughout the process of writing about him I have grappled with my memory of him in the nineties, when I thought he was some kind of rescuer.

When I was a kid my dad had a refrain: "These bills are breaking my back." We weren't poor but we were living in a big house, beyond our means. My mother had grown up wealthy—a house with an elevator, ballet and piano lessons, parties where kids rode ponies. My father had grown up poor; his dad died in a single-room occupancy hotel. Sometimes it seemed like my father was trying to make a princess life for my mother, but he couldn't afford it on his salary. He ran his own advertising business, but sometimes the ads didn't come, or the clients didn't pay.

When I met Dana, money was my source of panic. Friends had intervened. I'd been told: *You really shouldn't worry about money so much, it's neurotic, it has something to do with your childhood.* But it was some kind of frightful god to me. I saw scarcity even when there was abundance. Dana was the opposite. He saw abundance even when he was staring at nothing, at a column of zeros.

Dana's optimism drowned out the voice of worry that was my native tongue, the voice that said, You are going to go broke, you are not going to make it. Dana explained to me that I was definitely, definitely going to make it and everything would sooner or later be going up. Often I couldn't understand what he was saying when he talked about the market, but I chalked this up to my own ignorance. There was something about the way he described the endlessness of money, the fervent quality of his speech, the leaning forward, the flushed face. I was ripe for some kind of conversion.

Many of his predictions came true: He predicted the market

would soar to 10,000 by the year 2000. He knew Leo DiCaprio was going to become an industry. Many of his investments made money, in part because there was no downward spiral; there hadn't been any bad signs for a long time. The nineties boom had gone on for so long, investors started to wonder if the old rules didn't apply anymore. This whole thing of crash and depression, it was all part of the past and there would never be a depression again.

Twice in our history Dana has approached me and asked me to write about him: once when he was sent to jail and needed letters of reference addressed to the sentencing judge, and once after he'd been in jail for a couple of years. When he made the proposal he said, "Maybe you should write a book about me." In the character reference letter I wrote that Dana was "a unique and generous person," someone who could bring a smile to the "most hardened, impenetrable faces." I asked the judge to have mercy on him.

What follows is another story of his character. In this story, he is not as pure as he was in my letter to the judge. He is not a misunderstood, innocent boy. This book was written after I interviewed family, friends, allies, victims, lawyers, and specialists, after I combed through court documents, excavated all my memories of him, and held them up to the light. Much of it was written during a period of suffocating financial anxiety brought on by Dana's actions and promises, by the vanishing of my husband's money, money Dana had promised was there.

The character in these pages was not someone Dana wanted to see. The last time we spoke he said, "I don't like the direction this is going."

Dana is a classic American dreamer who doesn't waste time thinking about the past. He is cut off from history, and in this cutting-off, he stays alive and protects himself. More and more he only wants to talk about what is next. For a while, parole officers called to check on him, and he had to submit to humiliating random drug tests—tests that tied him to his old disasters. But he believes the old disasters can fade and soon he will be redeemed. He believes the day is just around the corner when he will live among the celebrities once again.

PART
ONE

On June 21, 1999, the Hollywood Athletic Club hosted a ball in Dana's honor. Rumor had it everyone was coming. Madonna in the wake of *Ray of Light*—a record on which her real voice was almost undetectable. Leo DiCaprio, riding on his *Titanic* fame. It was the kind of night gossip magazines wait for. For a member of the paparazzi, a photograph from a night like this could bring in three months' rent.

The Hollywood Athletic Club is located at 6525 Sunset. It resides in a fairly desolate neighborhood, a few blocks from the Avenue of the Stars, near a run-down hotel called the Mark Twain, down the block from the hulking black CNN building. On any given day you will find homeless people making their way down the sidewalk, dragging suitcases or pushing shopping carts. Yet on certain nights the block becomes a swarm of limousines, private security shooing the homeless away as cars pull up. The HAC has an old Hollywood feel, and people like to throw celebrity events there. In the gilded interior, stars are allowed to feel like stars.

The full title of the event was the Sweet Relief Medicine Ball to benefit the Sweet Relief Musicians Fund. Dana had organized the fund with musician Victoria Williams, a soulful, birdlike country singer who'd come down with MS. Hospital bills had nearly bankrupted her—*Sweet Relief* was the name of one of her records. All the proceeds of the night would go to musicians and artists who fell ill. Dana had worked hard getting donations for Sweet Relief, helping them set up their business. People said: *Without him, this never would've happened.*

Although Dana was the hero of the evening, he wasn't someone the waiting fans would've recognized. He was part of the inner circle, an A-lister, but as high up as he was in this rarefied atmosphere, he was essentially a member of an entourage. Part of Leonardo DiCaprio's "team." A name sometimes mentioned in the *Post*'s Page Six, but really only famous to insiders. A middleman, a conduit. Someone who could disappear without a lot of fanfare.

Good deeds were in the air. At these celeb-filled charity functions the mood tended to be both humble and self-congratulatory. Tables cost upward of $2,500. A tax write-off—a way to give away your money and save it at the same time. In Hollywood, charity balls were part of the regime of being a star. Dana attended many of them—for breast cancer and AIDS, for diseases and cures. He once told me a proud story about outbidding Harvey Weinstein at a benefit, although he couldn't remember what the benefit was for.

The Victoria Williams event was clearly a good cause. She was an authentic person, living far from Hollywood in the desert of Joshua Tree. Her music was ethereal and soothing, yet there was a current of panic running underneath the night. Power was already slipping away from Dana, even though he was the guest of honor. People took out full-page ads in the program—a twenty-eight-page, glossy booklet. But according to one source, a number of these people did not pay for their ads. Sweet Relief never saw the tens of thousands the program was supposed to raise.

The program ads were all about Dana's generosity:

Yo, D, Well Done, From the Mitchell K. Blutt and Margo Krody Family Foundation
(Blutt was a powerful banker who'd recently joined Dana in a venture with Chase Manhattan Bank. His wife, Margo Krody, ran a foundation that gave money to scholarships and ballet troupes and hospitals. Their names often appeared in the New York society pages.)

Man of the Millennium: Dana Giacchetto
Paper **magazine Loves You!**
(*Paper* was a glossy nightclub calendar Dana had been affiliated with from the beginning of his rise. They had a hipster credibility. There were always transvestites at their parties.)

Dana, Congratulations From All Your Friends at Creative Artists Agency
(Dana had been riding alongside the powerful men of this agency for many years: Mike Ovitz, Richard Lovett, Jay Moloney. There were scandals: talent-poaching, threats like *I will ruin you. You will never have lunch in this town again.* There was a major suicide in the works. But at the party people didn't want to talk about it.)

A glossy center spread featured a picture of Dana with one of his cockatoos, Angel, an enormous white bird with a sharp black beak and a habit of biting people. The text read:

A bird in the hand, sweet relief for the band
Congrats from all of us at Phish and Dionysian Productions
(Phish had subsumed the wandering fan base of the Grateful Dead after the death of Jerry Garcia. They had invested at least $4 million with Dana at this time.)

On the inside cover, the charitable mission was described:

Sweet Relief provides financial assistance to musicians of all kinds for medical expenses, alternative therapies, treatment for alcohol or chemical dependency, prescriptions, and living expenses if the artist is unable to work.

By the time of the ball, Dana had moved very far into the interior of power. He'd met Bob Dylan and the pope; he'd spent long weekends with Mike Ovitz, a frightful warlord among Hollywood agents, a guy who could poach all your clients away until you were left with a sorry B-list. The editor of *The New Yorker* drank in his living room. Magician David Blaine came to his parties, starlets like Cameron Diaz and Courteney Cox told him *I love you* every time they saw him. His networking had become feverish, like a condition. The condition of knowing this person who knows this person who knows this person.

The ball started early in the evening, when the sun was still hot and there was plenty of light left for viewing celebrity faces. Autograph hunters clustered on the sidewalk across the street from the entrance, waiting for limos to appear. They'd heard about the event through Internet fan sources, through the whispers of the celebrity underground, and they were not disappointed. Down the street came Madonna's car, as she crossed the cusp of middle age. She had donated significant money to Sweet Relief and she had a crowd-pleasing story about the night at Dana's loft when Angel bit her on the nose. Then there was Leo DiCaprio—so famous by now, the air around him had altered or sweetened; his fame was like a trippy artificial atmosphere. *Leo, Leo, Leo,* the girls called, as if he were drowning and they were going to save him.

Dana was someone Leo depended on. They'd met in 1996, and over the past three years they'd become inseparable. Dana handled a large chunk of Leo's millions. He invested it in stocks and private deals, and sent Leo statements, telling him what his money was doing. It was a close friendship—dinners, vacations, helicopter rides. Through Dana, Leo could keep his money in sight. Dana was the embodiment of his money, its messenger. At any point Leo could ask: "How much am I worth again?" Leo had been raised in a struggling middle-class family, so the *Titanic* money was unbelievable. *Unreal.* Dana could report from the other side of this unreality. "You are worth $20 million per film now." Once Dana took him on a tour of the stock exchange, just to show him how this almost primitive system of money worked.

Dana was as tall as Leo, and he liked to say they looked like brothers. "Actually, a lot of people commented on it," he told me. But Dana did not have a screen face. He looked like an ordinary person, unintimidating. The kind of person you might ask for directions if you were lost.

The night of the ball, Leo and Dana were accompanied by their parents. Leo's father, George, was a Southern California hippie in his fifties, passionate about environmental disasters and underground comics. Dana's father, Cosmo, was nearing eighty. He'd been raised working-class Italian, had a thick Boston accent, short and loud, with a drifting eye and thick white hair. He frequently lapsed into Italian. The two fathers barely understood each other.

Dana was as loud and open as his father, but he was a nineties' man—spiffy and gelled, cologne and body scrubs— while his father had the feeling of an old or vanishing world about him. At events like this, Dana sometimes wondered if his father was going to behave, or if he was going to say something outrageous that nobody understood. (He'd been mortified when Cosmo met Ovitz and immediately told a cryptic mob joke: "Italians don't die natural deaths. They are visited by a man in a black hat.")

Dana's mother, Alma, was dressed in a gown Dana had bought for her. "This was the most expensive gown I had ever worn," she says. Alma was a fragile lady who wore coats with fur collars and often checked her hairdo. Next to the loud men, she was the quiet one, the one who kept track of time. At a certain point, Leo hugged both Cosmo and Alma, and congratulated them on their remarkable son. Leo called Dana "the Don," as if they were brothers in a gangster movie.

Cosmo and Alma didn't recognize the celebrities in the room. Yet the famous people had certain tribal markings. They had tan, worked-on faces. Their teeth were impossibly white, as if lit from behind (it was the beginning of the era of laser teeth-polishing). There were models walking through who looked like they needed vitamins—toothpick ankles and transparent skin.

Do you know who that is? Dana asked Cosmo, as a woman walked past. Cosmo had seen her in perfume advertisements but her name escaped him. Helena Christensen, Dana said. *That is Helena Christensen.* The name hung in the air. The name had almost escaped but Dana caught it.

Dana wanted to be a source of happiness for his parents. He

had a younger brother, Russell—a walking disaster, in and out of jail since he was sixteen. That June he'd just been released from a one-and-a-half-year stay in the Concord State Penitentiary. Because of Russell, Dana had seen his parents worry and it was not a pretty sight—they were expressive people and he could see pain in their faces. He could tell exactly when his father was about to cry.

Whenever he told them about his famous clients they seemed truly happy. They would say things like, *I can't believe our son knows such powerful people.* They treasured the program from the evening, the huge advertisement from Leo that read:

To the Last Real Don:
Congratulations, Dana
Leonardo DiCaprio and Birken Studios

("That 'Don' didn't sit well with the Feds," Cosmo remembers. "They did accuse him of money laundering, after all!")

As they settled into dinner, Cosmo stole a glance at Leo's stepmother. "She seemed really unhappy, the boy was ignoring her," he says. By dessert, Cosmo says, "you could cut the tension with a knife." The stepmother stared at her illustrious stepson, but according to Cosmo, the son would not look back. George DiCaprio seemed oblivious to it; he was busy telling Cosmo about a trip they should all take to Africa together, a safari. Cosmo sat there in his new suit, reeling a little, and he said, "'Sure, let's go on a safari. . . .' But really I didn't want to go. I was just lying to him." The truth was, Cosmo didn't like leaving home. He would leave for a ball in his son's honor, or a big anniversary date, but otherwise, he wasn't going anywhere. Certainly he wasn't going to Africa with a bunch of movie stars.

For Cosmo and Alma the night was about their son but in a way their son seemed scattered and far from them. A whirling dervish, impossible to pin down. They wished he would stay still, remember the past, come to Medford, and stay for a while. "Sometimes he seemed so high on everything it was scary," Cosmo said of this time.

During dessert various friends and clients of Dana's took the microphone and offered toasts. They talked about him as the most generous person they'd ever encountered. Cosmo had a toast in his mind he wanted to give. He wanted to talk about where Dana had come from, what he was like as a boy, selling magazines door to door. The powerful people kept parading up to make their toasts—there seemed to be some unspoken order and Cosmo assumed that sooner or later he would be let in on it. But he wasn't. He waited and waited and he was never asked to make his toast. "I was pissed off," he remembers.

Cosmo had his doubts about the crowd. Once he'd warned Dana, "Those people could eat you alive, watch out." He thought they might profess love for his son one minute, and try to bury him the next. Because Cosmo considers himself a person who sees "everything in shades of gray," he tried to reassure himself that this was just this gray voice talking. Surely Dana would be all right. But Cosmo couldn't shake the bad feeling. Nothing could be this perfect—all this money and praise, champagne flowing. He was waiting for the dark to show itself. He didn't have long to wait.

Within a month of the ball in his honor, Dana would be under formal investigation by the Securities and Exchange Commission. A file would be started on him by a young attorney named Alex Vasilescu, a man of burning ambition who was looking for his big collar. By July 1999, Vasilescu was contacting many of Dana's clients, warning them about fraud, describing unauthorized transactions that had happened in their accounts, transactions that added up to a $20 million theft.

The SEC believed they had stumbled on a true criminal; someone who should be taken out of society, rather than be embraced by it or toasted by its power elite.

Later, Dana would use the program of the Sweet Relief Medicine Ball as evidence of his goodness, submitting to a judge who was sentencing him. The judge looked at the program, but the celebrity names failed to trigger his mercy. He handed down the maximum term. He said, "I am troubled by this young man's apparent lack of remorse."

1978: Dana was fifteen years old, a learner's permit in his wallet. One foggy afternoon he asked his father for the keys to the station wagon. He was almost a junior in high school and he hadn't been much trouble so far—he was the son who carried in the neighbor's groceries and helped his mother clear the table. Cosmo told him: I will trust you with these keys but don't let anyone else drive. You hear me? You hear me?

Dana and his friends took the car out into Medford, a suburb of Boston where the Giacchettos had lived since Dana was a boy. Dana's date that afternoon was a judge's daughter. "She was really built," Cosmo remembers. This built girl sat next to Dana, asking for the keys.

Finally Dana relented and let her drive. As she cruised along the border of town, she lost control of the car. They flew off the road and crashed through a guardrail. In the passenger's seat, Dana ducked as the rail shattered the windshield, just missing the top of his head. The car had to be towed out of the ravine, and a police officer came to take reports. The kids kept the fact of the driving girl a secret from the police. It looked like a terrible accident but it wasn't. Everyone rose up and walked away. The policemen said what they often said: *Consider yourself lucky. Take this as a warning.*

"Goddammit, you could've had your head chopped off!" Cosmo roared when Dana returned home. Yet the boy came away with nothing more than a dashboard bruise on his forehead. The girl was as intact as she'd ever been. Cosmo met with the girl's father, the judge. They agreed that they didn't want anyone to get in trouble—the car insurance, the girl driving, etc. They agreed to keep it outside the law and the bureaucracy, to keep the whole unfortunate event among themselves.

Stories like Dana's Car Accident were repeated and repeated in the Giacchetto family; history lessons the kids might be tested on later. The stories were usually started by Cosmo but at any point they could be completed or embellished by Alma. Often she would chime in with her version of events: It wasn't Easter, it was Christmas. It was not my sister, it was my cousin. The girl was not built, she was petite.

The primary stage for the telling of these stories was the dinner table. At the Giacchetto house, dinner was religion. They began in the living room with appetizers—spiced cod, a drink or two or two and a half. Shrimp cocktail, antipasti, pungent cheeses. Then they moved into the dining room: homemade pizza, pasta with crab, meatballs and spaghetti, more wine.

Cosmo is the king of his dinner table, the sun at the center of the orbiting family. He has lessons, lectures, nostalgic stories, bitter questions, things to get off his chest. "His mouth works faster than his mind," says Russell. He is full of digressions. A story that begins in the present can suddenly flash back thirty years. Cosmo has a photographic memory; he can describe in detail events that happened decades ago. If the eyes of his audience glaze over, he will try to speed it up, saying "to make a long story short."

One afternoon as I sat with them, Alma interrupted this refrain: "To make a long story short, don't tell it!"

He laughed and smiled at her, then finished a story about a childhood fight in which he almost lost an eye. He rendered in gory detail the act of pushing his own eye back into its socket. Soon after, he launched into a lecture on the reasons that lettuce should never come first in a meal: "It is virtually indigestible, so should never be eaten on an empty stomach!!"

Growing up with Cosmo, Dana and Russell learned to look like they were listening. Sometimes they tried to get a word in but often the word met the air and no one responded to it. Sometimes they protested: Cosmo, we have heard this story. But they couldn't compete with the motor of Cosmo's voice.

Everybody knew Cosmo exaggerated, that his stories changed depending on the drinks and the number of people in the room. Yet there was this violent beauty in the telling:

"I grew up in a cold-water flat, no running water!" he told me. "My grandmother was always mumbling prayers to us in Italian . . . 'May God reign eternally.' I took it slowly in my mind. I remember a cold spell. She had a woodstove, put on some kindling, got a fire going, boiled water so she could pour it on the frozen faucet. The bathroom was a common bathroom with another apartment in the hallway. The crapper was frozen! I remember my grandmother coming in one time, mumbling something, she's got a rat by the tail! He came up in the bathroom on the pipeline, there were big holes in there. And she is chopping him and killing him with her hands. Eee, eee, eee, and she flips the carcass out the window."

Then there was the story about a fight with black kids from a neighboring town:

Sparky, my best friend, stumbles, falls down, the guy is over him with a knife. I take a rock and hit the guy flush on the jaw, I think I broke his jaw. He was a big big black guy maybe 200 pounds, like a football player, I was 150 pounds. I put him down then I feel something hot on my arm, and I am moving around punching and I am picking Sparky up. He is almost unconscious. But we go running like crazy. We run all the way home and I take him to his house around the corner. I go upstairs and my father sees me, aghast, what is this? Blood running down my hands. Somewhere I had been cut and didn't even know it. He filled a tub with hot water and put some alcohol in it or something, and he put my arms in the water and used compression to stop the bleeding. The knife almost got all the way through my arm. But I healed. No antibiotics or nothing. Here, look at the scar.

The scar is a thin blue line across his forearm. At the time I hear the story, the scar is about sixty-three years old.

Blood is everywhere in Cosmo's stories. He remembers looking out the window of his grandmother's apartment: "I saw a guy disemboweled out on the street, his guts had been cut out with a banana knife." He remembers a crazy girl he slept with: "She had an Olds and she tried to run me down with it. I jumped in the bushes and got all scratched. I ran to get a cab and I was bleeding. The cabbie was afraid." He says this girl came to his house and tried to hit him in the head with a frying pan. "I threw a defensive punch I heard a click and I thought I broke her neck. Her tongue popped out of her head and she fell down."

The girl did not die but the story kept proliferating; the image of her with her tongue popped out of her head, the moment when Cosmo does not know if he is a murderer or not. The story gained velocity over the years. Cosmo says: My life was like something out of Mario Puzo! Like *The Godfather*, Cosmo saw his life as an Italian immigrant epic of violence and sex. He had encountered racist neighbors who thought Italians were natural criminals. Cosmo makes clear to me: We were not mafia!

Nevertheless the mafia keeps coming up in his life; he tells me he knows people who know the actual Corleones *The Godfather* was based on. When Leo started calling Dana "Don," treating him like a Puzo character, Cosmo was not surprised. He thought of his life as an endless novel. "If you wanted to write my story," he tells me, "it would take about 20,000 pages."

Cosmo Giacchetto was born in 1928 in Boston, and spent most of his life in East Cambridge. His parents were from Sicily, landing in East Boston Harbor as part of a wave of Italian immigrants who were crowded out of Ellis Island. The block that ran through the center of Cosmo's life was called Warren Street, a narrow cobblestone avenue, one of the oldest streets in the city. Irish and Italian men nursed drinks at bars across the street from each other. Warren Pals was a windowless men's club most Italians belonged to. The rule was you didn't tell your wives what was discussed in there.

Warren Street was a haven for bookies, for small-time gamblers making one-cent bets, for people who couldn't afford to go to the races but nevertheless believed in certain horses. Bets that could turn a quarter into five dollars, maximum. According to Frank Frameuni, a childhood friend of Cosmo's—"There was a betting pool called the 'nigger pool' because even the poor blacks could afford it."

Cosmo's family owned and ran the Warren Baking Company, and they lived in an apartment above the shop—a family of seven children. Cosmo was the sixth child, a little sister after him. The family was overcrowded, not enough beds for everyone. Because Cosmo was a boy, they believed he would be strong enough to live with his grandmother down the street.

"I was shipped off!" he says. "My sister wasn't, because she was cute." So he lived with his grandmother, the one who prayed in Italian and killed rats with her bare hands.

From the time he was twelve Cosmo worked for his father at the bakery. "My father thought the bakery was high art," Cosmo says. "He was very proud of it." Weekdays at 4 A.M., Cosmo walked down the street from his grandmother's flat and reported for work. Together he and his father prepared the ovens, baked the bread so it would be ready when people emerged from their houses and apartments and headed to work. Over the years the business grew, incorporating new recipes, bread trucks, and pastries. Employees were hired who were outsiders to the family.

As an adolescent Cosmo felt proud: He was part of a successful family business. His father had done something important on Warren Street, and nobody could deny it. His father had fed the entire block at one time or another. Yet the success didn't seem to make his father happy, and Cosmo started to wonder if the man was too nervous.

"He was real uptight. He didn't even eat meat. He was real strict with himself. He liked to eat mushrooms, only, said they were the same as meat. We went on a walk and the mushrooms he picked were enormous, like umbrellas. He said to me, 'Cosmo, you eat a cow every month.'"

Cosmo's father expected his son to go into the family business, but Cosmo started to dream of uprooting himself, of being the first Giacchetto to fully escape the family. When he enrolled in college at Boston University, he didn't tell his father. He feared angering him, and he didn't want the old man to feel abandoned. He worked at the bakery in the mornings and attended college in the afternoons. At the bakery he seemed so tired, his father started to wonder. "He was furious when he found out I was in college but then he was proud," says Cosmo. His father bought him a suit from the finest tailor in Boston. Cosmo guarded the suit like a treasure and kept it covered in plastic.

Cosmo finished college and entered law school at Boston University, majoring in criminal law. He dropped out a little less than halfway through. Law school was a race he didn't want to run to its finish, but he was glad he'd enrolled because he learned the way the laws worked, the holes that existed in them. After law school, he felt like a walking encyclopedia. His family called him "the professor," or "esquire," marveling at all the information he had at his fingertips. All the words he used! "Anathema." "Prophylaxis."

In 1959, at the age of thirty-one, he was hired by a soap company as a "sales associate." His assignment was to travel to New York to offer settlements to Puerto Rican families who were threatening a class action lawsuit after they had been poisoned by free samples of laundry detergent. The directions to the detergent were in English but the plaintiffs spoke only Spanish—they used it like hand soap and burned their palms.

During the day he wrote out $50 checks to the (mostly) women with burning palms. He found it depressing, but at night the city was a source of enchantment. He stayed at the St. George Hotel, a few blocks from the East River. He remembered:

> We had two bedrooms and there was a living room . . . double twin beds . . . a fold-out. . . . There was a beautiful swimming pool at that hotel. One of the largest indoor pools in New York City, fed by salt water just like the ocean! The ceiling was all gold glass and they had sun lamps all around. We were making out like bandits. We met a bunch of Jewish girls. They came to see us. You see, at the Saint George the BMT line had a stop that came right up into the lobby. So the girls got off the train and came right up into the lobby. Our rooms were upstairs and all night you could hear music and tinkling plates until two or three in the morning.

But the whole thing ended when his mother called and told him she needed him. The job became a dinner table story, the moral was "I could've been a different man." Cosmo worked for Warren Baking Company for the next twenty-five years. He said when he thought about New York, "Sometimes I wondered if it was a mistake to come back." By the time he was a teenager Dana knew the soap company story like the back of his hand; he knew the story of the St. George Hotel and the freedom it represented.

Medford was one town away from the birthplace of Horatio Alger. In the mid-1800s, Alger published a series of books for boys with titles like *Strive and Succeed* and *Struggling Upward*. In these books, humble, poor boys worked hard and, through perseverance and pluck, rose into the upper classes. Dana knew you needed to pull yourself up by the bootstraps, climb the ladder of success, etc. These American imperatives were always in the air.

Alma was born in 1927 in Medford, the third in a family of six children. Her grandparents had immigrated from Sicily as part of the same wave of immigrants as Cosmo's family, but her mother was born in America, so she thought of herself as second generation. Her father worked in a bicycle repair shop, and her mother worked in a chocolate factory. In December, they sold Christmas trees out of a downtown parking lot.

At age three Alma was diagnosed with polio. "My sister noticed I had one leg thinner than the other. So my mother took me to the hospital. The doctor asked: 'Was she ever sick with a fever?' but my mother said, 'It was only one night!' After that I went to the hospital all the time." The kids on the playground jeered: "One leg skinny, one leg fat!" Alma remembers being seven years old and sitting in the doctor's office. A little girl sat across from her, braces on her legs, stiff and sick. This girl's body was an obsolete machine. "See my daughter?" said the girl's mother. "Don't let that happen to you!" She turned to Alma's mother and said, "She was like your daughter before the operation. Now look at how she ended up!"

No operation was performed. They told Alma's mother that her daughter would always be cursed with an atrophied limb. The doctor predicted a girl's life of braces and crutches. Yet both Alma and her mother rejected the advice of the doctors and the polio information pamphlets. She never stopped skating or riding her bike as they told her to; she continued to act like a girl who had nothing atrophied about her. In 1945, at the age of eighteen, she won a jitterbug contest. "I came home and woke up my mother at one A.M. to tell her. She was so excited."

Her leg was always weak and small, but she found ways to hide it. She felt stronger because of the ordeal, like she had conquered something. She'd won this contest her body had brought to her. Later she would become a gambler, a frequent visitor to Vegas, an expert at poker. Gambling required a similar kind of faith in the future: *I am a lucky person. I have been dealt a hand of cards and people think I cannot win with it but I can.*

The Medford Alma grew up in was not so different from Dana's: St. Joseph's Church, narrow cobblestone streets, the confused town square where nobody knew when it was safe to cross the street. The town is situated on the banks of the Mystic River, a ten-minute drive from Boston. It's a middle-class, mostly Italian suburb of well-kept houses and chemically enhanced lawns. The historical society offers pamphlets on now-defunct Medford industries: clipper ships, rum, crackers, and bricks. Paul Revere passed through here, warning everyone that the British were coming. His route has always been a minor tourist attraction.

From the time Alma was fifteen she took the train into Boston to work as a salesgirl at Filene's—a department store with a vast bargain basement. She worked in the housewares department, guiding housewives to the right appliances. She knew she was a natural saleswoman. She quickly picked up the technique of the gentle, hard sell. She was the kind of salesgirl people didn't want to disappoint.

She believed she would always be working, taking care of herself. She didn't envision a future of kids and a breadwinner husband. When she looked into the future all she could see was her mother. "I was very close to her, I never wanted to leave her side," she says. Her father was stiff and quiet and didn't know how to entertain his wife. Alma decided if this woman were ever to have fun, it would have to be in spite of him.

She lived with her mother into adulthood, even after she had left Filene's after working there for ten years, from the ages of fifteen to twenty-five. She went to school and became a medical assistant. She and her mother went to dinner together, or to the Suffolk Downs racetrack, or shopping for dirndl dresses for Alma to wear to the dance halls. Any boy who asked Alma for a date soon learned her mother would probably be coming along.

Alma heard about Cosmo before she met him; she heard about this loud young man whose parents ran a bakery. She first laid eyes on him at Inman's Social Club. It was 1950 and they were both twenty-two. According to Alma, he was wearing horn-rimmed glasses and a natty suit. "Is he Jewish?" she asked her girlfriends. No no, that is Cosmo, they told her. He was one of those Italian East Cambridge boys, coming into Medford looking for girls, trolling around the dance floor with their shoes polished and their radar out.

"I noticed her high lifted breasts," Cosmo says. "I was a sucker for breasts."

On one of their first dates, Cosmo took Alma and her mother to meet Jimmy Durante. He'd come up with a back-stage pass through a friend of a friend. Alma's mother loved Durante—the sound of his voice and the ridiculous lyrics to his songs. He was part of their tribe: His father was a barber in Somerville.

That night Alma and her mother placed their faces up next to Jimmy Durante's and Cosmo took a photograph. Alma kept the photograph in a scrapbook. Over time it became faded, but when she showed it to me I could still make out the joy in the women's faces, the look of *I can't believe we're here*.

Cosmo always called Alma when he was off work from the bakery. She liked the quality and intensity of his attention. They were competitors; and he often talked about how she was the brains of the pair, she was the real professor.

By Labor Day, 1958, they had been dating on and off for almost eight years, dancing at places like the Flamingo Club. They decided to take a trip to the racetrack with Alma's mother, to celebrate the end of the summer. As he waited at her house, standing in the kitchen while the women put the finishing touches on their faces, the phone rang. It was a friend of Cosmo's from Cambridge. "Something happened to your father, you'd better come home," the friend said. "I can't tell you on the phone."

Cosmo remembers: "I went straight back to the house, and I ran upstairs. There were a lot of police around. I looked into my mother's bedroom and I see blood on the floor. The room is starting to spin, I said, '*Where* is my father?' A couple of cops took me to the hospital. The room was literally spinning—it was like a whirlpool. I go to the hospital and I go into the room and say I want to see my father. His head was swaddled; they said, 'We couldn't save him.'"

Cosmo's father had shot himself. According to Cosmo, he'd been in pain for years from glaucoma, crying as he put the drops into his eyes. The suicide became vivid in Cosmo's mind, a slow-motion drama he could describe in detail:

"It was twelve noon—my mother is in the kitchen cooking something. . . . He goes and puts a gun to his head near the window. The bullet passed through his head and into the steam pipe. I'll never forget it. Until the day we moved out and sold the house that mark was there. The police took the bullet out of the wall but the mark was still there!"

Alma helped him through the suicide, and he cleaved to her. They were married two years later.

Cosmo showed me a video from the shower before the wedding. It is a crowded room in an old, dark Italian restaurant. The kind of place where the bread never stops coming. Cosmo points out his mother, a stiff and proud-looking woman with her hair knotted in a tight bun. "She has a plate in her wrist, got caught in the bread machine," Cosmo explains. He pauses the tape and points to her wrist.

After the wedding they honeymooned in Rome. "We got a private chauffeur. A rainy cold spring. Cats all over Rome." Cosmo took nine rolls of Super 8 film during the honeymoon, and when I visit in Medford, he has recently delivered it all to a video production shop to have it restored, given it a musical background: Sinatra and Tony Bennett and the cha-cha. It is this restored version of the honeymoon he showed me. He tells me he wants to find a shot of Alma in front of the fountain of Trevi. He fast-forwards the tape, rewinds it, curses the video machine. "Where is that shot?" he mutters. "You have got to see this, you can really see how beautiful she was that day."

Alma and Cosmo wanted children but it wouldn't be easy. First there were two miscarriages, then finally a full-term pregnancy when Alma was thirty-three. This baby, a boy, came after a difficult labor and he seemed to thrive. Cosmo bought cigars and distributed them around the hospital. Yet something happened on the second day—the boy just died. Cosmo yelled a question into the hospital corridor, "What have you done to my boy?"

Alma conceived Dana at the end of 1961, a year when Cosmo was moonlighting from the bakery selling swimming pools, and Alma was working in a doctor's office giving shots and taking blood. The pregnancy moved forward without trouble, and Cosmo and Alma felt their luck was turning. That winter Cosmo wrote a novel, and he describes the period as a kind of creative high—Alma's belly growing as the pages of his book pile up next to his typewriter. "The book was finished in a hundred days!" he crows.

When he finished, he titled the manuscript *When the Act Accuses Him,* and signed his name Cosmo Gia, cutting off the last two syllables. He made a cover design: a pair of large red lips with a sword running through them. To Cosmo the design symbolized the idea that "People get into trouble when they talk too much."

The novel is the story of Vin Tosi, a corrupt councilman in a fictitious Boston suburb. The opening reads:

> Machiavellian: One who is characterized by political cunning or bad faith.
>
> Such a man is Vin Tosi. Here is Vin Tosi's philosophy as he might state it:
>
> "The American public is like a big whore. It likes to lie back and get it, but good. I'm here to see that they get it right, right up to the hilt."
>
> Herein is related the story of his rise to power, and of those people he loves and hates and betrays.

The book is dominated by sex; characters never go long without some sort of sexual episode happening to them. On page 155, Tosi's wife, Rena, is accosted by a neighbor woman:

> How she wished her husband were home to save her from this disgrace! Could she ever wash it away? This feeling! Though her body responded to the sensuous kissing and other sensory stimuli, her soul was revolted, and her struggle was a futile one as muscles not knowing whether to respond to the call of the mind to fight off this assault or to

accept the ingratiating stimuli and give herself up to it. Rena resigned herself to the idea that the woman at her feet was sick beyond the call of ordinary words. Rena had fallen back against the sink. In a wire mesh box on the sink were the utensils which she had left there to drip-dry. Rena groped and found the large handled knife which she used to cut cheese or bread. Her first impulse was to grab the knife by the handle and plunge it into the back of this woman who was violating her body. She shrugged off this idea. She could not take another's life despite the provocation.

When Cosmo talks about the book, he describes it as a thing that could've gotten him into trouble. He says, "Immediately, people saw similarities between my character and the mayor of Boston." He believes if certain powerful people had read it as a roman à clef, they would've been outraged. At the time, he anticipated an enormous outcry.

When he tried to find a publisher, he was rebuffed. As he saw it, the publishers didn't understand what was in front of them. One of the publishers, it seemed to him, was threatened by his ways with women: "I had a cousin who worked for Mizener and Company so I thought I'd try them. When I went to the offices there was a girl there, she was attractive and I took her to lunch. The guy rejected my book and I think it was because he was an old guy who was a head over asshole in love with this girl! My cousin told me I made a mistake by going out to lunch with her, because she came in raving about me and what a gentleman I was."

Eventually Cosmo printed five thousand copies of the book himself, hiring a local printer and naming the enterprise "Soliloquy Publishing Company." He told me: "The book cost five bucks retail and $1.15 to make. How did I do it? I went out and

I found paper that was a distressed lot! There was a fire on a railroad car and I went and I bought the paper for two hundred bucks. I am not kidding. The paper I got was number one!"

For his author photograph, he sat in front of a Smith-Corona typewriter, staring into the camera, a notebook open on the desk. It was an author photo in the style of *I am a great writer, and you will hear more from me.* Confidence. A particular Hemingway-influenced arrogance. *I can write but I can also box.* In the spring and summer of 1962, Cosmo undertook his own publicity campaign. He made flyers promoting the embattled "best seller" and distributed them around Medford and Boston.

Read it and discover for yourself WHY *When The Act Accuses Him* was not sold by one of the largest department stores in New England (located in Boston) after they received delivery . . . WHY every Greater Boston newspaper failed to print a review or even an announcement of its publication . . . WHY notwithstanding the foregoing WHEN THE ACT ACCUSES HIM by COSMO GIA is still the best-selling clothbound novel around Boston. WHEN THE ACT ACCUSES HIM by Cosmo GIA is the one EXCITING PROVOCATIVE novel you MUST READ!!!

The flyer included a cutout form for ordering the book through the mail. "We sold a few that way," Cosmo says.

Alma believed in the book as fervently as Cosmo did. She told her friends, "It is an Italo-political-romantic novel." She remembers passing out flyers in Harvard Square when she was seven or eight months pregnant with Dana. People stopped for her in her fragile state. They took the time to read Cosmo's urgent message for her sake.

Cosmo would always regret the fact that he'd never written another book, and over time those hundred days of pure writing intensified in his mind, an interval when a different self emerged. The book often came up after a few drinks. If there were guests, it might be pulled out of boxes and into the light. "Here it is," he would say, offering it up. "Take home two copies."

Dana was born on October 15, 1962. He was premature and spent a month in the hospital. When the nurses put him on the light table, Alma could see all the way through his ribs. Although he had asthma, his breath kept coming, unlike the boy before him.

From these frail physical beginnings Dana grew strong, sleepless, a darling. "Everybody loves you," Alma remembers telling him. "It is impossible not to love you." She stayed at home with him while Cosmo worked in the bakery at night, rising at 3 A.M. so he could get to Cambridge in time to start the ovens. Then after the bakery, it was time to sell swimming pools to rich people.

Alma saw how hard Cosmo worked and she started to wonder if she could reawaken her Filene's salesgirl and save the day. She began pursuing a real estate license. She read up about the properties in Medford, how everything was going up in value. She noticed there were no Italian Realtors to sell to all those Italian families.

She was hired by a local real estate agent. Soon he realized Alma could sell anything. She was demure but also impatient. She remembers selling a tire shop that had been on the market for almost a year. "I was famous for selling Mystic Tire," she says. After that, everyone in Medford real estate started taking her seriously.

Through her real estate connections, Alma learned about a piece of land, a 28,600-square-foot lot at 39 Winford Way, on the edge of a lake and a nature preserve. There was not much going on in this neighborhood, but rumor had it there would be soon. Soon people would want to live here; Medford was about to boom as people were priced out of Boston. Cosmo and Alma paid $5,800 for the lot, and took out a $35,000 construction loan.

Cosmo said, "Don't worry! I can build a house with that money." Yet after the foundation had been built and the hole for the pool had been dug (his fellow pool salesmen gave him a cut rate), after the bare walls of the rooms had been erected, the money ran out. They needed to take out a second mortgage. "It was scary," Cosmo says. The house leaning down on you, still just a skeleton, already asking to be paid for.

Yet they were proud of the house when it was finally finished. Alma had the shower in the master bathroom tiled with Cosmo's lips-and-sword design. They were proud of the hallway where you could hang your coat; the kitchen with its large walk-in cupboard that could hold enough food to keep them through the winter, the sliding doors out to the pool, the pool itself, which made them feel rich even if they were just getting by. There were a few complaints: Sometimes planes flew a little too close. Otters killed the geese. Snow could keep you home for a week if it was deep enough. Yet when they looked out the window and saw the trees, the birds circling, the lonesome pine isolated from other trees, they felt a surge of luck. *No one can build in front of this view!* Cosmo would say.

The house was a perfect setting for long parties, and Cosmo and Alma threw them regularly: cocktail parties, poolside extravaganzas, kid birthday blowouts with cartoon themes. Dana was three years old when Cosmo had an afternoon party for the boxer Rocky Marciano—in the fifties he'd won the world heavyweight championship four times in a row. He was the "Brockton Blockbuster," raised in Brockton, Massachusetts, a few towns away from Medford. He told reporters, "In the ring, I never really knew fear."

At that party in 1965 he was retired, and he sat on the Giacchettos' couch talking about where he might invest his money. Cosmo remembered one guy at the party was talking up this land in Texas, where you could grow potatoes and make thousands of dollars.

Cosmo made meatballs, sausages, and a lasagna dinner. "I had four or five gallons of homemade wine," he says, "but they drank everything in the house! I went to a neighbor to borrow a bottle of gin." As the party wore on, Cosmo thought Rocky's wife was losing it: "She was almost frothing at the mouth!" he says. They sat out on the deck, and Alma realized Marciano's wife was afraid of birds. When a bird flew too close, she dug her nails into Alma's hand and broke the skin.

Cosmo says: "They kept wanting more to drink but I didn't want to talk about how really bad off I was. Because I was counting the pennies to buy the booze. We were cooking for hours and they were eating like fiends!"

At some point in the epic evening Rocky Marciano held baby Dana in his lap. Alma remembers that she wanted to take a photograph, but thought it might be gauche to ask. So the moment passed undocumented. Later when he understood how famous Rocky Marciano was, Dana would say: "*I can't believe we don't have a picture of that!*"

In 1966, Alma decided it was time to start her own business. She settled on the name and wrote it down: *Gia Realty.* She designed business cards, Cosmo's lips-and-sword design was her logo. Her intuition that Italians would want to buy from Italians was right. Soon she was making so much money, Cosmo joined her, quitting the bakery and the pool-selling business.

On March 1, 1967, Alma gave birth to another boy. Like Dana, Russell was thin and precarious, confined to the hospital before coming home. Yet he didn't look anything like his brother—he had dark hair and eyes, while Dana was blond and light. Russell's personality was darker, too. He was quiet and sat in the corner, playing by himself, sometimes coming out of the corner to cling to his mother. Dana was out among the adults, a showman, acting like he already had a plan in place, anxious to get outside. Russell's sole intense attachment was to Alma. He always wanted to sit on her lap, and he always wanted to hold her skirts even when she was trying to move around the house.

Because she'd waited so long for her boys to arrive, Alma says she overprotected them. She wanted to be able to find them at all times, to know what they were doing. "I didn't want to leave them with sitters," she says. "I believed they should always be with me."

Alma decorated the house in an ocean theme: nets, shells, plastic lobsters. A glass coffee table with tile fish below the surface. She collected fragile dishes and trashy souvenirs and displayed them alongside one another. She couldn't walk by a bin of plastic toys without picking out something. One late evening, she went to the china cabinet and pulled out an X-rated plastic Santa Claus to show me—his penis came out of his red suit if you shook his hand.

It was the kind of house that is almost too alive. Kids running up and down the stairs. A pinball machine and a Ping-Pong table. Everywhere photographs, lists of things to do written in a scrawling pencil, dishes to be washed, tomatoes to be peeled, garlic to be mashed, a television to turn down or turn up, a record to play one more time, a cat to let in or let out (finally Cosmo built the cat its own ladder so it could come and go through an upstairs window). "What an idyllic childhood," Alma remembers. Their neighbors were the Gortons, heirs to a fish-stick fortune.

As he grew older, Russell revealed a reckless streak. He rode so fast on the rocking horse, they wondered if he would throw himself off. After a while they put the horse away.

On the edge of the pond Cosmo and the boys built a watch-tower. Some afternoons they'd pretend they were soldiers and enemies were advancing across the water. When otters came up out of the pond, Cosmo gave the boys permission to shoot them with BB guns. "Their teeth are like razors," Cosmo says. "They would kill all the geese if they could."

In the Giacchetto home there was always a very good reason for cocktail hour, and there was no law against starting it early. It could start at four instead of five, or at noon on Sundays. A flock of aunts and uncles lived in the vicinity. It was not uncommon to be sitting in the dining room with twelve relatives milling around.

Dana's closest cousin was Donna, Alma's sister's daughter. She was a tiny, dark-haired child, no brothers or sisters. Sometimes her mother drank too much and swerved around in her high heels at the summer barbecues. Another close cousin was Gale, daughter of one of Cosmo's sisters. Dana saw one or the other of these girl cousins every other day for many years. The girls felt an intense attachment to him. They both describe waiting to go over to his house, missing him when he was gone, wondering when he might come through the front door and save them from a boring day.

By the time he was eleven or twelve Dana had taken enough piano lessons so that he could play by heart Elton John's "Don't Let the Sun Go Down on Me," with its vaguely apocalyptic lyrics: *Although I search myself it's always someone else I see/ . . . But losing everything is like the sun going down on me.*

Russell accompanied Dana to his piano lessons, and the teacher tried to show him how the piano worked. But Russell says Dana was always the only one who could play. "I was never any good at it," he says. "I felt like a broad taking piano lessons." He waited for Dana to be finished, and he remembers sitting around, talking to the piano teacher's girlfriend. He remembers her as barely wearing anything.

In 1975, Cosmo bought a building called the Hazlett House, an antique Greek revival building in Cambridge, right near MIT. He paid $16,500 for it, which he considered a steal, even then. He planned to restore the place and rent it out to students. For the renovation he employed Dana and his army of friends. The boys tore down drywall, carried old refrigerators downstairs, pulled nails out of the wall, and demolished kitchen islands. Cosmo paid them a bare minimum wage. Sometimes he bought them beer. "Sweat equity!!" Cosmo reminded them, when they looked like they were about to complain.

Cosmo thinks the year was 1977 when Dana found out about his grandfather's suicide. "He must've been around fourteen. He confronted me about it." Cosmo had tried to keep the story of the suicide from his sons. He considered it a story too dark for them to know. As he saw it, that kind of self-destruction unsettles people. People never see you the same way once they know about it, once they know your father stood in the window and blew his brains out.

People know things like this and they start to see darkness everywhere in your history and your family.

But Dana had heard the rumors, traveling among the cousins. Cosmo says that they both cried as he admitted the truth. When I meet Cosmo, the suicide is one of the first things he tells me about. It is a piece of ancient history that has never receded from the forefront of his mind.

At the time Dana was growing up there, Medford was a mostly dry town. A restless teenager in a dry town quickly learns the signals of the underground. Drug dealers flocked to Medford and it became a teenage drug mecca. "You could get anything," says Dana's friend Jim McSweeney, "coke, mescalin, pot, acid, mushrooms." There were certain corners, certain times. Boys would leave the party and come back with the powder everyone was craving.

On November 14, 1977, *Time* magazine ran a cover story on "High Schools in Trouble." It was an exposé of three American high schools that were supposed to represent the deviant teenagers of the era. One of the high schools chosen for this honor was Medford High, Dana's alma mater. According to *Time*, the sheer volume of drugs flowing through Medford High defied all statistics. The school was presented as an extreme case:

. . . [At Medford High] vandalism is a problem. A favorite prank is to smash the school's two story glass windows, which cost $700 each. Last year's damage bill came to almost $30,000—close to what the school spent on textbooks.

So many students have taken to alcohol and dope that Medford has set up a special office for drug and drink consultation. Discipline problems haunt the school's five miles of corridors. Under an "open campus" scheme that permitted upper classmen to roam throughout the school during certain periods, most respected the privilege. But some smoked joints or whooped it up in the halls.

Dana's cousin Gale Rapallo said that when the article came out, it was as if Medford High had been chosen, it had become an emblem of some kind. Gale saved it for her scrapbook, even though she was part of the very drug culture the magazine was panicking about.

"There were these pits in the back of Medford High School," she says. "Big concrete pits meant for kids to study in. That's where everything happened."

I could not envision what she was talking about so I visited the campus and walked around while the students were in class. This strange, late seventies design was still in place, concrete pits with steps down into them, shelters out of the wind, like craters, only with hip-high walls around the rim so no one falls down into them. The designers of the school, with their money and architectural ambitions, had an idea in mind of using all available space for homework "pods." Yet they had unwittingly made a perfect place for kids to light a joint even when the wind was blowing.

1978: The same year as the car crash. Dana told his family, "You need to get out of Medford for a few days." They needed to get to Orlando and see Disney World. Dana was proposing a trip on the "Auto Train," where your car is loaded onto a container, and once you arrive at Disney World the car belongs to you again. He spread out the brochures on the table: pictures of the inside of the train, the dining car. He gave a presentation, like a salesman. He made a case for the fun that could be had, if only his parents would make this Auto Train investment.

Cosmo and Alma figured a boy who put so much effort into his amusement park dream should be indulged. They said, Yes, absolutely we will pay for it, we will go.

When I visited the Giacchettos in Medford the subject of this trip arose a few times. Russell talked about a shooting range, where he and Cosmo stood alongside each other, blasting targets into oblivion. Cosmo recalled about the excellent prime rib they ate on the train. "And it was all Dana," Cosmo says. "Dana made it all happen."

Weekends Dana often dropped acid with friends. Weeknights he worked bussing tables at Rustler's Steakhouse, a tacky, western-themed place where all the waiters and busboys were required to wear plastic cowboy hats. His friend Jim McSweeney worked there too. "We were living for the stadium shows," he says. They wanted to be liberated from the steak house and achieve a derangement of the senses.

Stadium shows cost as much as $25 a ticket, and fans would often find themselves way back in the bleachers, the singers so far away they were like hallucinations. Dana and Jim saw the Cars, who sang, "Let the Good Times Roll," in robot voices, and the J. Geils Band who sang "Love Stinks," the singer wearing tight, horizontal-striped shirts, his arms the size of toothpicks. Afterward, they went to parties in friends' houses where parents weren't home.

One night, McSweeney remembers, they burned all the furniture in a kid's house. "He was a pathetic sucker," says McSweeney. The furniture burning was the kind of thing that happened to a kid like that.

Teenagers wanted to be over at the Giacchetto house. It was a place where anything could happen, where the grown-ups were always in the mood for an adventure. Cosmo led tours of the garage, showing off his illegal fireworks. It wasn't difficult to drink or smoke pot—there was so much land a kid could go out into the night and light up a pipe looking out over the pond, then come back without anyone asking, "Where were you? Are you all right?" (Occasionally Alma might say, I think I smell something! Wagging her finger.) More often than not there was a $20 bill in the dining room drawer, inside a special purse—allowance money for the boys. Back then, $20 was enough to take two or three friends to the movies. Dana and his friends saw *Jaws* and *Midway* and *Star Wars*.

Russell was not adventurous the way Dana was. At ten, he still sat in his mother's lap, even in front of guests. Alma's girl-friends said: He shouldn't be doing that, that's clingy, it's weird. Alma said: "If that is what he wants to do, that is what he will do. I love him. I gave birth to him. I am not going to push him away."

Russell thinks it happened in 1979, when he was twelve years old. His mother gave him a first-day-of-school gift. It was a sweater, a $100 thing, something she could afford now that Gia Realty was a going concern. This sweater had patches on the sleeves made out of genuine suede. Russell hated it and thought it seemed like something meant for a girl. But as he tells it, she insisted he wear it.

Walking to school, he took the sweater off and threw it into the bushes. Later he told her what he'd done. When she tells me this story, it seems she still can't quite process it. "That beautiful sweater, what did he have against it?" she says.

"The sweater made me think she wanted me to be a girl, she would've been better off with a girl," Russell says.

This was one of the fears propagated in the family: the fear of being a girl. Cosmo sometimes wondered if Dana was a little effeminate, "effete," never showing an interest in sports or even throwing a ball across a lawn, playing those cheesy piano songs written by fags. But Cosmo reassured himself: If the boy was not exactly a man's man, at least he was loud and fired-up, enthusiastic about the most mundane birthday party. He was Johnny-on-the-spot. He was always in motion, yet he was not the kind of boy who would disappear on you.

If Cosmo had any religion besides dinner it was the Fourth of July. On that day the Giacchettos threw a poolside blowout; a party that started at noon and lasted into the following morning. Guests could get drunk and sober up two or three times, diving into the pool to regain their senses. Cosmo started cooking days ahead. The basement filled with cases of vodka and beer. Enough red wine to fill the pool. "A goddamn gorge fest!" Cosmo says.

In a home movie from one of these parties, Cosmo announces the guests as they arrive, and they wave into the camera. Big-haired women in bathing suits and shimmering cover-ups, men with distended tan bellies. Cha-cha music plays and Alma's sister Anita totters around in gold heels and short shorts. There is Dana, whose assignment is to synchronize the Boston Pops broadcast with Cosmo's fireworks. There is Alma, dancing for Cosmo when he directs the camera at her.

More and more, it seemed like there was something to celebrate. Money was coming in from Gia Realty. The Hazlett House was proving to be a good investment. In 1980, Cosmo shared in an inheritance after his mother died, one-seventeenth of 1.5 million. Cosmo started doing commercial appraisals of real estate for a fee. The days of worrying about money, of being bankrupted by the party, those days seemed to be over.

Russell entered Medford High in 1981 and headed right for the pits. Just as Dana had before him, he found a world of kids who wanted to escape the noise of self-consciousness: coke, pot, acid, prescription drugs stolen from medicine cabinets and brought to school in backpacks. Russell skipped classes, went on drug runs, returned to math class so high his name was like an abstraction to him. He had a different relationship to drugs than his brother; drugs were like his great faith, a kind of calling. He was always tempted to go a little deeper. He didn't want to be a few steps away from reality, still in its vicinity, buzzed. He wanted to obliterate himself. He wanted the buzz to overtake everything until there was no sound left but the buzzing itself.

Russell was beautiful: high cheekbones and half-lidded eyes. Girls hovered around him as he crossed into adolescence and his voice descended into his throat. In one movie from the Fourth of July, I watched as a red-headed girl stared at him, waiting for him to look at her as he walked around the pool, which he rarely did. Instead he riled Cosmo, flipping the bird into the camera. "That is just rude," Cosmo can be heard saying. "That is not good behavior at all, not at all!!"

Cosmo wondered if darkness was inherited, part of a kid's DNA. "This kid, he was irrational," Cosmo says. Russell kicked holes in the wall of his room. Driving down the highway, he proposed to Cosmo: "Why don't we cross into the oncoming lane. A big accident could get us insurance money!" Schemes like this made Cosmo wonder if Russell was right in the head. He wondered if there was even a way to reach such a boy, or if the boy was genetically unreachable.

One year Cosmo told the assembled Fourth of July guests: "I am going to show you what an atomic bomb looks like!" He walked down to the edge of the water and lit the fuses on a homemade concoction of fertilizer and dynamite. Cosmo describes a wall of water emerging from the pond, the stunned kids, the acrid bomb smell in the air for hours afterward.

Dana learned from his parents what a real party looked like, how it evolved, how just when the excitement dissipates and people are staring into space, dreaming of going home, the right song or another shipment of food and drink can bring about a second wind.

When I met Dana, parties were his specialty; it seemed counterintuitive for him to throw a bad one, and he threw them all the time. It was only when I met Cosmo that I realized the host gene was something he'd inherited.

Here is Cosmo describing a Fourth of July party in the mideighties, as he shows me the home movie: "There is a man who played guitar like an angel and died too young. There is a girl who was a nympho and asked Russell into the woods."

He is eighty as he tells the story. He tells me about how happy he and Alma felt after the party, energized for weeks. The party was replayed over the rest of the summer until the summer turned the corner and the weather shifted. Then you almost couldn't see the old party anymore.

Russell has some grim theories about Medford: "The kids who grow up here and stay here either end up in jail, dead, or OD'd." He talks about Medford as if it is a geographic and emotional destiny, a curse. He tells me: "I think from the beginning I was the black sheep."

I see how he might feel like the black sheep. Whenever I visit, there are very few photographs of Russell in the Medford house, but many photographs of Dana. Even though Russell talks to Alma on the phone a few times a day, and has dinner at the table at least three times a week, all the pictures in the house are of Dana. Yet Dana is gone, Dana is hard to find. So maybe Russell was not the black sheep, in terms of being exiled, not welcome. But he was exiled in the story of the family, as it was told through photographs.

I am talking to Russell in a motel room, the Amerisuites on the edge of Medford—a place of oddly stained carpets and buzzing fluorescent light fixtures. Occasionally he leaves our interview to inhale lines of coke, returning agitated and apparently truthful, as handsome as a movie star, only a little too thin—what his cousin Donna calls a "drug ghost." He is thirty-six and has been in and out of jail for years on petty crimes. For most of his twenties, he was a heroin addict. He is a compromised person, drugged legally and illegally, someone you would never want behind the wheel of anything. (At the time of our interview his license has been revoked and will probably never be reinstated.) He talks in a voice so low and an accent so thick I can barely understand him, and I must constantly ask him to repeat himself.

When I meet Russell it is after I have known Dana for many years. It is after I have embarked on the project of writing about him. In all the years I have known him, Dana has never given any clue about his brother's chronic troubles. When I ask him about Russell he says, "That whole thing is not very interesting, maybe only on a psychological level, but I hope you write about all the A-list people I know."

PART
TWO

1980-1991

IN 1980, DANA GRADUATED FROM HIGH SCHOOL AND enrolled at UMass Boston. Each day he took the train into the city. Walking around Boston, he saw his destiny manifest itself. The voice of fate said: *You are a cosmopolitan person.* Soon he became an expert—studying the landmarks and neighborhoods, the museums and galleries. Medford friends grew accustomed to his soliloquies about the city—how cities are the only place a person should live, the rest of the world is so boring, cities, cities are the reason to exist.

The city offered itself as an escape, and in the closed Italian community of Medford, a kid who escaped was talked about for years. "Medford was a place you never left, even if you wanted to," says Dana's cousin Gale Rapallo. "For the kids in those families Medford was like a ball and chain."

Dana decided to form a band. He'd been talking to his friend Jim McSweeney, who knew how to play guitar. Dana played keyboards and sang and wrote all the song lyrics. It was understood from the beginning that Dana would be the band leader. They decided it would be called Breakfast in Bed. Other possible band names that were proposed and discarded: Jungle Bird, Baby Boy. Jim and Dana started practicing and asking kids they knew to play the drums: in the final arrangement it was a three-some, Dana, Jim, and a drummer whose name Dana can't remember. Their first record was called *Australian Coffee*.

I have not heard any songs from these early records but I heard songs from later ones. My impression of the music was New Wave, i.e., that hollowed out, synthetic sound exemplified by the Cars. Dana sounds nothing like himself; he seems to have an English accent. Lyrics are confrontational and impenetrable: "Brick bat, I will hit you with my brick bat."

Cosmo thought of Dana's bands as "arty." He showed me a film Dana made during the era of Breakfast in Bed. As the film opens, a girl walks mysteriously into a fog. The music is tinny, ominous, Gothic. The girl wears a transparent dress. Sometimes she is right side up, sometimes she is upside down. Cosmo says of her dress: "You can see right through the thing!" Cosmo seems proud of the idea that his son could get a woman to make a spectacle of herself like that in front of the camera, showing almost everything.

Dana was strongly influenced by a band called Liquid Liquid, which sounded like the Cars except even more surreal, even more like robots with electronic souls. His heroes were Echo & the Bunnymen; haunted, death-warmed-over British boys who sang songs with lyrics like "Shiver and say the words/Of every lie you've heard." The music had a sadness to it, a sleepwalker's determination and resignation, and it would eventually find its full expression years later in a film called *Donnie Darko*, where a boy rode his bike through the suburbs, fast asleep.

The Boston punk scene was thriving in the eighties, and

Dana became a denizen of it. The prevalent ideology in the scene was that you didn't need to be an expert, you didn't need to know how to play your instruments. The more abrasive the music, the less polished, the less articulate, the better. It was about articulating things that were beyond speech. It was about being possessed, out of control, anarchic, etc. The stars of the show were Mission of Burma and The Pixies, a band that wrote dreamlike songs combining the dark wall of sound of punk with the wide-open permissiveness of surf music, a wall going up and coming down at the same time. Later Kurt Cobain would say his hit song "Smells Like Teen Spirit" was merely an imitation of a Pixies' song.

Almost everyone was white, and most of the singers were men. One exception and one of the most miraculous bands in Boston at this time was an all-female group called Dangerous Birds, fronted by a feral woman named Thalia Zedek, who sang as if her voice was about to propel her off the stage. Zedek was someone who seemed like she couldn't hold anything back, even if her life depended on it.

Dana was inspired by these musicians and their burning life. He watched the lead male singers and wondered if he could be like them. The guy from The Fall—he just stood there and shouted into the mike. He was from Manchester. He treated the songs not as if they were sacred things, but as if they were a bad taste in his mouth.

Some of the truisms of the scene:

Do It Yourself
Read about the Situationists
Day Jobs Suck
Read *The Society of the Spectacle*
Read *A Confederacy of Dunces*

Dana returned from the Boston shows ready to leave Medford behind for good. "Sure you can stay in a place like Medford where everybody knows you and you are part of the local society," Dana says. "But if you stayed in those places, nobody who mattered knew who the hell you were. I didn't want that. I didn't want to be some suburban person."

He combed his bangs over his eyes, bought vintage shirts, and in band photos he cultivated a defiant, bored expression, an angry seriousness that was never part of his demeanor otherwise. He started reading expensive magazines that only came from overseas. Cosmo declared, "There is something snobby about that kid." Dana started to criticize the furniture. He told Alma the chandelier in the entryway looked like it came from Kmart.

By the middle of his freshman year at UMass, Dana was growing restless. He didn't belong in the dusty hallways. He was not impressed by the rigmarole of turning in a paper so it could be read by one tired teaching assistant in the middle of the night. It felt unimportant, somehow. A charade of power among the powerless.

He needed to make something happen.

Sometime in 1982, he applied for and was given a job at Boston Safe Deposit & Trust, a downtown bank in a shining skyscraper. It was one of the city's oldest banks, with plush offices at the center of the financial district. His first position was as a full-time mail boy. He soon became so absorbed in the bank that he quit school, promising himself that one day he would go back.

Dana says of his days at the bank: "Everyone loved me there and they saw what I was capable of." From the mail room he was quickly promoted to the bond cage. Customers came to the cage to have their bonds clipped after turning them in for interest. The bond was a piece of paper sometimes fraying at the edges, sometimes kept in moldering safe-deposit boxes, often retrieved by relatives after someone died. Dana would slice off the end of the bond like clipping a coupon, and declare the interaction finished. The clipping of the coupon might mean hundreds of thousands of dollars for the person passing it through the cage.

There were a lot of rich people in Boston. Ladies of the small-dog school with flickering, entitled WASP accents. Maybe they were Daughters of the American Revolution. Maybe their ancestors had come in on the *Mayflower*. Boston was full of these *Mayflower* people.

One day an old distinguished lady presented a coupon to Dana; it was worth a million dollars. Before he clipped it, he made a copy on the Xerox machine. He brought the Xerox home to show Cosmo. They marveled over the way this little piece of paper meant a life of leisure for the lady it belonged to. Small as a greeting card, yet it cast a spell on the world and caused the world to set you free.

In Medford, Dana initiated conversations about money with the man next door, Luigi DiPietro (aka Louie). Louie was considered the economic sage of the neighborhood, a guy who never lost on his stock bets. He'd immigrated from Italy as a little boy, and he still had a thick accent. When he held forth about money his voice was low and considered. He spoke slowly and deliberately, with a wry grin on his face. His advice was: Watch your back. The thing you think is new is not new at all. The thing you think is necessary might not be necessary at all.

He told Dana to stay close to home. To remember his mother and father. To read Warren Buffett.

Warren Buffett, the "Oracle of Omaha," was at various times the richest, or second-richest, or third-richest man in

America. His philosophy was one of investing in reliable, well-established companies for the long term, making conservative bets on things people needed, not extraordinary bets on things people might never need. So he bought a textile company: Berkshire Hathaway. He preached the gospel of Coca-Cola—people would buy the stuff even if it cost more than generic cola. He was famous for his plainspoken letters to Berkshire Hathaway shareholders, sprinkled with family anecdotes:

> *You will be pleased to know that Mrs. B continues to make Horatio Alger's heroes look like victims of tired blood. At age 96 she has started a new business selling— what else?—carpet and furniture. And as always, she works seven days a week.*

> *Of a certainty, it was in 1936 that I started buying Cokes at the rate of six for 25 cents from Buffett & Son, the family grocery store, to sell around the neighborhood for 5 cents each. In this excursion into high-margin retailing, I duly observed the extraordinary consumer attractiveness and commercial possibilities of the product.*

At Boston Safe Deposit & Trust, Dana charmed the brokers and the secretaries. More and more they rewarded him by letting him out of the bond cage. He tells me that he was one of the first to use a Bloomberg machine, "the machine that would revolutionize the stock market." Bloomberg machines promised up-to-the-minute financial data, 24/7. They were big, clunky computers: forty-five pounds. As *New Yorker* writer Ken Auletta described it: "The Bloomberg machine is a dedicated computer and color coded keyboard which is leased to companies. It generates real-time, worldwide pricing of bonds, stocks, commodities, currencies, money markets, and mortgages." The Bloomberg machine could deliver the statistics on over 65,000 corporations. Dana called it his oracle. Until the Bloomberg numbers were running, the day was on hold.

Dana couldn't stop thinking about the bank and the tides of money, how he might figure out the patterns of those tides and become rich. He had this affinity for the white-collar life, the life of the boiler room and the exchange, yet he was still part of the punk rock scene, where everyone said Day Jobs Suck. In the rock scene Wall Street morons were almost like enemies. Not very many people in that scene knew what a Bloomberg machine was. And few employees of the bank knew who the Dangerous Birds were. Maybe one or two guys, but only because some weird girlfriend had taken them slumming.

In 1982, Breakfast in Bed put out a record entitled *And Now What?* They pressed it themselves, with some of the Giacchettos' money. Cosmo and Alma put *And Now What?* on display in the living room. The more they listened to the record, and the more they talked to Dana about it, the more they wondered if he might become a star. Cosmo was proud of the boy's undefeated attitude. It reminded him of himself, printing his book. To believe the world was going to listen to you, "That takes balls," he said.

Jim McSweeney remembers, "From early on Dana wanted to be a celebrity. He never believed there was anything he couldn't do."

Breakfast in Bed practiced in the basement of the Medford house where they were surrounded by weather-beaten yard furniture, Alma's plastic swimming pool alligators, and her jitterbug trophies.

The vibrations from the bass guitar rattled dishes in the

upstairs cabinets, but Alma and Cosmo didn't mind. They liked the idea of their house as a hive of industry and productivity. They liked the noise. They believed in it.

One night as the band rehearsed, police knocked on the door. Cosmo saw the patrol car out the window and told the boys: Stop playing, be quiet. He let the bell ring a second time. When he finally came to the door, Cosmo remembers a small woman cop stood there. She said she'd heard complaints about noise.

"I don't hear anything, do you?" he asked.

I guess not, she said.

She stood there and listened. Sorry to bother you, she said.

Cosmo tells the story with relish; the cop drives away, and as soon as she rounds the corner off Winford Way the band starts playing again, louder than before.

Dana was twenty and he wanted out of his parents' house. He had a different stage set in mind for his life. Something more streamlined, more European. Classy. A living room free of dust. Photographs in frames, not spread out all over the table. He wanted his world to look like the world of a metropolitan person.

He pulled together enough money, through salary and credit cards, to rent an apartment in Boston. The apartment was condemned, and Dana made an under-the-table deal with the landlord. "Basically it was a squat, with really low rent," says Jim McSweeney. It was a spacious, windowed loft with faulty wiring.

At Boston Safe Deposit, the young employees clustered in packs in the corporate cafeteria. Here Dana was the ringleader just as he had been at Medford High. He formed a finance club. They held weekly meetings, arguing about which stocks were winners and which were losers, debating the shape of the future. Following Buffett's example, Dana rooted for Coca-Cola, Disney, Kellogg's. Things people know and need. Drug stocks, because people will always be getting sick. Gillette. People will be shaving forever.

Dana met the girl he calls his "first great love" at a club in Boston in 1983. Artemis was wearing yellow earrings and dancing to Echo & the Bunnymen. She had streaked hair and a low, insider's laugh. She was from a wealthy Boston family—her mother was head of a hospital and her father was a judge. She was a Wellesley girl, studying philosophy and film. The kind of girl who probably couldn't run out of money even if she tried. He showed her his apartment, and soon she was visiting all the time. They constantly interrupted each other. They spoke in raised voices. Later Artemis would say: It was definitely not boring.

Dana brought her home to meet his parents. They were aware this girl was class. Rumor had it her family was listed in the Boston registry. Cosmo also learned that her family might be tight with the heirs to the Sweet'N Low fortune. Later Dana would tell people: I fell in love immediately, and she did, too.

In 1984, Boston Safe Deposit & Trust merged with Shearson Lehman, and Dana was promoted to account executive, making almost 70K. He had his own corner cubicle, far from the cage. He could afford a couple of new suits. He had a small, multiplying portfolio, and he says he was making money on the markets even then.

That same year, 1983, Breakfast in Bed released their third record, *Lust Drive,* on a label called Crunch. They booked a few shows around Boston. (Years later, after Dana was released from prison, Breakfast in Bed would reunite for a one-night stand in New York at Joe's Pub.) They were not big shows—early, and in lesser known venues, but still, *We have a show!!*

Russell volunteered to be a roadie for Breakfast in Bed. Alma encouraged Dana to bring him along: Come on, it will make your brother happy to have something to do. She was always worried about Russell. He didn't seem to see where he fit into the future. Time just came over him. He didn't separate the hours into missions to be completed, goals to be met. He followed his appetites. Or his appetites followed him.

For Russell some days would be fine—out in Medford, hanging out with his friends. Other days he'd feel like he was doomed and he needed to get as high as possible. Dana's bandmate remembers him as "a roughneck. Always in trouble."

T.T. the Bear's Place was a downtown Boston club where many punk bands played; Dana called and convinced them they should let Breakfast in Bed play there, that they were the next cult thing. Russell was a roadie for this show and he remembers it as a violent night. A sparsely attended show. Soon he drifted into the other room to play pool. He noticed a kid with too much attitude at the pool table. He remembers the kid as a "stupid little dick." The kid left for the bathroom and he was gone too long, so Russell finished his game for him. When the kid returned, he looked at the empty table.

Fuck you, he said to Russell.

"I smashed him," says Russell. "I could tell he thought he was a hard guy and I was a little sissy. But I smashed him so his tooth fell out and his lip was bleeding. I am not a violent person but he was asking for it."

Dana says he doesn't remember this night, he says sometimes Russell exaggerates.

Russell says, "What I am telling you is definitely true."

Jim McSweeney thought both Russell and Dana were pretty far inside their own worlds. "What Dana believed and what was actually real could be quite far apart at times," he says. "Russell could not accept reality, and Dana had this whole different reality. For instance we'd be out one night at a club. Some guy would be there. This guy might be a famous music scene figure, a royal hipster. The next day Dana would say we'd met him and he was really great. But we hadn't met him, we'd only been in the same club with him."

Breakfast in Bed shows that McSweeney remembered as mediocre Dana would describe as "mind-blowing." Were they at different shows? It was *bad*, McSweeney would say. No no no, it was good! Can't you see?!? Dana proclaimed. Some nights they only made eight dollars. Yet Dana was sure they would soon be on the radio, headliners. His belief inspired the people around him. "He'd see it as true because he thought it should be," says McSweeney. "I wouldn't argue with him. It's hard not to go along for the ride because he's very convincing."

He remembers Dana saying: "I don't follow trends, I invent them."

In 1985, Dana became a senior analyst for Boston Safe Deposit/Shearson Lehman, making $85,000 a year. He combed through annual reports and sales numbers, determining whether a company was a winner or a loser. He was regularly flown to New York to work in the research department on the 106th floor of Two World Trade Center. Often these were one-day drips, returning to Boston Logan around 8 P.M. and getting a car service. Maybe he would go into Boston and see Artemis, or out to Medford to meet his band and practice in the basement, arriving still wearing his suit, taking over the keyboard.

Breakfast in Bed fell apart as Dana's attention scattered with all the travel. There were no shows or practices for many months, and it started to feel like last year's project. When Dana was in Boston or Medford he called the former band members and had meetings during which they revived the rock star dream. *Okay, Breakfast in Bed may be over but what about a band called Patio Act?* Dana would say. The bands were businesses, enterprises. Ads were placed in the *Boston Phoenix* classifieds—*Drummer needed. Cars-influenced.*

Guys answered these ads but often didn't show up for the interview. Or they might show up, but never return for a second interview. Yet certain musicians stayed with Dana, became acolytes.

Russell Shoal (Patio Act, Waterworld):
"Dana and I went on a couple of clandestine tagging campaigns. We made Patio Act stencils and got out of the car on dangerous places like bridges in Boston spraying the name . . . it never flowered into a full-fledged graffiti media campaign. I remember driving by and seeing them a short while later."

Mike Gleidman (joined in 1986, for Waterworld, and showed up for numerous Waterworld reunions):
"Dana was definitely the personality in the band. You know, he just makes you laugh because he is so Dana. You can't take anything personally. We used to call him Mr. Trendy because everything was the hippest *this* and the hippest *that* and he was always flinging back his hair. He wanted to grow his hair completely over his eyes."

Sam Jordan (Waterworld, Big Catholic Guilt):
"He was shooting back and forth between NYC and Boston. He would jet in, do a rehearsal and leave the next day. Running up countless frequent flier miles,

because AMEX particularly in the eighties was handing out these miles. He would have all these miles and he would say OH MY GOD, I AM SO CLICKED."

These were the young men Dana would call and say, It is time for a rehearsal. They might resist, they might drag their feet, but soon they would show up in the Giacchettos' basement, thanking Alma for her hospitality.

The neighborhood around Two World Trade Center was called a canyon because buildings blocked out the sun. During the day, sidewalks flooded with executives in pressed suits, secretaries in running shoes, speedy delivery kids. At night the place emptied out and rats rustled in the garbage cans.

Dana was always long gone by the time Wall Street became a ghost town. He was part of the business class shuttling between Boston and New York; mostly men with *Wall Street Journal*s under their arms and peanuts on their breath. Once the plane almost went down, and he remembered the black water of the harbor coming too close to the window. He never took that airline again.

As if doing homework for the jet-set life, Dana memorized plane schedules. A friend in Boston remembers, "If you were ever going to New York you would not call a travel agency you would just call Dana and he could tell you when the next plane flew out." He knew exactly how long it took to get to the airport, and he was never early. He was the opposite of that nervous traveler petrified by the takeoff and landing. He saw the planes as inventions that made his life possible—the faster, the better.

Artemis stayed with him most nights—she became the girl

he was coming home to, the mythic Penelope weaving and unweaving his departures and arrivals. Sometimes she went with him on his trips, although she didn't have much of an appetite for it. She would come into Boston from Wellesley with a stack of homework assignments. She told Dana or whoever was listening what books they should read. She went to museums and pronounced the shows Brilliant or Lame.

Just as Dana believed in Artemis, Russell believed in Lisa. With Lisa, he says, he had found the girl of his dreams, the girl who eclipsed all others. Lisa was a pretty brunette, a heavy metal fan he'd met at a party in 1985. She worked in downtown Boston for the Boston Tea Party Ship and Museum, telling tourists about the moment when they threw the tea into the harbor and America was born.

"I don't know about those two," Cosmo would say about Russell and Lisa. They were too intense, staring at each other and whispering on the couch. Cosmo felt like shooing them out of the living room. He thought the girl was out of her tree.

Lisa made good enough money off the tourists to buy drugs for them both. They were heroin addicts together and the more the heroin permeated his system, the more Russell felt like she was the girl he'd been waiting for since the beginning. He tattooed her face on his back so it covered the entire right shoulder blade.

He grew pot in the closet of Lisa's apartment, and showed photographs of the plants to his friends. He collected guns. He had dinner at his parents' house most nights, although the tension between father and son was so palpable sometimes dinner was cut short—scooting a chair away from the table, *That's it. I'm done.*

One night after a Fourth of July party, Cosmo was making a speech. Russell can't remember what the speech was about but he remembers deciding it had to stop. The talk had to stop. Cosmo had to calm down. Russell slipped some Valium into his father's beer. "I just crumbled it up," he says. "It turned the head of the beer blue." Forty-five minutes later the house was quiet. All that could be heard was the lull of the television. For the life span of the tranquilizer, the Giacchettos had become an ordinary suburban family.

Alma knew something had happened to Cosmo. "What did you do to your father?" she asked.

"Why do you ask?" Russell replied. "He's acting normal, isn't he?"

"Yeah. He's sitting in the parlor watching TV."

Russell told her the truth—that he had dosed his father and made him artificially normal. Alma acted angry, but Russell knew she would forgive him. She always had and she always would. He was her beloved black sheep. She believed the black sheep needed to be held close and constantly forgiven, because he stood out, because he was the one who did not belong in the flock and if he was not held close he could wander off for good.

Alma still dreamed of Vegas. She didn't allow too much time to go by before she made a reservation in the city of light. She says, "I tried to go there at least once a year"—slots, small bets that became courageous as the night went on. Caribbean poker. A cousin with a condo outside of town, and then a bus or a rental car to take her to the Strip. In the eighties, there were many casinos with penny slots. By 2000, pennies would be obsolete.

Although Cosmo claimed to hate the place, Alma convinced him to join her in Vegas on their twenty-fifth wedding anniversary. It was 1985. They went to see Charo perform and sat in the front row. Cosmo drank so much he marched up onto the stage. Charo put her arms around him and took his shirt off. "Her tits were *out to here*!" Cosmo remembers. "She whispered in my ear that she loved me."

Once when Dana and Russell were kids Alma brought them on one of her Vegas trips—sneaking them into the casino, hiding them in the forest of slot machines so the security guards wouldn't find them. I asked Dana if he remembered that trip but he says he doesn't, and he wonders what I am trying to imply, talking about his mother and Vegas.

Yet like his mother Dana had a gambler's confidence, the market was like a game of blackjack where he was continuously winning, his portfolios rising, an overheated feeling about the world, Reagan making senile promises. He ran up his credit cards, certain that sooner or later the money would come back in his direction. He was not the type to believe in the warning: The house always wins.

In October 1987, Dana was twenty-five years old and the economy had been soaring for many years, at least since 1980. Soaring all the way through his adolescence and adulthood. But there were triggers at work, hidden from view, triggers of doubt. A newly computerized trading system sent stock orders through automatically—basically, the automatic order commanded: If it hits a certain low, sell. In mid-October a violent storm in Britain made it difficult for the brokers to get to work, so trading was thrown off. Maybe the storm was the final unraveling. Recession fears were already entering the zeitgeist. On Black Monday, October 19, the Dow Jones Industrial Average fell 22.6 percent. The fall inspired panic in markets throughout the world. The computers kept selling, until they had to be shut down.

Panic selling: I may lose. I need to get out with what I have.

The casino goer who decides: Cash me out. I'm going back to my room to sleep it off.

Dana saw Black Monday empty out accounts at the bank. He took the crash as a revelation of a great uncertainty—watching all this currency suddenly become as worthless as confetti. After the crash he didn't believe in the bank so much anymore. He didn't think these men knew what they were doing. They were stuffed shirts who couldn't see the future even as it rushed right up to their windows. Dana decided he didn't want to work in skyscrapers anymore. He called them "behemoths."

He says, "I wanted to actually connect with people."

Dana had this idea: an "alternative" to the whole oppressive bank atmosphere. I mean, he would say, why does it all have to feel so intimidating and oppressive? So formal? He envisioned an office where girls could wear jeans. Where the money guys weren't so pasty, as if they hadn't opened a window in years.

In early 1988, Dana reenrolled in school to bone up on business and economics. He took extension courses at Harvard. His favorite classmate was a sarcastic, raven-haired girl named Joyce Linehan. They quickly became close friends. She considered herself a punk, too. Alternative rock. Not this baby boom shit. She was a band manager, and she needed business courses because she wanted to start her own record label. She was a den mother to various punks, an intimidating hostess who threw kitchen parties where people stayed much longer than they had anticipated.

Joyce told Dana about Sub Pop Records in Seattle. She said this label was the next big thing, something new was happening there. She told him if he ever wanted to cold-call them, he should drop her name. The guys there knew her and listened to her.

In the evenings when he was not rehearsing with his band,

he hung out with Joyce, or went to dinner with Artemis. If Artemis's confidence was dragging, he told her she was brilliant, the most fantastic girl, a girl who could rule a place like SoHo. She rolled her eyes, asked the waiter for the check. He talked to her about his strategies for transforming himself into a money man. He knew people were afraid of investing in the market after the crash, and perhaps they needed a different kind of adviser.

He read more Warren Buffett—tales of boyhood days selling *World Book Encyclopedias* door-to-door. The basics! This was Buffett's mantra. It was not so different from the punk DIY aesthetic—this idea of keeping it simple, stripped down. Don't venture into anything too complicated, too prideful, and too ambitious. Don't start to believe you can do anything, fill up a stadium. Try to stick to the same three chords, the same cluster of reliable investments, otherwise you'll be brought down.

The idea of hubris before the crash was as old as the Greeks. Eventually Dana settled on the name the Cassandra Group, after the Greek goddess who uttered true prophecies no one believed. It was a way of implying: You'd better listen to me, the other money men are false prophets. Dana had always liked the sound and subject of the Greeks. Ivy League, important, the beginning of high culture, etc. Also, he liked the idea of a woman crying in the wilderness. It was dramatic, almost sad.

He knew the key to success was *understanding your target market*. He decided Cassandra's target would be artists. "Since I was an artist myself, with my bands," he says, "I thought artists could really connect with me. Because I was like one of them. They could trust me." He wasn't the New Wave singer anymore. He was the president and founder of Cassandra.

He had a business card printed up: The Cassandra Group, Inc. Investment Management for Those in the Arts. In the background was a sketch of a Greek hero in a crown of laurels. The Cassandra logo was a half-lidded eye with rays of light emanating from it. Dana drew the logo on scraps of paper all over the apartment, in charcoal, pencil, erasing and starting over. He planned to imprint it on stationery, key rings, martini shakers.

He was going to rock the boring, puritanical culture of money! He wrote a paragraph about vision:

> A Cassandra is often equated with one who knows the future but is never believed. However, the characteristic that we identify with most was the strength of her independent voice in the absence of support. The Cassandra Group, Inc., carries on in her tradition by maintaining a sound and independent voice in the world of investment management.

He wrote down a series of promises:

> We are dedicated to providing the arts community with the highest quality investment management at the lowest possible rates. . . . We believe in a clear, pragmatic approach that allows clients to fully understand their investments without complicated financial jargon.
> We promise significant return with minimum risk.
> A portfolio may be designed that emphasizes environmentally safe issues or invests in companies that have a history of supporting the arts.

Cassandra's mission statement was printed on fine paper, decorated with the same cartoon Greek busts that had adorned the business card. One bust had a speech balloon coming from its mouth: "Artists come! Lose your leaden brushes. Run wild with tumescent grapes of ecstasy. Beneath the golden laurel tree I priestess call on thee." In a remarkable paragraph, Dana presented The Cassandra Group as a solution to a problem that had plagued civilization since the days of Troy: "In the days of Troy creative financial solutions for artists and galleries were simply considered anathema. Fortunately things change. Now there is a registered investment advisor committed to providing quality investment management at competitive rates."

Artemis helped with the look of the brochures—she told Dana what worked and what didn't. She could be withering: Now *that* is just dumb-looking. But Dana didn't allow doubt into his vocabulary. In this way, he was like the boys in the Horatio Alger stories, where all endings were imagined (or reimagined) as happy, and all beginnings innocent.

I looked over the Cassandra brochures with Dana and I asked him about how he came up with the money to start the company and rent the office. He said: "I had savings. I was savvy in the market then and made money. I had a couple of partners on and off." Whenever I talk to him about amounts, about the origins of his money, he is vague like this. In his version it is like the money was just there, ready to multiply.

Cosmo and Alma tell me a different story. About how they emptied out their savings accounts to help Dana start Cassandra, "Almost $200,000," Cosmo says. "We cashed out these stocks of Alma's that had done really well, these T-bonds that had matured." They said Dana brought them the idea for Cassandra and asked for a loan. He laid the brochures out for them, just as he'd presented the trip on the Auto Train. They decided if anyone knew what he was doing, Dana knew what he was doing.

* * *

Cassandra launched in 1988, Dana was twenty-six. They rented an office at a tony address on Boylston Street, and threw a party with top of the line hors d'oeuvres. The first person he hired was Donna Wong, his former boss from Boston Safe Deposit & Trust, a Harvard girl, Chinese, second generation. He remembers paying her around $50,000 to work as an analyst, putting through orders, taking care of clients once he had reeled them in. She was happy to leave the bank, and she believed in him. She was only a few years older than Dana and wanted to experiment before the bank became her life.

Dana made it clear to everyone he worked with and everyone he cold-called that Boylston Street was only the first of Cassandra's offices. Cassandra was growing, diversifying. Soon, he said, there would be offices in SoHo and Los Angeles. Not only stock investments but merchant banking ventures, private buyouts.

Dana didn't have trouble attracting clients, even over the phone. At gallery openings, he might pass out a dozen business cards by the end of the night. He soon recruited the artist Oliver Herring, German-born, who made sculptures out of mud and wire; an Australian woman journalist who thought Dana was a great story; an aristocratic British collector who spoke in pounds instead of dollars; film and video producers; cult comic book publishers; old families, friends of Artemis's parents. It almost felt like giving your money to a nonprofit. A Good Cause.

He called punk labels that represented bands he admired. He said, *You could be making a lot more money than you are making. You need me to translate the world of money to you.* He called Matador, Sub Pop. Both of these labels eventually signed on as Cassandra clients.

Dana and Artemis had parties in their apartment. They invited art world people who they hoped would become Cassandra clients. Jon Imber, a popular, decorative Boston painter whose canvases sold for $20,000 and up; Hannah Barrett, known for her portraits of distorted old people sitting in chairs, seeming to melt into everything they touched. Hannah helped Dana figure out who the *real* Boston artists were, the ones who might soon be noticed by New York.

Hannah remembers Dana as the ultimate eighties guy. I ask her what she means and she says, "The New Wave, the exposed brick, the sushi!"

The offices on Boylston Street were small, minimal, decorated with a couple of abstract paintings. A wall of windows. Alma says, "I was impressed." She was impressed by Donna Wong, by the Rolodexes, the ringing phones, and the tidy bathroom.

When clients signed up with Cassandra they signed a contract, allowing Cassandra to take 1.5 percent of all earnings. Whenever a trade was made, too, Cassandra was paid a nominal fee. All of these interactions had to be sent through the fax machine or over the phone: The Internet barely existed. The primary bank Dana dealt with was Brown & Co. From early on in his relationships with clients, Dana presented Brown & Co. as the bank that could "take custody of their money." Brown & Co. could be trusted; they'd been around for decades and they weren't going anywhere.

New clients were given a Brown & Co. account number and their money was wired to that bank and its vaults. Each month, they would receive a statement from Brown, showing the investments Dana had made. For some clients, Dana did not need to have investments approved. They trusted him to move their money; to park it in a better spot. Others wanted to know every plot twist in the story of their money.

* * *

Sometime around 1988 or 1989, he can't quite remember when, Russell worked at a flooring and laminate company, showing people samples and explaining the virtues of various plastics. In the back room, he and his boss got stoned. Afterward, he met Lisa and they'd go looking for heroin together. Driving around Medford, Russell kept getting pulled over. Insurance violations, tickets for operating after a revoked license, moving violations that brought up the records of other moving violations. He was building up a wall of debt around himself just trying to get through Medford. He resented the stories of Dana's success, delivered at the dinner table like punishing sermons.

Dana heard about Russell's trouble over the phone, and he tells me he always felt an emptiness around it. He liked to tell his male friends, "We are brothers." It was a phrase that came to him naturally, indiscriminately.

Craig Kanarick met Dana in Boston in 1990 and he remembers him saying, repeatedly, "We are brothers." Craig was a twenty-one-year-old MIT student who needed to find a place to live. He saw an advertisement on a telephone pole: ROOMMATE WANTED. At the loft Dana welcomed him inside and offered a gimlet. Craig said, "I can't believe it, that is my favorite drink." In the background Dana was playing Blue Nile, Craig's favorite band, obscure New Wavers only known by certain people who read ten-dollar music import magazines.

Craig remembers feeling like he knew Dana even though he'd just met him. He remembers the way Dana came close to his face, and kept asking: "Are you all right? Is there anything you need?"

Craig was a punk rocker and a thrift store shopper: scuffed

shoes, trench coats, a little bit of *whatever* always in his eyes. But he found it hard to find any ironic distance from Dana. He fell for him. Like Dana, Craig had dreams of taking over and leaving his mark on the world. He was a math whiz who knew the inner workings and private languages of computers.

It would be two years until the term Internet was officially part of the American lexicon, but Craig was already starting to see the Net the way an explorer sees land on the horizon. Young men like Craig were just beginning to realize they had a secret and esoteric knowledge that was of unimaginable monetary value. The older generation of businessmen did not understand this Web language, this Net. They did not understand how to "make a presence on the Web" or "restore lost data." It was a dramatic generational shift, this new tech language. It was a form of gold.

Craig and Dana were similar types: both hungry for recognition, itching to establish a network. They asked each other: Have you heard of Mission of Burma, Dangerous Birds, Sub Pop? Each band or record label that you'd heard of was a door further in, a further way of cracking the punk rock code.

Soon, Craig became Dana's roommate and constant companion. He remembers Dana and Artemis as immaculate hosts: Their parties were never too crowded or too small, the food was brought out at just the right time, the wine was good, and Dana never stopped making cocktails. Dana and Artemis worked as a team, quietly controlling the pace of the evening, the music.

Dana had more credit cards than anyone Craig had ever met. "A whole pile of credit cards inches thick," he says. With the cards Dana shuffled money, one card to the other, redistributing the maximum balances so the debt was always in motion. The purchases made on the credit cards—restaurants and office supplies, cash advances for rent—all these purchases added up to frequent flier miles. Dana had so many frequent flier miles, he could've flown to Mars.

Craig noticed the way Dana and Artemis always seemed to be on their way somewhere: suitcases by the door. Maybe the frequent flier miles created a need to go somewhere. Hurry, before the miles expire.

At the time he met Dana, Craig was one drone among thousands of MIT students glued to their computers. Herded into enormous lecture halls, anonymous. Dana's spontaneity and attention galvanized him. "Dana would decide we had to go to a movie five minutes before it started. Come on, come on. We would rush out the door. He would decide the morning was right for Bloody Marys, and he would start mixing them. He would decide to read a passage aloud from Aeschylus, everyone be quiet, just listen, this is amazing!"

In 1990, the *Cassandra Art Newsletter* was conceived. Although it was essentially an advertisement for the Cassandra Group, it didn't mention money until the last pages. The rest of the newsletter consisted of interviews with Boston and New York artists. These were earnest, admiring articles burdened by a term paper tone:

> It does not seem that Jeffrey Ringdahl finds these materials alienating, instead they serve to reify a cyclical theme that recurs in much of his work, seed-birth-growth-rust-decay-death-rebirth . . . there is an unleashed physicality that delineates much of his work . . . a blue landscape with a sexually charged chasm.

In the newsletters, it was as if it was vulgar to mention money right up front. This was the philosophy that would ultimately ruin Dana: the idea that money could be talked about later, after the talk of art and philosophy and film—the idea that money was somehow a given, no need to dwell on it when there are more interesting things to dwell on.

Like Warren Buffett, the economic advice in the newsletters aimed for a casual, familiar tone. From a section called "Market Beat":

> Disney: Mickey has lots of news imbedded [sic] between those big black ears.
> Kellogg's: Home of that ultrapremium confectionary dazzler, Pop-Tarts.

Cassandra recommended Hollywood stocks, based on forthcoming films: "At Paramount Communications there are high expectations for *The Addams Family* and *Star Trek VI* films." At Time Warner, "There are record home video sales, and strong box office from *Robin Hood*."

Other recommended stocks: Pepsi. Clearly Canadian. Sara Lee, "which also owns L'Eggs and Isotoner gloves."

Dana conceived a mass-mailing of the Cassandra newsletters to arts organizations and galleries all over Boston and New York: the Nielsen Gallery in Boston, and Mary Boone, Castelli, and Pace in New York. He was determined to get his name out there, in front of the eyes of New York tastemakers. He was like Cassandra. *Here I am. Listen to me.* He was confident that he would make a connection, that his visions and promises would be understood.

Cara and Robert Ginder are married artists—sometimes he paints realistic, empty Art Deco bungalows. Places that look like a starlet could've died there. Sometimes she paints white-wine glasses floating in a field of black—if you look closer, there are shimmering diagrams buried in the background, astrological charts. At the time they met Dana, she was in her thirties and he was in his forties. Robert was thinking: Maybe the world needs to quiet down. Maybe a kid. They had a regular gallery, OK Harris. Dana had sent OK Harris some of his Cassandra materials. "Somehow through the mail or at the gallery we received these Cassandra pamphlets," says Robert. "And we loved the homemade quality of them."

They had been thinking about finding a money guy. They owned a co-op in TriBeCa, but the co-op meetings were driving them mad. Maybe they should sell, go upstate? Their money fantasy was modest; they wanted to afford top of the line art supplies, buy nice shoes for their kid if they had one. Ideally they wanted to have the worry of money banished from their days so all their paintings could be finished.

Cara remembers: "He was such a happy-go-lucky guy on the phone and so nice. We ended up meeting; he came over to our house he was like Oh, I love you guys, I love artists! You know he gushes over everything."

Bob: "At the time people in the arts, hardly anyone knew what a mutual fund was. Dana came around just before people started to think about that, kind of like a translator."

The Ginders gave Dana $50,000 of their savings. Cara Ginder remembers: "He made sure to tell us that the money would go to an established Boston bank, and he would never take custody of it."

Dana became fast friends with the Ginders and he put their paintings up in his office. He said things like, *You guys are exactly the kind of clients I am looking for. People who are also friends. We understand the same taste and the same artistic vision. We are all going to have a great future together.* They felt an exhilaration with him, just as Craig Kanarick had, just as I would when I met him a year later.

By 1990, Russell and Lisa had been raiding her salary from the Boston Tea Party gig for four years, buying heroin in the suburbs and riding back into Boston. "Back then it was like fifteen bucks a bag," Russell says, "I paid $110 for a bundle. But it would last a couple of days. I was doing it a couple of times a week." He had another part-time gig spackling and painting the interior of a nursing home. "You know," he said, "there are a lot of old people in there screwing up the walls. When I wasn't doing a job I would go there and put in hours, talk to the nurses."

Russell describes the onset of true physical addiction; the moment when the narcotic stops becoming something you want and becomes something you need: "My back started to hurt. I was like, 'Why does my back hurt?' And why am I wicked depressed? My friend was like you're chipping!" *Chipping* is the moment when the addict crosses over: You will only feel better with the drug. "Right before you have a habit you get a chip. I got off heroin a million times," Russell says, "but I always went back on. Eventually it is a full-time job. What are you going to do? People would ask, and I would think: Be a dope fiend. I was a dope fiend. My girlfriend was too. Doing twenty or thirty bags a day—two hundred bucks a day."

One afternoon Russell was out of money and he asked his mother for help. He told her, "I am a junkie and if you don't give me money I am going to get really sick." He remembers she said to him, Oh, Russell. "She cried her head off, she is an old Italian mother, what do you expect?" but she gave him the money. He promised to go to rehab. And he did, for a little while. He went to a clinic, he waited at the counter, took his methadone. But he hated the NA meetings, the people who said they were giving up their power to God. "I am a leader not a follower," he proclaims on a regular basis.

In 1991, Dana was making enough money in Boston that the New York move seemed inevitable. He was in control of around $10 million. Art collectors, rich clients who followed him from the Boston bank to Cassandra because they missed his voice. With commissions from trades, plus his 1.5 percent, he could afford to pay himself a living wage, and still there was more than enough, or almost enough. He hired a woman named Regina: she had a Yale degree. Rich remembers her as "super stylish, like Hong Kong–style." Databases were created. Did we call this person? Did we follow up? Did we follow up again? Salaries were $75,000, or $60,000; Dana won't be clear and the records of the company are private.

The Cassandra SoHo office at 579 Broadway opened in early 1991. The rent was around $4,000 a month, and usually Dana worked there alone. But if you could write BOSTON and NEW YORK on your business card, if you could say in your company letters: "We are proud to announce the opening of our New York office"—if you could deliver news of expansion, clients tended to trust you a little more. He opened an 800 line: 825–4ART.

Dana believed SoHo was where the real artists lived. Others would argue that SoHo ended in the late eighties, when money started to pollute it. They would say, there are no real artists in SoHo anymore. Nevertheless he was enthralled with the place, and he often slept on the floor of the new office, awaiting the inevitable day when he could afford a SoHo apartment, too.

Now who is *he,* people asked as he appeared at New York gallery openings, gesturing flamboyantly, his laughter reaching a feverish pitch rarely heard at such functions. He caught the attention of Marc Glimcher, who ran the Pace Gallery, one of the most powerful in New York. It was a place where corporations went to buy Picassos. Where rich Midwesterners went to buy art for their mansions. Schnabel. Longo, Bleckner, Salle. Something dramatic to cover an entire wall.

Glimcher liked Dana and he vowed to tell his friends about him. Dana had a premonition that soon Glimcher would introduce him to major artists and hotel owners, and he was right. He had this idea: "One day, every single person in New York will know who I am."

In June 1992, the *Boston Herald* featured an article about Dana. It was a perfect press release for his business:

Musician/Businessman Links
Arts Community to Stock Market

Dana Giacchetto has watched dancers break out in hives when the talk shifts from pirouettes to portfolios. And he's known painters and sculptors who carry on as if they're allergic to treasury issues and corporate bonds. But as a former artist himself, Giacchetto says he has a remedy.

Five years ago he started Cassandra Group, a Boston-based investment-management firm founded with the belief that people who work in the low-profit or nonprofit arts sector have unique financial requirements and need an investment adviser who speaks their language.

The article announced the offices in Boston, New York, and a "just-opened Los Angeles branch." (This office was actually a middle-aged woman he'd hired to answer phones in her apartment. She was the former manager of the Dangerous Birds.)

Dana told the *Herald*: "People have every right to be skeptical" about his motives and added, "It takes time to build a community's trust." The article described the "excellent results" the Cassandra firm was getting on its investments.

After the article came out, the phone at Winford Way wouldn't stop ringing. Cosmo and Alma and their friends read the *Herald* faithfully. The messages filled up the answering machine tape: "Oh, your boy is a wonder. He looked so handsome in the photograph. He is famous!"

Sometimes Russell found ways to be rescued by his brother's light. One night, he remembers, "I was extremely high, and out of nothing I saw the cop lights behind me." In the glove compartment: a hypodermic needle and a brick of heroin. He had to think fast even though all his reflexes were operating at half speed. As the cop came closer in the side mirror it came to him: he would pretend to be his brother.

"I don't have my license, Officer. My name is Dana Giacchetto and this is my parents' car. They live on Winford Way, Cosmo and Alma."

The cop walked back to his car. Russell waited, something he knew how to do extremely well. He was what his friends called a "cop magnet." As if the cops were irresistibly drawn to him just like the girls were.

The cop came back after looking up Dana's name. There was no bad history attached to it—no warrants, no rap sheet that set off the system of police procedures. He told Russell: I will let you off with a warning, son, you are free to go.

By pretending to be Dana Giacchetto, Russell had escaped himself. He'd become a person who only needed a warning. He had moved out of the periphery of the police-car lights under cover of Dana's impeccable history.

PART
THREE

1992–1996

DANA FIRST ENTERED MY LIFE IN EARLY 1992, WHEN he flew out to Seattle. He was there to visit Sub Pop, where my boyfriend Rich worked. I was twenty-six and living in a dark, ground-floor apartment. A hippie lived directly above me; he claimed he could move televisions with his mind. I was as broke as it was possible to be without calling my parents to ask for money. Rich didn't fret over money the way I did; he'd written a bad check on our first date, $15.75 made out to Thai Heaven. "Don't worry, I'll take care of it at some point," he said.

Sub Pop was a record label started by a Rich's friend Bruce Pavitt in Olympia, Washington, in the early eighties. Rich and Bruce had both come to Olympia for college but soon became full-time participants in that town's thriving punk rock scene. They were believers in what they sometimes called a punk rock revolution. The scene was another manifestation of the scene Dana was part of in Boston: mostly white male singers, a reverence for anarchy, nihilism, negation, a sense that Reagan's

America had been a fascist state—all of it bound up with an old-fashioned American desire for success, a need to be appreciated and recognized, to be number one, to be adored.

Rich was a well-known performer in Olympia. He sang a cappella in suits or hand-painted T-shirts, elliptical poems with lines like, "I am an animal, an animal, a rude and righteous animal." Often he made up the lines at the moment he was singing them. People said, "That is really punk." Fanzines wrote articles about him. A record label called K released a Rich Jensen cassette called *Two Million Years,* and on the inside flap Rich wrote: "I used to think songs were stupid so there are almost no songs on side one. If you have to hear songs, fast-forward the tape and listen to side two first."

Through his tapes and performances, Rich became close friends with Pavitt. They formed a mutual admiration society. Rich liked the way Bruce was always inventing things: Subterranean Pop, shortened to Sub Pop, all black and white. He made stickers and buttons imprinted with the logo. Bruce found a business savvy partner, Jonathan Poneman, and they figured out how to create a record contract. Poneman was dapper and punctual. Pavitt was a charming space case, the "creative one," the kind of guy who was often asked the question *Did you hear what I just said?*

The bands out of Olympia at this time were Beat Happening, the brainchild of Calvin Johnson, who sang in a low, handsome voice lyrics like "Breakfast in cemetery, boy tasting wild cherry." Then there were The Wipers from Portland, fronted by a thin, bald, ageless man named Greg Sage. One of their greatest songs was called "Dimension 7" and Sage droned these lyrics: "Reject reject, not straight not so straight, defect defect." Mudhoney from Seattle had one of their first underground hits with a song called "Touch Me I'm Sick." In 1987, a band started playing Olympia house parties—everyone was talking about them. They were called Nirvana. People who saw them or heard them had a hard time forgetting them.

Sub Pop released Nirvana's first single, "Love Buzz," in 1988, distributing it through their mail order network, the Singles of the Month Club. In 1989, they released their first full-length record, *Bleach*—Kurt declaring, "Give me back my alcohol give me back my alcohol," and "Daddy's little girl ain't a girl no more." Rock critics talked about the remarkable guitar fuzz and drudge. Someone said "grunge" and it seemed like the right name for all of it.

I was taken in by Nirvana and grunge when I met Rich in 1989. I had never been part of a crowd like this, and it felt like something that could change me or something that could last. I think I worshiped Nirvana in a way I'd never worshiped anything. I watched the stage divers as they floated over the crowd, believers at a baptism.

The band and the label were becoming a cult for tens of thousands of white, disaffected kids all over America and Europe. In the Sub Pop mail order offices the names multiplied each week; letters came in on childish stationery or three-ring-binder paper: Add me to your list, let me into your club. By this time they were selling respectable amounts, enough to break even, maybe: 50,000 Mudhoney EPs, a tour of Berlin, in which a loud, roaring man named Tad became a minor superstar. Backpackers made pilgrimages to the cluttered offices. Twenty-year-olds moved to Seattle from New York and Los Angeles, tired of cities everyone knew about, hoping to be part of a new scene.

The city was teeming with young hipsters, the kinds of kids who never woke up before four in the afternoon, layers of fading door stamps on their wrists. Boys wore black jeans, rancid polyester cardigans that never released the smell of sweat, and T-shirts with obscure band names on them. Girls powdered their faces so white they looked like they'd just come aboveground after being buried alive. The style of speech was monotone one-word answers, don't talk too much, don't ask questions like "What do you do?" Just nod at each other, offer cigarettes, drink beer. Remember old television shows and their theme songs.

When I first met him Rich was part of the Sub Pop scene, working as a bus driver, going to shows at night. Sometimes his route took him past the house where I rented a room. If I wasn't working at my office job I would wait out there for his bus to come along. When I boarded we would pretend we didn't know each other, and I would stay on the bus until the end of the line. If the bus was empty, we would talk about the day, and he would sing some of his absurd songs into the bus microphone.

Rich had a mind for numbers. He knew what spreadsheets were, and at thrift stores he liked to buy accounting books. Bruce Pavitt knew this about him—everyone knew Rich was a math geek. In early 1991, Rich heard through the rumor mill that the Sub Pop bookkeeper had been fired. He said, "I am going to go down there and pitch myself." He presented himself to Bruce: a friend who wouldn't always need a paycheck. "Maybe I can help you out of this mess."

Rich found that Sub Pop's accounting was in shambles, they'd defaulted on an American Express bill, their credit was ruined, and they were on the verge of bankruptcy. He found files stuffed with old bills: the ink becoming redder and redder, as red as blood. PAST DUE. Notices from printers and designers, bands asking for royalty statements.

Rich tried to reassure Bruce: "I know I am not a CPA but I can fix it."

At Sub Pop they made jokes about the label achieving "world domination," but the rumor mill flowed with stories of impending bankruptcy. SUB PLOPPED? read the headline in the local free weekly.

Since *Bleach,* Nirvana had been working on a new record that came to be called *Nevermind.* The band felt a loyalty to Sub Pop, but they were tired of late checks and overheated vans. In early 1990, Geffen Records offered to buy Nirvana out of their Sub Pop contract. The offer stipulated that if *Nevermind* became a hit, Sub Pop would earn a quarter for every record sold over 250,000 units.

Nirvana left Sub Pop, attracted by the Geffen health insurance benefits, described in little binders. Tour buses where the seats folded out into beds and the bathrooms smelled like Glade.

By the time Rich came to Sub Pop in 1991, Nirvana was another failure story the men told one another. *If only we could've made them into the Stones, the next Creedence, the next Whatever. Then they wouldn't have left us for Geffen. Geffen is going to ruin them.*

During the period when Bruce was Rich's boss, we spent a great deal of time with him and his wife, Hannah. We smoked pot and turned records up really loud and didn't talk about much of anything. Not only were we broke but everyone we knew was broke. We drove around listening to *Bleach,* looking at the unrenovated buildings going to dust.

I now realize we were living in a bust time, a depression. Nirvana and Microsoft and Amazon would change all this and Seattle would become a city of rich, urban, international people.

Sometimes it is hard to remember Seattle before it became a

city featured in the fake backdrop of national news broadcasts. *We are broadcasting from Seattle, an important place.* A center of power. People who matter live here.

Rich felt he was at Sub Pop working on a life-or-death rescue, bailing out a ship that was about to sink. He worked long hours and tried to get the files in order. He became so committed to Sub Pop he quit the bus, and I soon missed the days when I knew he would be driving past my house in his brown polyester uniform.

The Sub Pop men didn't seem like future millionaires and moguls. Although Jonathan had a certain suave quality, mostly they seemed like what they pretended to be: losers (Sub Pop's bestselling T-shirt had the word *loser* emblazoned across the front). Bruce had never learned to drive, and everyone was grateful for this fact. Drugs were everywhere and always. There were walking casualties, walking dead: for example, a kid named Dylan, an infamous junkie and one of Kurt's best friends. The kind of person about whom people said, *Is he still alive?* A guy capable of brilliant conversations whose band Earth would play one note for ten minutes straight. He had track marks on his arms and pupils with that junkie's "pinned" quality, like a cat who can't see in the bright sunlight.

The scene was characterized by a fierce regionalism. According to the regional code the place was as important as the noise coming from it—the climactic conditions made the noise possible. Rich was a tour guide to this underground: There was the studio, where this song was recorded. There was the former location of the printing press, where a certain brilliant poster was manufactured. Seattle was a desultory, gray place, where it seemed possible to live as an artist. It was the kind of place where you could pay $350 a month for your own room and bathroom in a decent house overlooking the water.

Bruce and Jonathan recognized this: You could sell a place as easily as you could sell a person. The place had all this darkness, and Kurt had all this darkness, and maybe you could package it to the dark people with disposable income. They wanted Sub Pop to be to Seattle what Motown was to Detroit. A music that evoked a geography. Bands posed for PR shots in flannel, holding chainsaws, evoking the Northwest's history of clear-cutting. The idea was to sell Seattle as a timber hick town, the provinces, remote and exotic. This primitivism would later be described as a "successful brand" by music critics.

The bestselling records of 1991 were from Madonna, Milli Vanilli, and New Kids on the Block. Michael Jackson was working on *Dangerous,* and he still looked like a black man.

The principals of Geffen agreed to the rules of the Nirvana contract because they didn't believe that in this bubblegum atmosphere *Nevermind* was going to be a successful record. They believed the Nirvana boys were too depressing, too unfinished. The kind of band parents would tell their children to turn off.

Yet, in Seattle we wondered: Maybe *Nevermind* would be a hit and Sub Pop wouldn't go broke? Rich and Bruce talked about it: If only we could keep the business out of bankruptcy for a little while, maybe?

We'd been listening to *Nevermind* all summer on bootleg tapes. Bruce knew I had "mainstream" tastes, and Rich constantly ribbed me for liking Bruce Springsteen. As a representative of the mainstream, Pavitt asked me, brightly, "What do you think?" I told him I couldn't stop listening to it. He said, "I think it is going to be a hit." We agreed there was something truly necessary in Kurt Cobain's raspy, stepped-on voice.

That September 1991, Rich and I went to the *Nevermind* record release party in Seattle, at a club called the Re-Bar, where drag queens tended bar and made you feel stupid for not being a drag queen. It was Indian summer, and the club was right by the freeway. There was Kurt Cobain, not talking to anybody, smiling as the music pumped out of the speakers. People approached him and said great, great, thank you. The way you greet someone who has come to liberate you.

Afterward, there was another party, an after-party, the crowd winnowed down. You were so close to Kurt you could almost touch him. I touched him on the shoulder walking down the stairs and said, "Thanks." He said, "Uh, thanks." In the living room a girl was crying in a corner; later I saw him trying to cheer her up, bending over her with very thin hands and that chain on his belt and a serious way of speaking—careful, measured: *It is okay really, you will know it is okay tomorrow.*

It took a few months before the voice on *Nevermind* really took hold. But in November it went gold, selling over 500,000 copies. Since Geffen had not expected this need for a new kind of music, they had only printed 250,000 copies. For a while there was a *Nevermind* shortage, the records rationed out to the kids in need. In December, during the Christmas shopping season, Nirvana went platinum, overtaking the number one space on the Billboard charts, which for weeks had belonged to Michael Jackson's *Dangerous.*

Bubblegum pop is over, said the punks. This is a revolution or something.

I was sitting at the Sub Pop reception desk answering phones the day *Nevermind* went number one. Jonathan marched through the room, rushing to answer phone calls from magazines. He was like a politician who'd won an election. It was strange: to have worshiped Kurt all this time, and then have everyone else worshiping him. He didn't belong to this small group of people anymore. You might even hear him in the grocery store.

At Sub Pop the major label representatives started coming around to shows, infiltrating record release parties, loud and nervous, big-game hunters. *There must be more where that came from.*

With the *Nevermind* deal Sub Pop hit the jackpot: quarters raining down. Geffen assured them the money was coming in. They made plans to move to the eleventh floor and take over the space. They could remodel. They could buy a really nice conference room table, handmade, one solid piece of wood.

In some ways they were like poor people who'd won the jackpot: They had no credit history, they were intruders in the realm of money. Their wealth was a fluke, not a product of good investment strategies and hard work and shoring up your savings. While Sub Pop waited for the money to come in, they were close to bankruptcy. Banks still considered them a risk, outsiders, people not to be trusted to pay their bills. Paychecks bounced. Rich would bring home his paycheck and say: "Let me just wait to cash it for a little while."

I said, "What about the electricity bill? They are threatening to turn it off."

On the floor of the reception area a band called the Dwarves spray-painted a message: YOU OWE DWARVES $$. The Dwarves were known for a guitarist whose name was He Who Will Not Be Named. This man played only in dirty white briefs and a hockey mask. Fans often emerged from the mosh pits of Dwarves shows with sprained ankles or bloodied faces. The Dwarves claimed Sub Pop owed them at least $5,000.

Dana called the Sub Pop offices at this time, when they were certain the money was coming in, but they were rapidly going broke. They needed someone to usher them into the world of loans and banks—of betting on the future instead of the past. Later a William Morris agent would say to me, "Dana was brilliant in that he saw the value that was in Sub Pop and they needed him and no one else had seen it yet. He got to them first."

One of the ways to get inside any subculture is to say, *We both know this person.* For Dana with Sub Pop this person was Joyce Linehan, the raven-haired girl from night school. "I know Joyce," he said to Rich, when Rich answered one of his many cold calls.

Rich remembers walking past the ringing phone, thinking he shouldn't pick it up. He thought perhaps he didn't want to talk to one more person today, perhaps he wanted to get out and smell the air. But the light flashed and the ringer commanded an answer. When he heard Dana's voice it triggered something in him, some automatic trust.

When Dana cold-called he was breezy and casual, never asking anyone to sign anything or agree to anything. Dana and Rich talked about Joyce and how great she was. They talked about Seattle and about how Nirvana might be kings of some kind. Seattle was no different from Boston. It was all part of the same underground. Punk had triumphed in the mainstream. What is the mainstream? they asked each other. It was the kind of question that made you want a drink. They talked about the Pixies—the Boston band Kurt had sworn his allegiance to, claiming in interviews that his whole sound was an imitation of them, and he would never live up to them.

The names were dropped, the faith to punk rock was declared, Rich decided: I like this guy. Now Rich often wonders: "What would our lives be like if I hadn't answered the phone that day?"

A few weeks later, around January 1992, Dana flew out to Seattle to visit the offices. He introduced himself to Rich, who worked amid towers of paper and CDs and empty soda cans. His was an office so dense with clutter he had been nicknamed PigPen by the staff. Rich didn't expect Dana to look so young, like a high school kid. He looked like one of the teenage fans who made pilgrimages to the office: thrilled and jumpy. Not like an emissary from the world of banks and balance sheets. Yet this was his language, and it was a reassuring language Sub Pop needed to hear as the paychecks bounced, waiting for the Geffen checks.

Dana had literature for Rich, sample portfolios, the names of safe, "blue-chip" stocks and "politically progressive" investments. Rich was impressed by the fact that Cassandra had more than one office. Boston, New York, Los Angeles, the business cards read. Dana implied they controlled $50 million.

"What we really need more than anything are credit cards," Rich confessed. Sub Pop was falling apart because they could barely send their bands on tour. The bands would call and say: The cards didn't work or the money didn't arrive. Sometimes they would spend their own money, and repeatedly ask Sub Pop for reimbursements.

Hotels, restaurants, drinks, a broken guitar or guitar string, a flat tire in the middle of the desert. A car crash halfway through the tour and no health insurance. A van so intensely foul it is decided you all need to go to the laundromat. You all need to stay somewhere nice, with a bath.

Rich and I were renting a house and he'd often invite bands over. Use the bathroom, freshen up, he'd say. We'll get some fried chicken. I'd try to be nice, although I couldn't figure out what to say. There was Mark Lanegan, who sang in a low and unmasked and destitute voice about whiskey, depression, a lost girl who was deep in the woods and never coming back. There was a roadie named Flood, who talked so fast it was impossible to understand him. He was the driver, and he seemed to be impatient to get back on the freeway.

The bands knew people loved them. The Sub Pop publicists were eager girls who said, "Fantastic, fantastic." The shows were always sold out. So where was the translation of this love into green?

Dana said he could make the green appear. Rich remembers him explaining that he knew his way around bad credit histories, he knew how to get the history forgiven or erased. He talked about health insurance for the bands.

On that first visit, Rich brought Dana around and introduced him to the bosses. They veered from money and talked about music; they talked about Liquid Liquid and how they were seminal, absolutely. Thomas Dolby, "She Blinded Me With Science," they laughed about this absurd song. The music was another language, like the language of money, and you either understood it or you didn't.

Rich walked Dana out onto Fourth Avenue and he took a cab back to the airport, this messenger who had appeared in the world of Seattle from the East Coast, promising a backstage pass into the realm of money.

In the next few years, there would be more money within the Seattle city limits than anyone had ever predicted. It would never be the provinces again. The two richest men in the world would put down roots across the water from the Sub Pop offices: Bill Gates and Paul Allen. Microsoft was Seattle's hometown industry, producing ten thousand millionaires within five years, yet there was something untranslatable, even secret about it. Microsoft people were like aliens, and they loved stories about outer space and close encounters. Allen had aspirations of "pushing further into space than any private citizen ever has." Bill Gates dressed up in *Star Trek* costumes.

Walking around Seattle, I often saw posters of Bill Gates on telephone poles—a grimacing cartoon face accompanied by slogans about POWER CORRUPTS, about Microsoft as some new fascist dictatorship. The town had its rich fathers, and the more you looked around, the more you realized everything was being built in their image. Both Gates and Allen had grown up here, but their workforce was assembled from around the globe. Microsoft brought flocks of rootless boys to the city, many who were hired before they finished college, or even high school. Those boys brought with them a certain climate of expectation, a certain rubric of desires. Eventually their desires would transform the landscape. Money would make new life forms grow within the city. Old buildings would be demolished to make room for these new life forms. By the time the money had finished with Seattle, the skyline was unrecognizable.

For people like me who had lived in the city for a long time without much money, things seemed a little off—not quite home anymore. I would come around a corner and a building would be gone overnight, or a store replaced: an old wig shop called Wigland cleared away for an upscale Home Comforts store. It seemed to me there was an uneasiness to Seattle at this time—like the city was the same person but now she had a different accent. She was always getting work done. Cranes everywhere, eighteen-story-deep pits where construction crews worked around the clock, at night a glow emanating from the pits like a UFO had landed there.

Dana called Rich from New York to deliver the news that the credit cards had arrived. The Sub Pop men couldn't believe such a reckless history as theirs had been erased, and they were free to move about among the creditworthy classes. Here were the cards with their corny nature scenes, the raised letters and numbers promising distant expiration dates. The line of credit suddenly stretching out in front of them like a road where all the lights are green. It was unreal, yet it was also commonplace. In Seattle, all kinds of awkward men who had dropped out of college and exhibited the behaviors of delinquency were rising to the top of the world. Bill Gates himself was a dropout with a mug shot in his past.

In late 1992, Nirvana released *Incesticide*, a collection of odds and ends and songs that hadn't made it onto *Nevermind*—critics were underwhelmed by it. The band appeared on the cover of *Rolling Stone*. Kurt wore a T-shirt on which he'd scrawled "Corporate Rock Magazines Still Suck" in black marker. He had already started talking about the way Nirvana was doomed, he was doomed, he should die before he's thirty, this was his rock star destiny.

The lost element in his voice had become a commodity, something to be imitated. You became addicted and you wanted to taste it everywhere. The generic, depressed, heroic flavor, a kind of fast food.

As grunge proliferated, Rich and Dana became more and more certain of their powers. I had never been remotely associated with anything successful, except my own straight-A report cards, filed in my memory: They meant, you are in order. Dana and Rich had this chaos about them—this loud, uncontrollable ambition. Their blustery confidence seemed to be working. Their conversations were so heated I shushed them in restaurants. They were living proof that disorder triumphed, and I should stop worrying so much. Dana's voice on the phone: *Em, Em, I miss you, everything is going great.* It started to be the voice of luck.

In the spring of 1993, Richard and I took a trip to Yosemite

National Park with Dana and Artemis. We drove through the forest in a rental car, and as we passed a burnt-out field Dana declared, "Here we go from the green to the death." This dramatic pronouncement was vintage Dana. Dana and Artemis were decadent and loud and they argued openly in the front seat. He packed a thermos of Bloody Marys. Every half hour or so he checked: Does anyone need a refill? I remember the reflex of following him, as if his voice had some kind of hypnotic music running underneath it.

Later the gossip columns would call him a "pied piper."

One of those evenings at Yosemite, we followed him into the forest. The trail had disappeared, leaving us to fight our way through dense underbrush. Dusk was coming down like a veil and we were listless from the Bloody Marys. The men walked ahead, while Artemis and I lagged behind. Sometimes the men waited, holding back branches as if holding doors open. "It's this way, it's this way," Dana promised, determined he knew how to find the motel, determined it was only a matter of time before the lighted windows appeared.

The forest grew darker. Nettles inflamed our shins. I could feel the mud seeping through the soles of my only good shoes. I wanted to get back and soak my feet and treat myself like a princess. I became angry thinking about the hot bath. "Where the fuck are we?" I asked Rich. "Shh," he said. "Wait."

Artemis and I read the men the riot act. We looked at each other like, *Where have we let these idiots lead us, and are we going to die out here?* When we found the hotel, about forty minutes into the meltdown, I felt like we had overreacted. Once again it was proven: The men knew what they were doing and they wouldn't lead us astray.

* * *

The Microsoft millionaires first became real to me in Seattle in early 1993, when I met one of them. His name was Thomas Reardon; he was twenty-two years old and had been hired by Bill Gates when he was barely twenty. He had an engineering mind that I couldn't fathom, patents posted on the wall of his office for certain operations he had invented, methods of entry into the Web, programs that made it possible for everything to happen at warp speed. He was some kind of mastermind, and he came on swaggering and full of himself, with hair down to his shoulders and model girlfriends. But it wasn't hard to pierce his ego. He'd endured a violent childhood and when he sunk down into his computer games, it was a way of circumventing time. He seemed like a child to me, and I felt motherly toward him. I felt like I wanted to give him advice. If I had believed in God I would've told him to go to church. Instead I said, "Take a walk, turn off the games."

Reardon would invite Rich and me over for dinner, and he would serve wine that cost $400 a bottle. But still he drank too much of it, still at a certain point he turned inward and looked like he was lost to us. My friend who worked with homeless men came to one of these dinners. He said, "He is like the guys in my shelter; he is right on the edge."

In September 1993, Nirvana released *In Utero*, full of references to heroin, poppies, and being buried in the ground. Kurt started posing for photos with a gun in his mouth. "He is being ironic," people said. He portrayed himself as out of control, almost lost. But it was supposed to be a joke. It was supposed to be *a representation*.

At Sub Pop the money was starting to come in from *Nevermind*, but Dana encouraged Bruce and John to think bigger, to move on, to expand their horizons. He started to talk to them about a deal. The deal would sell a minority share of the business to a major record label, and Sub Pop would be infused with cash and resources while still technically "independent." "It could be worth millions," Dana said.

"It sounded good to me," says Bruce Pavitt. "Dana seemed like a very talented art enthusiast. It turns out he knew more about art than financing, and was clever enough to understand that many people involved in the arts are not necessarily very sophisticated when it comes to investment."

In 1993, police raided the apartment where Russell was living with Lisa. They found a forest of pot plants in the closet, and a sawed-off shotgun on the desk. Russell says "a stoolie" had tipped off the cops and set the whole thing up. He tells me he threw the gun out the window, but the cops went down into the courtyard and retrieved it.

Russell was committed to MCI (Massachusetts Correctional Institution), Norfolk, a medium security facility about twenty-five miles southwest of Boston that usually houses around fourteen hundred inmates. Russell was busted for fighting soon after his arrival, and he was placed in solitary. Alma visited. He was shackled, his hands in cuffs chained to his waist, another set of chains running down to his ankles, which were also in cuffs, the chains just loose enough to walk in. Alma couldn't help it and she started to cry. Russell said: "You need to get over it. This is the way it is. We can't talk about the way it is supposed to be; we need to talk about the way it is."

Russell was twenty-six years old. The guys he met in jail spoke his language and taught him things: how to break into a place, how to steal an identity, how to become someone you are not. They became his dear friends and his mentors, the people he would hang around with for years. So it was not like he was rehabilitated so much as initiated into a vibrant and eventful world.

Rich had been promoted far into the interior of Sub Pop. By early 1993, he was general manager, and he'd had a card made up that called him Puppet Master. They manufactured jokey stationery: "Celebrating Several Years of Record Making." I think it was around the time of the new stationery that I realized there was a world of things Rich wasn't telling me. I decided not to ask. My attitude was: *whatever.* Phone calls became heated and whispered, urgent. He would be talking to me and then he would drift off, as if replaying a scene in his head, almost talking to himself.

Now I know it was the deal he was whispering about, the deal had become a secret life. The millions the deal represented shimmered on the edge of Rich's mind, like a mirage, and he couldn't quite pay attention to anything else.

Dana flew to Seattle for long afternoon meetings with the Sub Pop men, trying to hammer out the deal's parameters. They met in the conference room on the eleventh floor. Out the windows there was a group of oil refineries—delicate, rusted cranes burrowed into the earth beneath the sound. Beyond the refineries, islands where the millionaires lived. The men were trying to decide what Sub Pop was worth. Dana kept telling them that they were sitting on a gold mine.

For Bruce, the idea of big money meant maybe he could retire, maybe he could grow a hippie beard, take psychedelic mushrooms, and build campfires.

For Jonathan, the money meant expansion of the business, offices around the world, employees paid enough to buy new cars and go on trips. Christmas bonuses. Parties with real food, instead of mountains of rotten hummus and nauseating dip.

In pursuit of the deal, Dana, Bruce, Jonathan, and sometimes Rich went on trips to New York and met with major label representatives in giant high-rises. "It was like a cartoon, or a TV version of deal making," Poneman says. Dana talked big, he said things like *Don't bust my balls,* and *Do you know how huge this band is going to be?* Pavitt remembers, "Dana's brilliance was that he did not hire a lawyer. A lawyer would've slowed everything down." Dana often kept meetings going for hours, acting like he was about ready to sign on the dotted line. Then he would say to Bruce and Jon: "We need to think about this."

He kept everyone hanging in this masterful way. To the Sub Pop men, it was clear Dana knew how to make the New York major label guys tremble in their wing tips.

Dana's great advantage was that Nirvana had appeared out of nowhere; they had surprised the major label moguls, who often sat in 58th- or 94th-floor offices and said, "I know this is going to be a hit." Nirvana destabilized the confidence of the hit-makers. They hadn't seen Kurt Cobain's voice coming. His voice had emerged suddenly, a sound in the middle of the night that could wake up a neighborhood. It had taken control of the airwaves; it had taken control of the eardrums of the masses. Dana was adamant with the record label stuffed shirts: *How can you even place a price on something like that voice?*

The labels would come up with figures: $10 million, and total control over the label. Dana would say $15 million, and no control.

In Olympia, the purist punks heard about Sub Pop's impending deal. Calvin Johnson had long warned his fans about the "advancing corporate ogre." Rumor had it: *The military-industrial complex is coming to steal your music.* There was this vague, prevalent desire to be independent. Corporate rock whores! They wrote in Olympia fanzines and in alley graffiti. Hatred of capitalism!

Meetings about the deal accelerated in early 1994; Dana had the interest of Geffen and Warner and Sony. He was hoping for $10 million, maybe. He used the tactic of: *I have someone else on the line.*

In April 1994, Kurt Cobain shot himself in the mouth. I was in Rich's apartment with the rain blowing in through a window; I was thinking about closing the window, about to walk over to it. Then I heard the news. The man on the radio, Marco, was one of those DJs who believed the rock stars were like friends. When he delivered the news he sounded shaken, choked up, like he'd just seen a ghost.

With the news of Kurt Cobain's self-destruction, the deal left the air. Rich says, "No one wanted to talk about it. It felt like we were preying on him." People had assumed the sound of Kurt's voice was the sound of the future, but really it was the sound of his soul getting away from him. I had ignored all the warning signs in his music. All that work, all that industriousness, and the whole time he was weaving a death shroud. It was almost like I'd been tricked. But maybe I didn't want to see what was right in front of me.

Later, people blamed his wife, Courtney Love; they talked about her like people in Salem probably talked about witches. Like she had the power to undo people.

In the weeks after he died I would drive past his Seattle house and there would be kids waiting down below, pilgrims. I was always driving so I could never get a good look—just a shock of red or orange hair or a kid sleeping in the bushes, dangerously close to the roadside. That summer, one of Courtney Love's bandmates, from her group Hole, OD'd in the bathtub, a girl who was about to make her own record, they said, a girl whose voice everyone was about to hear and adore. She took the wrong mix of tranquilizers and her heart shut down. Then a quiet kid we knew from another band called the Tree People went home to Idaho, quit drugs, and in his new sobriety decided to shoot himself.

So the drugs made you do it or the clarity without the drugs made you do it. Take your life, that is. The suicide story was all around us, a bad scene. At the time it felt like an epidemic.

Dana put the Sub Pop deal on ice. He had other deals going: He was talking to the record label Matador about the same kind of sellout. Get out while you are on top, get a cash infusion. Like Sub Pop, Matador had ideals of independence: They wanted to control the label, but they were tired of the grind of keeping it alive.

Matador was a New York label and Dana was mostly a New York person by 1994. He'd shut down his Boston offices, moved into the back space of a friend's art studio, big and roomy and a place Artemis could decorate so it felt like home. His client list was growing. Marc Glimcher had signed on with him, investing a significant amount which Dana will not disclose. Glimcher told people he was charmed by Dana; he thought he seemed like a breath of fresh air. Soon after Glimcher came George Condo, whose canvases were selling for half a million dollars out of Glimcher's Pace Gallery. Condo usually painted large canvases that would take up half a wall, and his mood was satiric, irreverent—a character from *Bonanza* superimposed over an Impressionist masterpiece. The *New York*

Times usually loved Condo, but a critic for the *New Republic*, Jed Perl, wrote: "No gallery show this season brought me quite so low, probably because I adore many of the styles Condo has done violence to. Condo doesn't understand that the closer you work to someone else's style, the more imperative it is that you be clear about who you are."

Through the art world connections of Glimcher and Condo and Ross Bleckner and David Salle, etc., Dana encountered a man named André Balazs, who would connect him to a world of hope and sun and man-made paradises. André was a powerful hotel magnate. He had revamped the Chateau Marmont on Sunset Boulevard in Los Angeles. He had been born New Jersey Italian, but when he spoke to Dana their accents bled into each other. André was often referred to as the Prince of Cool. He was enchanted with Dana, and he felt from the beginning as if they were old friends. ("I felt I have lost an old friend," André said, after Dana was arrested.) Dana and André recognized each other: Someone you would see on the block growing up. Someone you'd invite over to listen to records. They had a good dialectic going: the Prince of Cool versus the Unrepentant Dork. Echoes and variations of the same homeland, far from home.

Dana and Artemis's SoHo apartment was noisy. Their days went on and on. Dana had one very expensive suit. Artemis had her family money. She was working on a documentary about geishas. Cassandra had almost completely stopped the production of the newsletters. Now the business was all about having dinner, saying I will call you tomorrow, here is my card. Dana did not want to come on like a desperate salesman. He wanted to be like the owner of a private club that everyone should be a member of. The kind of place where you would need a password.

In 1994, Dana met a guy who introduced him to a world of

private dance clubs and whispered-about underground happen-ings. His name was David Hershkovitz, and he was the pub-lisher of *Paper* magazine. *Paper* was written in the same elitist, were-you-cool-enough-to-be-there tone as the British music magazines Dana had devoured as a teenage New Waver.

Hershkovitz remembers: "I met Artemis and we started talk-ing. She was a big fan of *Paper* so she was excited about meet-ing me. She said, 'We subscribed in Boston, you should meet Dana,' so she introduced this guy Dana. He was an investor for people for whom money wasn't their thing, that was his niche. . . . He was interested in *Paper* and suggested we get together at some point, and of course I was like well that is great, but I had heard that before, didn't know if it was going anywhere. Eventually we got to be friends. . . . With Dana it is very ADD-style friendship. You know he had a way of feeling very close with whoever he was with. But out of sight out of mind, if you weren't in his radar you couldn't get his attention no matter what."

Dana knew that in the world of hipster Manhattan where all the young authentic artists were required to live, he needed to be ready to throw a party at 3 A.M., after the bars closed. He needed to be part of the 3 A.M. nomads, the ones who could be heard yelling in the street, Come on you can't go in yet, we will find a place to go. A band called Nation of Ulysses had even written a manifesto against sleep. Sleep was not cool, it was not something to admit you were into. Dana knew some hardcore all-nighters: Greg Dulli of the Afghan Whigs, a white man who sounded black. Radio people sometimes said he would be *the next Elvis. But modern. Elvis after black music.* Sometimes Dulli's performances felt like minstrel shows.

A story Artemis told me, which stayed in my mind: It was a night when she'd made Dana swear not to bring anyone home.

I need to be by myself, she said. It is vital. There are all these things going on for me. Yet at 3 A.M., Dana and Greg Dulli wandered into the apartment, talking loudly about how great the show was and about his future as the black white man. When she heard their voices she was incensed. She marched out into the living room and told them to get lost. Artemis's voice had this undeniable authority. She was not the kind of girlfriend who drifted in and out of the room like a minor character. According to her version of events, they were gone in minutes.

It seemed more and more dull to her. She talked to me about it, circling around this unavoidable idea: He did not listen to her, he did not hear her, she might as well have been talking to the air.

One client Dana pursued at this time was the Spanish director Pedro Almodóvar. Almodóvar had a success in 1988 with the film *Women on the Verge of a Nervous Breakdown*. When Dana contacted Almodóvar, he was making a film called *Kika,* about a cosmetologist, a corpse that comes to life, and a violent rape. What if Sub Pop did the soundtrack? Dana proposed. It could be a deal to benefit everyone. You are cool, Sub Pop is cool. It is a winning combination.

Kika debuted in February 1994. It was not a hit. *The New Yorker* wrote: "The movie feels hammy and strained, and the details are chucked in your face." The soundtrack was forgotten. I remember Rich and I flew out to New York and went to the premiere. I can't remember the movie at all. But I remember how odd it was to watch it a few rows behind Almodóvar and his actresses, the women staring up at themselves, fifty feet high, their red-coated lips as large as highway billboards.

Dana's friendship with André Balazs had become a loud,

true thing. Partners, compadres. A shared sense that they were put here to turn things around. The two men could be insufferable in restaurants. Taking forever to decide the order. Arguing in such a way that the waitress has to wonder if someone is going to leave the table. Yet enormous tips and a kindness in their eyes. Princes was the exact right word.

Behind the chatter they built plans, and in early 1994 it was a plan for a refinancing of André's Mercer Hotel, located in SoHo. The Mercer was hemorrhaging money, but its buzz was just beginning. Dana could organize a refinancing—private citizens loaning money, knowing that it would be paid off. Celebs who hung out at the Mercer seemed to know it was a place of inevitable significance: These black dining rooms with their waiters in heavy eyeliner. In the world of André's hotels a refinancing would pay for things like: lavender-cucumber soap, maids who could be models, art books, rugs that look old but will take a beating.

In the summer of 1994, Rich and I were married and Dana and Artemis flew out to Portland, Oregon, for the wedding. The night before the ceremony we met them at their hotel, and they took us out for drinks at Trader Vic's. We ordered one of those party rum drinks where everyone slurps out of the bowl from straws. Dana pleaded with the waitress to give us the bowl the drink came in. It was Polynesian-themed, topless girls leaning down over island scenes. Dana begged. The waitress hesitated. He said, "I will give you twenty dollars," and she agreed.

The next day, still a little unsettled from the sickening bowl of drink, we were married in the house where I grew up, an old rambling mansion on the hill, a place that signified to my father that he had arrived in the upper classes, a house that had been redecorated and redecorated until we'd begged my mother: "Just keep it the way it is."

In the provincial world of Portland, Dana was exotic; he was someone my mother pointed out to her friends, a high-powered person from Wall Street. Portland society ladies muttered "Wall Street" as they looked in his direction. Artemis seemed exotic, too, smoking her cigarettes and blowing the smoke straight up into the air, bending her neck back.

I'd told my mother about Dana and his important job. I suppose I wanted her to be impressed, to see that I was not only from here anymore, that I was from somewhere else, too. I had another geography and maybe I was going to be redeemed by it. I pointed him out to her. "There he is," I said. He was standing in the corner talking to the Sub Pop men.

My grandmother said, "He is really from New York? . . . Oh my, the people you know, you go everywhere. He is really flying back to New York? Won't the plane make him tired?" She'd lived in New York once in her early twenties, when she was awarded an opera scholarship at Juilliard. After that she'd moved back to Portland, and sang occasionally for the symphony. For me, her imperfect mezzo-soprano was riveting. Dana thought so, too. When she performed at the wedding Dana said to me afterward, "Oh my God, I cried!!!"

This was before the deal had been finalized and before I knew anything about it. But looking back and sorting through the photographs from the wedding, I can detect the deal hovering around the men, making them sweat a little as the rain tried to break through the thick and stubborn cloud cover.

In the fall of 1994, the Sub Pop deal came back to life; Kurt had been dead long enough that the deal could be talked about, the way you eventually talk about what you are going to do with a dead person's furniture. In the wake of his suicide, his value only increased. He'd become a legend. A true life story with a terrible ending, constantly told and retold.

So the price went up, like bidding at an auction—$15 million, 16, 17, 18, for a 49 percent share of the label. During the 1994 holidays the deal slowed down but in January 1995 the Sub Pop men were flying to New York constantly. They were disoriented and decentered.

Rich remembers the huge reception desk at the Time Warner center. Each time he walked by, he'd think, The desk, the desk. The whole capitalist pageantry was a little surreal to him: He'd grown up on welfare, with a back-to-the-land hippie mother. She'd invited Tibetan monks to live in their house, and over breakfast one of them told Rich, "The best thing to do is to realize all life is suffering." By the time he was six Rich had mastered all the variations of Hamburger Helper.

Rich owned a 2 percent share of Sub Pop, so depending on the size of Dana's "cake," he could be out of the forest of financial worry forever.

The long haggling narrative of the deal came to its conclusion in January 1995. Some details:

On January 10, 1995, the parties closed the transactions provided for in the Asset Purchase Agreements and made the contributions of cash, assets, and liabilities to the joint venture called for in the foregoing agreements. In addition to the exchange of documents called for under the Asset Purchase Agreements, Warner Music wired an aggregate of $18 million to Sub Pop Ltd and $2 million to Sub Pop Music Ltd. In accordance with the Asset Purchase Agreements Warner would purchase: "an undivided 44.1 percent interest in the

Assets of SP . . . Buyer and Seller are entering into a Joint Venture Agreement (the "Joint Venture Agreement") pursuant to which they shall establish a joint venture (the "Venture") to engage in the music business and related businesses . . .

Translation: Warner now owned a percentage of Sub Pop's assets. These assets included: "All audio and video master original recordings ("Masters") owned or controlled by Seller, whether on magnetic recording tape, film, disc, or any other substance or material used in the manufacture of the recordings of the masters ("Recordings") . . ."

Books and financial records were part of the deal, too. Everything was turned over to Warner for an audit. Warner brought in their own people to make sure all the ducks were in a row.

Rich had overseen the books and records, and he was grateful to give them up to someone who wore a suit and had the time to untangle all that bullshit. He wanted to write songs, anyway.

He was glad not to have to worry about it for a while:

Amount Due:
Amount Past Due:

Over and over he read the sentence: "The initial payment in the amount of $18,000,000 shall be paid by buyer to the seller on the Closing Date." He looked at the number and found it unfathomable.

Buried in the contract, there were caveats: If "you should become physically or mentally incapacitated," the deal is off. And this: "You shall keep secret all confidential matters."

The deal went through. The price agreed upon after twelve hours of negotiating was $20 million. In a few weeks the money came over the wires. Dana called Rich to say: "Check for your money, your money is there." Jon and Bruce walked away with $4 million each. Dana made a million. Rich walked away with almost $500,000. Here was the money, free and clear. Here was the money, coming through for the bad check written in a Thai restaurant for $15.75 five years ago or a lifetime ago.

After the Sub Pop deal, Dana rose up in the entertainment and art world—the deal amassed a certain cultural capital for him. The deal was the passport into a realm of respectability he'd been seeking ever since he'd started cold-calling. Now all his calls were answered. Now there was only a short pause before the rich person was on the line.

Some of his clients or almost-clients around this time, early January 1995:

André, the gatekeeper to models and Hollywood

Artists:
Ross Bleckner
George Condo
David Salle

Gallery Owners:
Pace/Glimcher
Mary Boone (trying)
Castelli (trying)

Film People:
Good Machine Productions
Pedro Almodóvar

Circling around him, waiting to sign on the dotted line: David Blaine, Fiona Apple, members of the band Phish, Courtney Love, Jesse Dylan (Bob's son), Courteney Cox. And then there were the numbers that came with these connections. Numbers of Hollywood agents and managers. People who lived inside fortresses of phone numbers.

All these people became more interested in Dana after the Sub Pop deal. The consensus was: This was a kid who knew what he was doing. That was a hell of a lot of money to pay for some degenerate punk rock label.

Obviously, this guy knew how to make a sale.

André and Dana agreed that wealth and its expressions had changed. Rich young Americans were of a different type than the previous generation, with different tastes and desires. It was no longer the eighties with shoulder pads and cocaine. In the nineties people were healthy: yoga classes available at all times. Healthy thoughts. There was a certain decadence that was passé. Now the prevailing style was "boutique"—welcoming but not overbearing. Practical, or at least a look of practicality and minimalism even if you were hemorrhaging money out your eyeballs.

André introduced Dana to Ted Demme and his wife, Amanda (brother of Jonathan, who made *Silence of the Lambs*). To Kathryn Bigelow (girlfriend of *Terminator* director James Cameron, who had made a confounding, surreal surf film called *Point Break* that would become a cult classic). Gary Oldman, who was headed for a career as a villain.

Dana added all these names to his Rolodex. He made a point to write down a spouse's name if he knew it. Whether they were married or expecting. A dog's name.

* * *

In late 1995, after everything had been signed and distributed and sent through the channels of the banks, Rich said, "Now we can buy a house!" I had nothing to do with the money: We were married, but we had always come and gone into our own worlds. As far as I was concerned the money was his world. Rich had been so secretive about the deal, I hadn't adjusted to the idea of it. I never saw the paperwork, and even when I finally did see it I didn't understand it. A house at this point was just an abstraction, something that belonged to parents, old people.

It was hard for Rich to believe in the money, too. When he was a teenager he'd traveled with the yippies, spreading their gospel against private property. Now at the age of thirty-two he was house-hunting—something neither one of us knew how to do. We simply drove up to houses with FOR SALE signs, took the pieces of paper out of the plastic boxes. Then we drove away and thought *that did not feel quite right*. The pieces of paper talked about the rooms, the full and half baths, the views. *Cozy up to a fireplace!* they read, inviting us into the interior of the property-owning tribe. I remember a Realtor leading us through the house of a dead man, stuffy and still, all his furniture in place as if awaiting his ghost, hospital equipment scattered in the garage. The Realtor stared at Rich's decrepit sneakers. He had this puzzled look on his face, as if he was wondering if this was a joke.

Eventually we found a house looking out on the water, a place where you could sit on the deck and watch cars driving across the bridge. The first morning we woke up there, I'd been dreaming of floods and earthquakes. I wondered if these dreams were premonitions and something was going to go wrong. I said to Rich, "Nothing is going to go wrong, is it?" And he said, "No, everything is going really well."

My dad wasn't so sure. He said: "That kind of thing just doesn't happen, that kind of windfall. There's got to be a catch."

Russell spent most of 1991–93 in Norfolk, after being caught driving a stolen car with drugs inside it. When he was released he took up with Lisa again, hanging out in her apartment. Alma always knew to call him there. Cosmo and Alma hired him to paint the walls of their rental properties. By 1995, he was proud to say he had been clear of the cops for almost two years. Okay, this is a turnaround! Alma said. Russell tried to behave like a boy in the midst of an awakening, a boy who was getting better, but he could not uproot his deeply rooted hopeless self, and he still loved the oblivion of heroin.

One afternoon he was shooting heroin with Lisa. Russell doesn't remember nodding off, but all of a sudden he was awake, an hour had passed, there was a paramedic in his face. His life had gone out from under him. As Russell discovered later, Lisa had seen him nod off and panicked, but instead of calling the ambulance she called the drug dealer. She asked him, What am I supposed to do?

The drug dealer said, Put ice in his armpits.

She said, I don't have any ice.

Use anything cold, the dealer said.

So it came to pass that Lisa placed scoops of chocolate ice cream all up and down her lover's body while he lay there turning blue. She called 911 and when they arrived, he was covered in the chocolate sludge. Russell remembers waking up and wondering why his skin was brown and why this guy was asking him, "Can you hear me?" He remembers it as the all-time strangest scene in which he has ever come back to earth.

Around this same time, the middle of 1995, Rich and Bruce were traveling to New York to talk to the Warner Partners, and they stopped in San Francisco for a hallucinogenic conference. It was called Entheobotany Visionary Botany Conference, and it was a pseudoscientific convention for hard-core hippies, inspired by the god of mushrooms, Terence McKenna. McKenna was the author of creeds that talked about the "twilight of civilization," and the need for a rebirth of shamanism. He believed that only in an altered state could the twilight of civilization really be witnessed properly.

At the conference, drugs were abundant, and Bruce and Rich bought DMT, a powdered substance that was known to insiders as the strongest hallucinogenic anyone could take. When you took it, you were supposed to see the other side. Rich told me about it before he took it. "Shamans did it," he said. You were supposed to be able to see the end of the universe, little spots, something like that. It was a short, intense high, a form of flying too close to the sun, I suppose. Together, Bruce and Rich laid down in the bedroom of a friend's house and took the powder. "I saw a whole bunch of spots, and I think I heard some alien voice," says Rich. "It was over in five minutes but I will never forget it."

I had to wonder: Could these guys take these drugs, could they escape the world so intensely, and still rule it? Could they still have cultural power in a culture they so diligently wanted to escape? Feeling powerful from the DMT, Bruce and Rich flew to New York to chat with the new partners and eat five-star dinners charged to the Warner credit card.

Once, Rich came into Dana's apartment with a piece of street debris in his eye. It turned out to be a paint chip, large and mean, "I think it was three quarters of an inch," Rich says. Rich could not open the eyelid without pain, and he was in a panic, helpless.

Dana went to the medicine cabinet and found some Vicodin and tweezers. He said, "Rich, sit here on the couch, lie still, drink this water, take this pill, I'm going to take care of you."

Oh my God, it hurts, Rich said.

It will be okay really soon, Dana said.

For a long time Rich remembered that act of Dana's, the way he knew exactly what to do, the way he became focused and authoritative, rallying his senses. He lifted out the paint chip with his tweezers and they marveled at its terrible size. The incident made Rich trust Dana even more. It was an act of love, impossible to dismiss.

PART
FOUR

1996

B Y THE MIDNINETIES, DANA'S ANXIOUS, COLD-CALLING energy had been replaced by a broad, confident, cruise-director warmth. When you were this far inside, you didn't want to seem anxious. Anxiety was not reassuring in a money manager. Dana knew this, and he told his clients to *relax*. He had a reassuring speech about the back and forth of money—he made it sound like a tide going in and out. If your stocks were dropping, he might remind you to lie back and take a breather, take a trip. *By the time you get back, things will be booming again.*

He became more and more of a global operator and the password into various closed societies was the name Glimcher, the Pace Gallery, the gallery where people could buy actual Picassos. Where people could buy actual great art. In Los Angeles particularly, these promises carried weight. Studio heads and agents wanted art in their mansions. If you had great art it meant you were really rich. It meant you really had taste. So it was as a guy from SoHo, who knew all the top, top galleries, the guy who'd made the Sub Pop deal and was close with Pedro Almodóvar, who had done all these hip and important things that had nothing to do with California: this was the story surrounding Dana as he entered Los Angeles.

At the Chateau Marmont bar, famous and powerful people sat in the garden on tasteful rattan chairs. They moved softly over the perfectly distressed oriental rugs, waited on by Mexican bus boys, by girls in streaked hairdos and vintage dresses. In spring, bougainvillea bloomed across the walls, and desert shrubs put out blooms like red bottle brushes. Palm trees sheltered the garden from the noise and smog of Sunset; sometimes you could hear the squeal of bus brakes, but you were mostly high above the riffraff, and it was possible to believe sitting there that the world of commerce was far away and manageable, something to reenter but only when the time came, whenever the check arrived, no hurry.

Dana entered this oasis on André's arm. At the Chateau, André always gave Dana a sought-after room, maybe one of the bungalows out by the pool. There were ghosts out there— comedian John Belushi, who died on one of those floors when a mixture of heroin and cocaine caused his veins to collapse. Even though the rooms had this destructive history, the Chateau had a way of banishing ghosts; the decor conspired to create a feeling of some rich grandmother's home: the worn writing desk with the old-fashioned stationery, the simple vase of flowers on the table. The kind of room that made a person feel protected and watched-over even if they had never been protected and no one had ever watched over them.

The next big hotel André envisioned was the Los Angeles Standard, down Sunset from the Chateau. He started talking to Dana about it during the Mercer bailout. It would be less expensive, a place that could take the overflow of tourists from the

Chateau, tourists who had come to Los Angeles to see celebrities in the flesh. Dana helped André pull together his business plan and find investors. They made a set of convincing spreadsheets. Dana promised the investors: The Standard will be another hit. (He was right. The Standard soon became a hotel guests needed to reserve months in advance. As of this writing, it is still a place of 24/7 celebrity sightings.)

André was married to Katie Ford, who ran a modeling agency. Consequently, the more time Dana spent with André, the more he was surrounded by models. Artemis often found them irritating, and she and I would make fun of them—leggy, impossible girls who stared at each other's clothes as if their lives depended on it.

Part of the plan for the Standard: Have a live underwater model staring out at you in a tank behind the reception desk, a mermaid.

Another part of the plan: The sign should be upside down. So the word is upside down. So it is like the Standard but reversing the standard. Isn't that cool?

Yes, I think so, the investors said.

Dana held meetings about the Standard at the Chateau bar, talking to rich people who knew rich people, talking around the idea of a private placement—a deal where you are getting in on the ground floor, where you are coming in by a hidden entrance, where your name is in the history of the hotel, and the hotel is part of history. You are not some common person, part of a public stock offering. You are one of the select few, offered a stake in the enterprise before anyone else. With these kinds of explanations, Dana was trying to convince investors to part with their money (often it was spoken of as "parking money"). André offered gifts: drinks on the house, free rooms.

We only need another $2 million to really make it happen.

Dana and André treated potential investors like old intimate friends. Have this room, have another Cosmopolitan, money is no object. It's on me. Come to New York, come to the Mercer. Tell the people at the desk who you are. André and I will meet you in the bar.

Jay Faires was a quiet, bearded man, suspicious of wheeler-dealers, a wearer of old T-shirts. But in his campaign to fund the Standard, Dana won him over. Sometime in 1995 or 1996, he remembers he agreed to invest $250,000 in the place. Faires knew André—he admired him. He says, "I couldn't really resist Dana. He was this really endearing dork, he really had the charm down." Faires looks back fondly on lunches in the Chateau garden, although now he says he thinks Dana is either mentally ill or a crook.

Faires owned a record label called Mammoth, an independent out of North Carolina. Like Sub Pop, Mammoth had discovered bands the majors had not seen coming: the Squirrel Nut Zippers and Pavement, a retro swing band and a cheeky, lo-fi boy band. Both were the kinds of bands who were never quite serious. Either the irony was a shield or the irony was all that existed.

When the men got together in the Chateau garden, they were monopolists, old-fashioned American optimists, looking for the next frontier. If it worked once, it would work again, on a grand scale. *The city needs the hotel. We are filling a need.* This was Dana's pitch. In the fever of his pitch, Dana moved further from the ideas of Warren Buffett, conservative and homey, and became more of a global operator, as ambitious as Paul Allen, who wanted to launch himself into outer space.

By the time Dana arrived in Los Angeles on André's arm, the Medford accent had almost completely left his speech. People couldn't tell where he was from anymore. He was a stranger coming to town, and all kinds of histories could be projected onto him. I heard he was from Jersey, or Queens, people said. I heard he was a new-age guy from San Francisco. There was a powerful strange inflection in his words, but it was hard to place. The rootlessness of his accent was part of his magnetism.

In Los Angeles, power had a different set of codes than in New York. Here, the power brokers spoke a different dialect. It was at once amorphous and rigid, wide open and mysterious. Dana was accustomed to people like André or Glimcher, who wore suits and always seemed to be working, always on the clock. In L.A. half the time they looked like they had just come in from the beach. In L.A. you were more likely to wait, to never bring up business at all at first. Decisions weren't made in conference rooms but on boat rides where everyone sat cross-legged on deck and imitated the posture of vacationers.

Los Angeles was often so hot and dry, the air itself made the citizens delirious, irrational. You could barely walk down the sidewalk because you were literally walking across a desert. It was like another planet, a polluted and possibly doomed one, yet a place that with its palm trees and red bougainvillea and bright pink smog sunsets, also managed to evoke paradise.

In the spring of 1996, Glimcher introduced Dana to a man who he would once again call his brother. Jay Moloney had more in common with Russell than any of Dana's previous surrogate brothers. He was an intensely self-destructive person, a guy who was constantly looking for drugs. Moloney was also one of the most talked-about celebrity agents in Los Angeles; he was the protégé of Mike Ovitz, who had at various times been designated the most powerful man in Hollywood. In the family language of Hollywood, Jay was Ovitz's "favored son."

Ovitz had risen to power as the head of Creative Artists Agency. The agency represented all the big names: Scorsese and Spielberg, Stallone and Harrison Ford. In a *New York Times Magazine* article, Ovitz told reporter Lynn Hirschberg, "I've always felt I can do anything." He'd left CAA in 1995 to help run the Disney corporation with an old friend, Michael Eisner. Both were men no one wanted as their enemy. Both were men always looking for enemies.

Ovitz was a superagent and the superagents were the keepers of rare and sought-after phone numbers. They knew the hidden phone lines of famous people—people who changed their numbers constantly, trying to escape calls from their fans. The superagents were the last people you encountered before you encountered the stars themselves. They spent their days driving up enormous driveways to have catered meetings in star homes. People called Ovitz names like "shark" or "god."

Jay was Ovitz's young and handsome favorite, and Ovitz's power attached itself to him like an incubus. When Ovitz left the agency for Disney, the gossips often talked of Jay Moloney as the next king of CAA, the inheritor of the power Ovitz had accumulated. In 1996, Moloney was thirty-two years old, and he had been working at CAA for ten years. From mailroom to agent: that ladder-to-success story. His role was to whisper to old agents the secrets of the young. *This person is a Raw Talent, but they could be turned into the next leading man.*

Moloney's father had been an aspiring screenwriter and agent. For a while, his father even represented Charo. In high school, Moloney would boast to his friends: I sat in Charo's lap! When he was a teenager his parents divorced and he moved with his mother to Newport, Oregon, a coastal town of foghorns and permanent rain. But Hollywood was always in his blood and he had a gift for it, a tendency.

When Dana met Jay they were both in their early thirties, blond and tall, with wire-frame glasses and fine suits. Both men were manic and captivating. Some people say that by this time Jay was already halfway gone, a coke-binger with an underworld of dealers and disappeared nights in his history. He'd already been in rehab twice. Gossips decreed: *That guy is probably hopeless.*

Dana says, "I saw no evidence of drugs in him." What Dana saw was a young man at the height of his powers, agenting the next generation of stars. "By the time I met him Jay was managing Leo and Cammie and Ben and Matt," Dana says. These were the first names of the new stars. The old stars: They were confronting the ravages of time. Jowls. Permanently frozen hairlines. It was time to cast these old stars as fathers, mothers, uncles. People who died in the first reel.

Dana and Jay name-dropped together. They linked one name to another to another, an endless chain of association that could go on for hours, years. They talked about who they thought was really going to make it. One name they agreed on: Leo, Leo. He has it. They agreed that there was no way the world would stop paying attention to Leo.

Through Jay, Dana met both Michael Ovitz and Leonardo DiCaprio: He was introduced to them as *a guy who could make you 40 percent.* Dana remembers his first meeting with Leo, which took place in Paris in the spring of 1996.

> I was meeting clients, I can't remember exactly who, and he was there and we set up a meeting. I was staying at the Ritz and Leonardo called me there to suggest the meeting place, the Musée d'Orsay on the left bank, which impressed me quite a bit.

He was remarkably erudite, charming, and we hit it off right away. Things I recall: discussing art, money and film, my fondness for Jay, his family background Italian/German, my family background Italian; socially conscious investing, beautiful Parisian women, acting talent, more art, more women, and then leaving the remarkable meeting feeling quite a strong bond. Interestingly, from that point on we often looked at artwork together, and he developed a keen eye for art.

Up until now, Leo had played a retarded boy and a boy whose father threw him across the room. In Paris, Leo was filming a trashy swashbuckling picture called *The Man in the Iron Mask,* which involved fencing and elaborate costumes. Before *The Man in the Iron Mask,* Leo had been in Baja, Mexico, filming James Cameron's *Titanic,* a $170 million production that had gone on too long—it was overbudget, the director needed everything perfect, all the way down to the silverware. The actors were unhappy, tired of treading water. The spring edition of *Baja Life* magazine reported on the local extras in Rosarito Beach who were playing dead bodies in the *Titanic* production: "More than 1,000 area residents and townsfolk— permanent and temporary—have died; and they will die many more times during the next three months."

Cassandra's business was growing and Dana signed on new clients every day, most of them investing over $200,000. Ovitz came on board along with his old partner, Richard Lovett, an agent who was almost as feared as Ovitz. Dana says by 1996 his client list had grown to over 100 names. Yet Dana could not figure out when he had time to grow the business in an efficient way, it just kept growing around him. He often said, "I really need to work on the infrastructure." But the infrastructure needed to wait, as three-hour dinners ate up the evenings. Trips to the airport wore out his nerves. Sometimes all he wanted was a good drink and music and Artemis telling him what to do.

More and more of Dana's clients had maids and drivers. They had assistants in multiple cities. This was not, as he told me, "some unknown actor with only $10,000." These were people who had so much money they forgot to cash checks. A check that says: eight hundred thousand dollars and no/100. For these kinds of stars, so many checks were coming in it was hard to tell what the checks were for. His clients included:

David Blaine and David Copperfield (magicians)
Marco Brambilla (director of ill-fated action films)
Benicio Del Toro (character actor)
Dan Cortese (star of Burger King commercials trying to become character actor)
Tim Roth (British import, brilliant in torture scenes)

It also included more powerful people:

Richard Lovett, head of CAA
Marianne Boesky, powerful gallery owner
Marc Glimcher, powerful gallery owner
And then Mike Ovitz, *for whom there was a litany of numbers in Dana's Rolodex*
    Mobile
    Fax
    Home
Also: Heather's direct line

Also in his Rolodex were the names of people he wanted to pursue, wanted to bring into the Cassandra fold:

Steven Spielberg (he had his number, that's all he had)
Martin Scorsese
Keith Hernandez, former Met
Jermaine Jackson (Michael Jackson's brother)

With money from his wealthy new clients, Dana moved into an office in the "Little" Singer Building on West Broadway, a former sewing machine factory turned into sleek industrial loft space. The office was a hive of ringing phones and bike messengers: anxious delivery boys carrying documents that needed to be looked over yesterday. Dana handled all of it casually, *Thanks, thanks, oh, great, I am glad it is here, I will read it tonight.*

One afternoon when I dropped by he introduced me around: I remember seeing good-looking people, with a style that was both edgy and prim, laundered. Depending on when I showed up, there could be six people in the office, or a dozen. Be nice to this wonderful woman, he told his employees when I visited. Her husband is like my brother, he is my great friend.

Stefania Fuomo worked there at this time. She knew Artemis from Wellesley and filled orders for Dana, took messages, promised people that he would call back, sent faxes when people called about discrepancies in their statements. Rich remembers Dana saying, "Call Stefania, she'll figure it out for you." Sometimes Rich wanted to know how much money he had and where it had been invested. "Tell me if she calls," Rich would say.

Stefania had an exotic phone voice. She said, "Your money is safe, it is at Brown & Co., you should get a statement any time." Rich and I met her a couple of times. She was pretty and serious, impressive. The kind of girl who would tell you if things were not as they seemed. Later she would want to put the whole Cassandra thing behind her. She would wish the whole sordid episode could be erased from her past.

Dana continued to traffic among the cool. He sold Matador to Atlantic in a deal similar to Sub Pop's: millions of dollars for a minority share. He bankrolled Me & Ro jewelry, a favorite of models and actresses. He met regularly with André about incursions into new hotel territories: maybe a hotel where mermaids waited behind every window. He befriended the actor Willem Dafoe and served on the board of his theater troupe, the Wooster Group. He volunteered for museum boards. He often said, "I really believe in nonprofits."

Craig Kanarick, Dana's former roommate from Boston, approached him about financing in 1996. He, too, was making a New York incursion. He'd started a company called Razorfish, whose mission was the design and control of websites. Their literature was about "creating a presence on the Web," and "taking part in the technological revolution."

Craig played up a punk rock attitude; once he showed up at a conference about "digital integration" in blue hair, a blue suit, and an orange shirt. According to *Wired* magazine:

"'Some square asked him if he wore the getup when he pitched to corporate clients.'

"'Sure,' Kanarick said.

"'Well, how to you get them to take you seriously?' the square asked.

"'I open my mouth,' Kanarick told him."

By the time Craig approached Dana for financing he considered himself an A-list person: he'd met Michael Stipe and the chef Mario Battali. He was no longer an anonymous MIT geek who needed an apartment; he was the subject of magazine articles, the boss of fifty employees. Yet Dana didn't treat him like he was on the A-list, and this bothered Kanarick. It bothered him that Dana didn't believe in the whole tech thing—the idea that websites were the new television. He saw

Craig as his old roommate, not as an equal in the world of power and names.

Dana was wrong about Craig. Soon this old roommate—who'd arrived in his life through a telephone pole advertisement—would have more money to his name than many of the celebrities Dana was so ardently pursuing. Craig started Razorfish at a time when certain words were just penetrating the language: interface, megabyte, hyperlink. Other words were taking on new meanings: crash, virus, worm. As e-mail proliferated, the desire for constant messages took root. Cell phones were large and ungainly but getting smaller every day.

Wired wrote this convoluted description of Razorfish's enterprise: "They are helping old-economy companies gain entry into the new economy by plotting a strategy (the consulting part) integrating their existing systems (the technology part); and building clean functional interfaces." The author described them as an "edge downtown operation" working on "the edge of digital design."

Edge, downtown. These words should've appealed to Dana but he was suspicious of Razorfish. He didn't want to advise his clients to invest in it. He was the same way about Microsoft. Rich remembers Dana sold his Microsoft stock before it started to soar: Dana thought it was a risky venture, not "real" like Coca-Cola or Merck.

Yet while Dana was conservative about the risk of tech stocks and the NASDAQ (the tech stock index), actually his investments were getting riskier by 1996. He'd started discussions with T. Boone Pickens Jr., the son of infamous Texas corporate raider T. Boone Pickens Sr. As a corporate raider, Pickens Sr. located weak or faltering companies and took them over, cleaning house, dissolving unions, changing names, changing locks on former employees.

Pickens Jr. came to Dana with a pitch, a deal he might want to get in on. It was about buying up public water utilities in Texas and privatizing them. According to one investor, the pitch went, "If you can choose your power or cable company, you should be able to choose your water company."

Could water be privatized, branded? Could a private company deliver water to your faucet more efficiently? Could your water come with a free magazine subscription, or a mail-in rebate? Craig Kanarick remembers, "Dana didn't really give me a choice. He just said you are in on the water deal."

Sometime in early 1996, Dana and Artemis took over the top floor of the Singer Building, above the Cassandra offices. He was making enough money now to pay rent on both spaces, $10,000 a month, and he claims at this time Cassandra was in control of $20 million. He was proud to be settling into the Singer Building, overtaking its top two floors. It was an architectural landmark, and sometimes clusters of historical society visitors stood outside, looking up into its windows.

This was a ritual being enacted in SoHo more and more as the nineties wore on, the rich person in expensive clothes, telling the industrial history, saying, "But look at this space!"

By the spring of 1996, Rich had been promoted to president of Sub Pop, making $100,000 a year. We ate in restaurants we used to only go to for birthdays. As Rich's bank accounts filled up with this absurd enormous salary, Dana invested $200,000 for him in various stocks. He started talking to him about a big private placement. Rich tried to explain it to me: It was going to be like a bond, it was our security for the future, it was the way you park the money and all the money does is sit there and multiply.

Bruce had mostly backed out of Sub Pop and Rich was working for Jonathan, who was manic and expansive—more employees, more desks, redecorate. Go on retreats where you talk and talk until your throat is dry, sleep in hotel beds, and grow tired of the other people.

Because Rich had a certain Zen hippie energy, he was assigned the task of talking to drug-addicted or alcoholic musicians, trying to help them straighten up. It was something he was good at, making people feel somewhat ridiculous for trying to destroy themselves. One Sunday afternoon he drove into the country to pick up a musician from rehab. The guy appeared in the waiting room two hours late, drunk, and when they pulled onto the highway he vomited out the car window. Rich turned the car around and drove him back.

Really, you should live, you have songs you could be writing. Rich told Dylan Carlson about his band Earth: Your records are beautiful, remarkable, no one has ever done anything like this. One junkie told Rich, "You should really be a dealer. No one would ever suspect you."

Rich's favorite band was Sebadoh, fronted by a guy named Lou Barlow. Barlow was a fierce romantic who wrote songs to one unshakeable girlfriend. Once Rich and I were sitting with Lou and his girlfriend in a club when they started to fight. Lou threatened to break his fingers so he could never play guitar again. "Maybe I'll just do it WHAT WOULD you think of that?" he said. It would be like Van Gogh, cutting off his ear.

Sub Pop could afford to fly Rich all over the place so they sent him to Europe when Sebadoh was playing there, to Germany and France. I suppose Rich was flown out there to check on Lou, to make sure he wasn't breaking his fingers. He served as the emissary from the label.

Packing was not something Rich could really fathom, so as

he rushed through airports he would always buy new deodorant and shaving cream, a new toothbrush. These items filled our drawers and cabinets. He traveled with falling-apart suitcases. He had one suitcase he'd had since Olympia, a hard plastic thing on which he had spray-painted *Life* in white and red, like the logo for *Life* magazine. The suitcase didn't have a handle so he strapped it to his back.

When Rich was gone he was truly gone. Many nights I would wander around the empty house looking for the cats, turning up the radio and television to drown out the silence. I was resentful and insomniac. I thought the men acted so important, as if they were building a bomb or something. Couldn't everyone just lower their voices and sit down to dinner? Did they have to make a federal case out of everything?

Sometimes I went with him on business trips. We stayed at the Soho Grand during a music convention. There in the bar was Gwen Stefani, an impossible figurine, a piece from a glass menagerie. There in the staircase was an LSD dealer with bright red hair who said, "You guys should come back to my place." We went to a little town in France and Rich said we would go to restaurants and stare at the water and talk about our love. But a guy who worked for Sub Pop Europe lived in this little town and Rich needed to meet with him; they needed to catch up on their accounting. The accounting went on all night. I stayed in the Sub Pop Europe boy's room. The sheets were gray and the wall behind his bed was stained black from hair dye. I went out into the town but the sky darkened and I was afraid of losing my way, so I went back inside.

When he returned from working on the books I was in tears. "Some trip," I said to Rich, my voice bristling. "Sorry, honey," he said. "Really."

Once he called to tell me a story: He'd been taking trains

through Germany and ended up in a small town, a run-down station, mean-looking characters, and long-destroyed vending machines. He decided to catch up on the Sub Pop bookkeeping by taking over a bathroom stall, turning it into his office. As he sat there with his broken suitcases and his laptop, he heard a group of men enter the stall next to him, and he could smell the burning of heroin. Rich cleared his throat so they would know he was there, packed up his things. As he was leaving, a man burst into the room with a gun and held it to Rich's throat. He said, *"Polizei, polizei."* Rich did what he'd done with so many of the Sub Pop musicians: treated this guy like his violence was ridiculous and kept walking. He gave the cop a baffled, peaceful look that probably saved him.

When he told me this story I said, "Please come home, I have a bad feeling." He said, "You always have a bad feeling."

Artemis and I commiserated about our loneliness. Neither one of us ever knew where He was. The men were nutcases. They were heavy in our lives. We were waiting for the day when the heaviness would subside.

Artemis had declared the apartment her fortress but it was clearly not her fortress. It was instead a shelter for partygoers who wanted to continue to talk and smoke and change the music. Who still wanted something to happen even though it was four in the morning. It was a place where Dana was always packing and unpacking, running around like he was trying to put out a fire—a place where the phone was always ringing but it was rarely a call for her.

Ever since Artemis had known Dana, he'd been going on trips. Now he looked tired, like the plane air was getting under his skin. All the people in his life were about the future but Artemis was an anchor to the past. The very sound of her voice was like a flashback of Boston, the old self. It was Artemis who had been by his side for fourteen years, more than five thousand nights. Ever since they'd met when she was wearing yellow earrings, listening to Echo & the Bunnymen.

They say money burns a hole in the pocket. From what I witnessed it seems money causes people to move around frantically as if to escape the burning pocket, the radical heat the money is generating. In the wake of the Sub Pop deal Dana and Rich seemed overheated and on the edge of burnout; Artemis and I agreed on this. We were widows of the deal. *I can't come home. I can't, I can't.* This was Dana and Rich's nightly refrain.

In the summer of 1996, Dana was part of a celebrity whitewater rafting trip down the Colorado River. It was a Save the World charity event, and it had been organized by Dana and Jay Moloney. The kind of trip where you paid enormous amounts of money to take part in it, to say you were there. Celebrities often took these trips, as did powerful executives. It was a way of going on vacation, doing good, and networking at the same time. Power brokers released momentarily back into the elements.

Along for the ride was Jane Pratt, who'd been the entrepreneur behind girl's magazine *Sassy,* and eventually *Jane.* These were highly successful magazines, in which skinny girls discussed the pressure to be skinny, and how it was OK to be fat. Jane knew the guys from R.E.M. as if they were her brothers. Also along was J. J. Abrams, who had made a universally panned movie (*Regarding Henry*) about a man who gets shot in the head but ends up happier without half his brain. Yet Abrams would go on to invent an addictive and hugely popular TV series, *Lost,* about people isolated on a desert island. He became the type of guy who has his own plot on the studio lot. Also along was Andrew Jarecki, a young man who'd made a fortune on an automated service that would tell you movie times at your local theater, so you wouldn't need the newspaper. Jarecki would ultimately direct a revered documentary called *Capturing the Friedmans,* about a rumored sex predator whose life dissolved around him as the rumors took hold.

And then there were Jay and Dana, the ringleaders. They would take care of everything. You could be quiet, you could almost listen to the stars or trees or whatever.

Often Jay and Dana would refer back to the white-water rafting trip as if they had been at camp together. Memories of the river were presented as anecdotes of purity in the power life that was beginning to engulf them. They would remember the water in their faces and the birds in the trees, enormous birds you would never see in New York.

Even before the trip was over, the gossips knew about it. Agents in New York and Hollywood burned up the phone lines. Did you hear who went away together? "I heard about how all these connections were made," says one New York agent. "It became legendary in certain circles."

One person who knew about the trip early on was *New York Observer* gossip columnist Nikki Finke. Nikki prided herself on knowing what powerful people were doing, even when they were hiding out in the woods. She believed the trip was an event of significance.

At the time of the rafting trip, Nikki was in her forties and she had perfected a caustic, aggressive form of gossip. She was not chatty; she was serious. She believed Ovitz was a homophobic creep and should be exposed and that a lot of these power brokers were so out to lunch, they belonged in an asylum. Dana often talked about Nikki in a similar way, like she should've been committed: "Why would anyone ever believe the words of someone like her, she is insane." Another agent said, "She is a complete maniac and shouldn't be believed."

Magazines who hired her were often threatened with lawsuits. She wrote about the inner workings of Hollywood like someone who was waiting for Hollywood to fall apart. Yet she was a skilled reporter who knew when to use words like "alleged." Very few people had ever seen her. There were rumors about her: she was a debutante, she had once been married to a wealthy banker. She was rich, she was poor. She was beautiful and trim, she was ugly and not trim at all.

I never met Nikki; in the course of writing this book, I tried at least ten times. She was living in Los Angeles. I would say, "I will take you to lunch," and she would say, "Maybe," and then she would describe the infernal helicopters outside her apartment.

Nikki described Dana to me as someone people were leery of on a physical level: "He came right up to your face!" one filmmaker told her. "He talked too close!"

But other people were drawn to this close-talking quality: like each word was an emergency or a promise. I know this close talk is something I liked about him. By the time I met him I had spent too much time among distant people and I needed someone who didn't care about distance, who acted like distance had never existed.

Dana flew the family to New York: Russell and Lisa and Aunt Anita, Donna, Alma. Everyone except Cosmo, who was rarely in the mood to travel. "He took care of everything; what a guy," says Aunt Anita. She is telling me this in the living room of the Medford house. She is wearing gold shoes, sitting next to her daughter Donna (pronounced *Donn-er*). She says: "The Rockettes were putting on a show, acting like bunnies, maybe it was Easter?" She talks about her ten-year-old niece, who danced in the aisle.

"Oh, have you *seen* Russell yet?" Donna asks. "Have you seen how handsome he is?" I tell her yes and agree with her that there is something devastating and crushing about his looks.

Later that night Russell will lean forward almost threateningly and say Dana was a great brother, the best brother anyone could ever have. "I have nothing bad to say about him. I don't think he committed any crimes." Russell talks about how Dana paid for him to go to rehab. He remembers it was a nice place, about a half hour outside of Medford. But he was really far gone by then. He knew all about the routine and didn't much believe in it: the methadone, a thin imitation of heroin, the pee test, and the 101 ways to trick the pee test. He knew all about promises you make to your probation officer when the officer says, "I never want to catch you using this stuff again."

"Certainly, sir, I have learned my lesson!!"

After enough visits to his various probation and parole officers, the workers at the Somerville Justice Center started to recognize Russell's handsome face. As he waited for his name to be called, he chatted up the secretaries and the janitors. A man who worked there had known Cosmo as a teenager on Warren Street. He would tell Russell, *Your dad, your dad was the hardest fighter on the block.*

Whenever Russell was out of jail Alma hovered over him. She told him it was time for a new beginning. He agreed with her at first and came home to dinner. Together they constructed elaborate shrimp cocktails in martini glasses. But drugs were a memory in his blood. Lisa was still everywhere in his thoughts and tattooed across his back. He had suspicions she'd cheated on him while he was in jail, but he couldn't be sure. He didn't want anyone to look at her. It was as if he wished the world was blind and no one but him could see her. He had violent fantasies about all the guys who seemed to be coming after her. Once, he says, he came after her old boyfriend with a beer bottle, ready to crash it over the guy's head.

He says he also came with brass knuckles, with a knife hidden in his boot, with a baseball bat.

Dana says, "Don't believe him."

Lisa and Russell would think about staying clean for a little while, and then they would banish the thought from their minds. He thought of himself as too wild to ever be clean. He started collecting guns again. I asked him why and he replied: "Girls love guns, they always have and they always will."

Russell's regular bar was the Red Hat, in East Cambridge. The bartender was a close friend who had once bailed him out. During the day he worked on Hazlett House, painting and applying flooring so Cosmo could rent the units to MIT students. The students would come sniffing through the apartment at the beginning of a semester, particular little scientists. In the evenings it was the Red Hat and girls. Russell's inner mantra became: Don't get pulled over. Don't start a fight.

But there was that other voice that said, People should not mistake kindness for weakness. He wanted to show the world that he wasn't weak, even though he was thin, with the face of an amazing girl. He wanted people to consider him a man. Fighting was his vice: He'd butt guys in the chest, or turn mean on a dime. Violence flickered in his eyes and muscles.

At one party I attended with Russell he circled around a guy: What did you mean by that, what did you mean? Russell thought the guy had said something about him being gay. The guy was drunk, he couldn't really answer, his face was blurred, and he was trying to flirt with a girl who kept walking away from him. Russell stalked him, cornered him: What did you mean? Pushing his chest out.

Finally I say, "Russell, it is nothing, and what is so bad

about being gay anyway?" This breaks the spell for a moment and he laughs. There is something he was trying to tell me but he can't remember what it is. We go downstairs into a hazardous half-finished basement, holes in the floor, and there is a guy with his eyes at half-mast in full zombie mode. Russell says, "Don't be scared, are you a scared type of chick?" On the ride home, he talks about the guy he'd almost beat up. He talks about the fight like it was something that should've happened, that would've showed me something.

Russell often came home to Alma with scars and bruises, but for her this was not extraordinary. Cosmo's life was a story of black eyes, knives in the arm and neck, the girl with a broken jaw, the guy with his guts sliced out with a banana knife in the middle of the street. "My uncle was a boxer," Cosmo says, "on my mother's side." Uncle Charlie taught Cosmo to fight off street enemies. Cosmo believes Charlie was the reason he won most of the turf wars he engaged in, dragging his bleeding friend Sparky home. Both Cosmo and Russell have a flair for describing fights, and usually in the end, the other guy is down for the count, a poor sap ready for the hospital.

Up there in his loft, Dana seemed as far from the street as you could get. There were never fights at his celebrity parties. There were hugs and promises. There was enough ecstasy to sink a battleship.

Dana took Russell to Madrid. Russell says they visited a sex club, and there were men standing around with rifles.

Dana says, "No, we just went there and had fun, brothers. I don't remember any violent sex club."

Lennee Chassee, a drummer for Waterworld, came out to visit Dana in SoHo one afternoon at the Singer Building. Lennee still lived in Medford, and he had been struggling with depression. Dana invigorated him and brought him back to the surface. Lennee says,

> One of the funnest times I have ever had was visiting him in SoHo. Artemis was out of town and we went out and went all over the place in a cab. I guess we went to about five bars and had dinner in the afternoon. Then Dana said, "We need to go back to the apartment and change because we are going out." With Dana it just all seems to merge into one thing and nothing is intimidating and everything is just like a ride. He always made me feel like when I was with him, this is fun, everybody is great, everybody has good qualities, and it's good to work on those qualities and not be negative. We went to his office. There was a Phish CD there and the next morning he got a call from the drummer of Phish!

Phish had been talking to Dana and investing money with him for about a year. They showed up at parties; they stayed at André's hotels. By 1996 Phish's money was pouring in. They'd struck oil when the Deadheads lost Jerry and needed somewhere else to go. These were concertgoers who would spend $300 without thinking: bootlegs, T-shirts, concert tickets, the new record that sounded reassuringly like the old record. It was harder and harder to find places to park all of the Phish money. They were his richest clients, and soon he controlled $4 million of their money, under the client name Dionysian Productions.

Like André, Phish was often surrounded by pretty girls. Hippie girls who didn't mind crashing on the floor, who never started fights the way the punk girls did. Phish money came from a completely different subculture than Nirvana money. The

Phish millions came from the pockets of fans who were look-ing for a positive experience, something like the sixties, some vague reenactment of free love and up-with-people.

Phish was loyal to Dana and always called him right away when they were touring and landed in New York. They liked his laid-back manner, the way he wouldn't turn down a joint if offered one, like most money guys. Even though they smoked the strongest pot known to man, Dana never lost his cool or acted like he was out of himself. The band and their entourage visited the loft, everyone sitting around, talking about what they might do that night and who they might meet. When peo-ple grew hungry, Dana ordered sushi to be delivered.

I was at one of those Phish parties. The pot people were smoking was the kind that made you think you'd said some-thing when you hadn't said anything. That night, the party kept moving. There were twenty or twenty-five people, but we moved in a flock, clamoring down the stairs and out into the street. We'd been at Dana's a few hours; Dana cornered me by a painting and whispered, "Ninety thousand dollars, ninety thousand, Em." I can't remember who the artist was, but I remember that $90,000, like three years of a teacher's salary, and it looked like elaborate mud. Then one of the Phish wives said to me, "Where did you get that dress?" But she didn't stay around for the answer. Eventually Dana announced the party was moving over to George Condo's house.

At the time of the party, Condo's vision was of one-eyed alien beings he called "antipods"; brightly colored blobs, enor-mous pupils staring out diabolically from canvas after canvas, invaders in a brittle cartoon landscape. Malignant smurfs. He took us on a walk through his studio. He offered drinks as the aliens stared down at us.

Over at Condo's, Dana played the piano: "Don't Let the Sun

Go Down on Me." Despite the night and all the substances consumed, the notes and the elaborate fingering had not left his memory since the time of childhood piano lessons. "Stop, stop," people begged, laughing hysterically at his Elton John impersonation. He played it so perfectly, it sounded like a wind-up piano. Condo drifted into and out of the room, a small, intense man with jet-black hair that needed to be cut, a look of mischief about him.

My girlfriend and I left the party and went upstairs to a lushly furnished room where we took cocaine she had brought with her. I hadn't experimented with it since college, and I started to feel too wild, my heart as fast as a rodent's. Rich wanted to get me out of there. For weeks afterward he would talk about how high I became over at Condo's, as if I was on the verge of some kind of collapse, as if I couldn't handle the stratosphere I was in, the five-hour parties. Was I all right? Was I self-destructing? "Because if you are, that is stupid," he said, "it's a waste."

I said, "Maybe you are talking to yourself, too."

Dana talked Condo up to Phish, and for a while afterward the band projected Condo paintings onto screens at their concerts—the antipods, floating above ten thousand hippies, $950,000 hallucinations. Dana and Condo decided a documentary should be made, a portrait of the artist. *Let's look for investors. Glimcher and his friends.*

Condo knew a director named John McNaughton—a guy who had made a murder movie called *Henry, Portrait of a Serial Killer,* a notoriously violent film. Investors were found and McNaughton agreed; Dana was executive producer. The film, called *Condo Painting,* was shot in Condo's New York studio and at his house in the Hamptons. Sometimes his wife and children enter the frame, but mostly it's Condo, talking about his process. Gloomy music drones in the background. He talks about how he believes TV characters have changed the history of art. He talks about painting as a long journey into nowhere. He says when you are painting you need to go into the "mental equivalent of Australia." The movie opened to bad reviews and went straight to video.

Condo had been mentored by Warhol, and Dana responded to the Warhol connection because more and more in his imagination he equated himself with Warhol. He thought of his apartment as the Factory, but a little less decadent. "Cross-pollination," he called it. Connecting "great people with other great people. I am an artist." He would say, "I am almost like a film director."

In Seattle our multimillionaire friend Thomas Reardon spent more and more time in his basement, playing games on his wide-screen TV, games where he fought his way into the interior and came out victorious, a winner. If it took three days to win, he would play for three days straight. He ordered all his food delivered and he said soon there would be no more books. People would just read books on a screen.

These end-of-the-millennium technological dreams were part of some unsettling sci-fi kid alienation and reductiveness, the idea of things disappearing instantly, like being beamed out of the starship *Enterprise*. Books would disappear. Trips to the grocery store would disappear: You could log on to www.homegrocer.com and check off your list. Trips to the video store would disappear: You could log on to www.mylackey.com, and they brought videos and food within thirty minutes. Piles of bills would disappear because you could pay them online. Trips to the record store would disappear because music could be downloaded straight off the Internet.

The boys were designing a world that would disappear but they didn't know what would appear in its place.

Down my street, I'd hear the rumble of the Home Grocer trucks. I'd wonder if this was the sound of the future: trucks rattling the windows, and no one going on errands anymore. I thought about my mother putting on lipstick to go to the grocery store, and I wondered if such social gestures were part of the past.

Bruce Pavitt finished his house on Orcas Island, a porch exploding off the side, metal, Gehry-inspired. He wanted to be in architecture magazines. Down below there was a sweat lodge, where he could take mushrooms uninterrupted by the world. Sometimes he would come into Seattle and go to the rock shows. Along with his foot-long beard, he wore a Fidel Castro hat. When he walked by people said, "There is that Bruce guy, he is rich."

By the fall of 1996, Kurt Cobain's imitators were in full bloom—boys who'd trained their voices to sound exactly like him, pampered boys with washboard stomachs and no demons. On the radio they filled in the empty space where Kurt's voice had once been. I remember boarding the elevator at the Sub Pop offices after a rooftop party. Once again, just as when Nirvana had first hit there were these nervous radio people hovering, they seemed like they were on amphetamines, but this time they were saying: *I don't hear any hits on that record.*

Huge record deals were made with bands that would never recoup, with bands that had started off as jokes. Even the Dwarves, who regularly pounded audience members in the head with mike stands—even they flirted with the major labels for a short time.

Dana came out to Seattle and visited our house. It was in a nice, mixed-race, middle-class neighborhood. People had lived on our street for many years, there were no renters, there was a Neighborhood Watch. Dana said, "Oh my God, you even have a white picket fence!" He screamed this down the street. The next day Rich was planting a tree in the yard and Dana crowed, "This is insanely suburban!" In the evening Rich and Dana drank on the deck and talked about schemes.

An Internet service where people could download movies.
A record label that would sign the great Seattle bands Sub
    Pop missed.
A television station with only really cool shows on it.

Dana told Rich that among André, Matador, Sup Pop, Ovitz, Jay, among all these powerful people he was in control of $150 million, at least.

No one could blame the men when they started to believe all their best possible futures would come true. They had been launched into the upper classes so quickly, it was as if they'd lost gravity. While our neighbors worked off thirty-year mortgages, we owned our house outright. It didn't feel like we would ever get back to zero again.

So there was this euphoria. You could feel it in the air at the parties. It was the drugs, but it was also history doing this to people, making them act this way.

In the winter of 1996, Artemis told Dana, "You take up all the oxygen in the room." He'd planned a romantic trip for them for New Year's Eve. He knew she was tired of the noise, so he'd bought first-class tickets to the Caribbean. He thought they could just lie on the beach and reconnect with each other and everything would be all right. He was certain she wouldn't be able to turn it down. But she did.

She said it again, "You take up all the oxygen in the room." She said she wanted to go work on her documentaries, be alone and think. After all these years of him, and now she was looking for the exit. He thought she seemed crazy and imbalanced. To him there was so much oxygen here, it felt like a person could never run out of breath. He thought she was jealous of his increasingly powerful friends. "God bless her, Artemis was her own worst enemy. She was making a film but she was not like people who had opened a movie at number one."

He called his cousin Gale Rapallo in Los Angeles. He was crying, saying, She doesn't want to be with me anymore. He explained to Gale that since Artemis had bailed out she could have a free trip to a tiny exclusive resort, a place that had been written up in the *New York Times* travel section.

"Get a plane from LAX, and meet me at eleven at JFK Airport in the Admiral's Club. We'll go from there."

Gale packed her bags, leaving behind her Los Angeles apartment and her job in the marketing department of Pepsi-Cola. She could call in sick, she figured. She could lose her job, but at least she would be with Dana.

They boarded in first class. Gale remembers how at the last moment a passenger came on board. "It was Mick Jagger!" Down the aisle he came, taking a seat next to Gale, trading the aisle for the window so he could sleep, "Thanks, miss," he said. Dana was across the aisle, and Gale says, "I switched seats with Dana so if he woke up he could talk to him." She realized Dana needed to meet Mick Jagger more than she did. "When Mick woke up he and Dana talked for the rest of the flight. He actually invited us to a party on his island!"

Dana and Gale roamed around the island and drank and talked. Dana was in a panic without Artemis. They befriended some gay men with powerful television jobs. The story of power kept washing up with the sea. New Year's Eve was at the end of the week: Would they be able to get across the water to Mick's party? The theme was twenties and they didn't have anything twenties to wear. They kept calling around, trying to find a private helicopter, a boat, something to get them over to that island, something twenties. But no one called back, the helicopters were off duty, there was no way to get across the water. "I almost felt like we should swim," says Gale. But they stayed put, and tried to act like it was all for the best. "It was terrible and I felt like I was missing something," says Gale.

Dana tried to cheer her up. He said at least they had met Mick, and they had really made a connection. It was a story they would be able to tell over and over to the family in Medford. Even when the celebrities were long gone, stories about them could always transfix the audience at the Medford dinner table.

After Artemis left, I felt protective around Dana—like he was a wounded bird. Dana claimed Artemis had turned on him and that he hadn't seen it coming. I was at his apartment when she came over to pick something up after the breakup. I was polite but distant, quietly bitchy. I'd taken sides. My friend and I put our arms around Dana. We were sitting on his modern sectional facing out to the view. We said: It is going to be all right, let's take a Vicodin, let's go to Coney Island. His apartment filled up with the noise of those birds: two cockatoos, Angel and Caesar, the latter he bought "for Leo." "This is Leo's bird," he would say, introducing the creature, its black feet curling around his finger.

Without Artemis, Dana was ungrounded. In the realm of reinvention, his last line to history was cut. No one around him had known him very long. Leo was his constant companion, and he stayed in his apartment when he was in New York giving interviews or shooting movies. He had only known Dana for eighteen months. They were living in a kind of limbo before *Titanic* hit.

In this limbo, Dana and Leo had parties. They had a Halloween party where everyone dressed up like KISS characters. Dana made a home movie of it, and there is character actor Lukas Haas playing "Hey, Jude" on the piano, while Dana and his friends dance around in their masks. Watching the film, I cannot tell which one is Leo, which one is Dana or Tobey Maguire. They are in hysterics. They have the whole night in front of them. The gossip columnists have started calling them "the pussy posse." Girls are always part of the night's plan.

Victoria Leacock went on a date with Dana shortly after Artemis left him. She was the daughter of famous documentary filmmaker Richard Leacock, who'd perfected the art of shooting with a handheld camera. Even when she was a little girl, artists bowed down to her because of her royal lineage. As an awkward teen, she was befriended by Andy Warhol. He invited her to hang out at the Factory after school instead of going home to her sick mother to watch TV.

Dana met Victoria when she came into his office to invest the proceeds of *Rent,* a musical she had coproduced which was starting to make money. She'd first taken her money to Merrill Lynch, but the office culture bothered her: She was too much of a bohemian, the fluorescent lights offended her eyes. "It was so strange all these guys in suits. I couldn't understand what they were talking about. I have never been able to understand money people. It is like I have a bias against them. Then I went to meet Dana, made an appointment. I went in, the beautiful space, in the Singer Building, into that office and there were these good-looking businesspeople, looked like you would like to have dinner with them, they offered a good cappuccino, there was a Calder on his desk."

Victoria was in her late thirties; she had worked as a party promoter and knew all the best drag queens. In the eighties she had seen many men and a few women die of AIDS, so her eyes had a certain hospital sadness. She wanted to find a husband and have children. She'd dated lawyers and directors. Dana was one date among a handful of these New York power types she kept meeting, but there was something she liked about him.

She tells me: "Nothing happened on our date, we fell asleep. But he told everyone I had sex with him."

He says, "That was a strange date."

In the office, people knew Dana had been on a date; they talked about it across the bright room. By early 1997, Dana had a half dozen employees and some hip interns: researchers and analysts recommending stocks, researching ways to lower taxes when a million dollars came in for a movie role (invest in a fledgling company—a hotel, a record label; once the money is invested, taxes do not need to be paid on it). There was a parade of girls who returned calls and said, *Dana just left the country but he will be calling in for messages anytime now. Would you like to leave a message?*

All these office workers were waiting to see what would happen to Dana now that Artemis had disappeared. For anyone who knew him, the idea of Artemis being gone was like a seismic shift. I was worried over things like:

Who will rent the car?
Who will answer the phone?
Who will make sure he is all right?

Even though nothing happened on their date, Victoria continued to invest with him. He kept returning with better and better news about what was happening to her money. Her money multiplied even as she slept.

Dana proposed to Rich that he invest $100,000 in the Pickens fund. He explained to Rich that he would be getting in on the ground floor, that the money would slowly accrue interest and could not be lost. He told Rich the same thing he told Kanarick: It was about privatizing water and electricity so people could choose their utilities. Rich said, "It is for our future. When we have kids." It was called a "corporate bond," which sounded safe. I remember we were standing in his basement workshop where he often sat in the clutter, conjuring up inventions: a globe that could shift borders in real time, an art project up and down the interstate. A regional manifesto. Lists covered his desk. It seemed to me sometimes he dreamed too hard, like his dreams were doing him in. But he said, "We are safe, this is safe, everything is going great." The next day he told Dana, "Let's do it." And there the money went, traveling down the wires into the "P Cap Fund." One assumed the wires could be trusted and the money was real.

PART
FIVE

PART
FIVE

1997–1998

IN 1997, DANA STARTED APPEARING ON THE CABLE FINAN-
cial shows. He was one foot soldier in an army of breezy
pundits who could be called on by *Squawk Box* or CNN
Financial Network or the Bloomberg Channel to talk about
what was happening with the markets. When the call came in,
he would take a cab to the studio and head for makeup.
Attendants moussed his hair and straightened his collar.
Beneath the show lights a host's skin often took on the color
of an old peach.

On an episode of *Squawk Box*, he argued with an attractive
young woman from Merrill Lynch. She was wearing harsh
grape lipstick. The hosts played them off each other, as if this
was an audition for a date.

Dana's recommendations were the same as they'd always
been: blue-chip stocks, established companies. Yet he made
grand pronouncements like: The market should hit 10,000 by
2000, and it will only go up from there. He said, "Even if there

is a correction, the market will always go up eventually."
Another argument: "Corrections are a good sign. All you need
to do is ride them out."

The woman in the grape lipstick said she was not sure that
was true. Maybe people should be more careful, and think
about investing in bonds.

When Dana called Medford with news of an impending television appearance, Alma alerted friends and relatives: turn on
the TV, set your VCR. After his segment was over, the phone
started ringing: the Maffos proclaiming: He looked so good.
Aunt Anita calling from Stoneham: I can't believe that is our
Dana!

Cosmo taped every episode. He labeled them and stacked
them in the television room. When, hours or years later, Cosmo
and Alma turned on a tape and sat in front of Dana's image,
they memorized his answers and repeated them to each other.

Investments were still handled through Brown & Co., in
Boston, even though Cassandra had decamped to New York.
Brown was the "custodian" of Cassandra money. Brown was
the location of the vault, the safe-deposit box, the FDIC-insured
bonds. Again and again Dana explained to his clients: I have
worked with Brown ever since Cassandra's early days. They are
almost like friends.

Sometimes I get this picture in my head when I think about
Dana and the bank where he was supposed to be putting the
money. I think there must've been so much money circulating,
it started to fall out of the vault. Or maybe someone forgot to
lock the vault. Someone forgot to tell us that even when the bank
says they have your money, it might be flying out the vault door.

Rich had wired Dana $100,000 for the Pickens fund in February 1997, but he had yet to receive a statement by the end of March, and he was getting nervous. According to the accounting books (the ones he'd bought in thrift stores), this lack of a statement was a bright red flag. He kept calling Dana saying, "Where did that money go and when can I get it out?"

Once I was in the kitchen while Rich was making one of these calls, hoping to turn the faucet of his money back on, since his money was running out. His voice became low and loud. He was almost yelling, but not quite.

When, a few weeks later, Rich finally received a financial statement from the Pickens deal, it came in elaborate packaging: glossy spreadsheets wrapped up in a box with a metal manhole cover on top. The manhole cover was supposed to say: Congratulations into your investment in utilities. But Rich was offended by it. "It must've weighed twenty pounds and it was FedExed," he says. "I felt disgusted. What a stupid waste of money. I just threw the thing away." He couldn't get Dana on the phone to ask him about the money, or complain about the ridiculous package.

Although he kept telling me: *It's okay, it was a good investment,* I could tell his heart wasn't in it. He walked around in a fugue state, forgetting to pull his cash card out of the cash machine, forgetting to close the front door.

Rich had invested in the P Cap Fund, but in his statements the name changed at some point to Great Southern Water. "Is this the same thing, this fund, this Great Southern Water? Is that where my $100,000 is now?" Rich asked Dana. *Oh sure.* But Rich had learned enough from the accounting books to know that when the name of your investment changes, and no one told you about it, this is not a good sign.

Intermittent waves of anxiety hit the market. Clients would call Cassandra, asking if their money was OK, if it was still there. Dana reassured them with the "10,000 by 2000" speech: You might've lost a little today, but it is low tide, and the high tide is coming along with the millennium. Keep your money in play. Don't get scared of the market, because the market is ultimately a win-win situation.

People were losing money with Cassandra and Dana wasn't telling them. He was a television soothsayer, but he wasn't telling the whole truth.

The list of celebrity names grew in his Rolodex. The Rolodex was a novel unto itself. Dana offered it to me when he was released from prison. We looked through it and he said, "Can you believe it?"

Ben Affleck, home fax
Macauley Culkin's manager
Jellybean Benitez (one of Madonna's early producers)
Good Morning, America
Naomi Campbell (model)
Helmut Lang (fashion designer)
John Hall (Hall and Oates, an eighties band)
Morgan Freeman, character actor
Lizzie Grubman (a publicist who would become
    momentarily famous after she ran over a group of people
    outside a nightclub)
Fred Schneider, B-52's
Michael Stipe (R.E.M.)
Uma Thurman, up and coming actress

By 1997, the "Rolodex" was actually a constantly updated computer file. Some were names of clients, some were people

Dana was determined to meet and bring into his web. The list was as neverending as the story of Scheherazade. To keep it expanding, he was industrious, subtle, like a good reporter. He could track down cell numbers, pager numbers, real, true home addresses—not the P.O. box. The number that would open the gate at the bottom of the endless driveway. Dana carried printouts of the Rolodex with him. He continually added notes, details: VERY GOOD FRIENDS WITH, or REPRESENTS SLY AND ROBERT D., or RELATED TO JOHN MALKOVICH.

Other entries included:

American Express Platinum Travel Services
Angel (cockatoo) Tag #
Bliss Spa
Blue Ribbon Sushi
Canibus

Living upstairs from the Singer Building offices, the difference between work and the party became even more amorphous. A typical afternoon in the Cassandra offices: It is dusk and some movie star has come to visit. Perhaps Leo or Cameron, the eternal blonde exclamation mark. Or maybe Lukas Haas, who had played a cute Amish boy overpowered by urban life. Or Tobey Maguire, who would later become a laconic Spiderman.

The movie stars were usually restless. They knew Dana could make things happen, he could pull a party together out of the uneventful afternoon. What is happening, is anything happening? Who is in town tonight? These were the movie stars' persistent questions and Dana learned how to answer them.

He determined where the party should begin. If there was no logical place to begin, it began at his loft. As the evening took shape, anticipation about the party replaced any shapeless, anxious, uncertain feelings. The party gave the partygoers an end to the story of the day.

In March 1997, Dana went out to Los Angeles to visit Jay Moloney in a house in the hills above the Chateau Marmont. They looked out over the city. It was a kingdom they'd talked about conquering together but Jay was losing his conviction. Cocaine was the center of his life now, it was the thing he would trade himself for, that high that took you so far up you couldn't see the future down below. Dana gave him pep talks, and Jay enthused about getting better. He said he was going to check into a rehab in Oregon and "rock the place."

While in Los Angeles Dana paid visits to Mike Ovitz. Ovitz was as worried about Jay as Dana was. For Ovitz, Jay was an estranged son. By 1997, Ovitz was a man with many enemies. After being hired by his friend Michael Eisner at Disney, they had quickly gone to war. Ovitz was fired after eighteen months, and he emerged from the bloodbath with a $20 million severance. Blacklisted, living in a house the size of a small country. In the gossip columns, he was a "fallen titan," or a "fallen king."

In the aftermath of the Disney debacle Ovitz trusted few people, but he trusted Dana. Dana was telling him, You are a genius, you have an amazing future, even as *The Hollywood Reporter* was narrating his doom.

With Ovitz, as with everyone, Dana was casual—sketching out business plans on legal pads or envelopes, his wild handwriting filling up the space. Later he would formalize these discussions in spreadsheets and investor proposals.

"What about a whole new agency?" Dana asked Ovitz.

They started to talk about it. Ovitz started calling Dana his "life adviser."

By 1997, Cassandra controlled around $200 million, according to Dana. Starlets left rambling messages on his answering machine, *Where are you, where are you?* The celebrities had arrived in Dana's life like a flock of migrating birds.

When Dana called Rich and me, he talked about how he had conquered, he had won. He said things were going so well it was time to start thinking about the politicians. He wanted to meet someone who knew President Clinton. To charm the preppie Washington crowd.

In the summer of 1997, Dana met a man named Jeffrey Sachs. They were both in the Hamptons, staying with movie people. Jeffrey had known the Cuomos since he was a kid. He had not settled into a career at the time he met Dana. He'd dabbled in financial management. But through the Cuomos his connections proliferated. He was like a connection machine. He knew a guy who controlled the purse strings of the biggest union in the country—Dennis Rivera, head of the hospital workers' union. Sachs said maybe if he and Dana worked together, he could convince Rivera to invest some of those union dues with Cassandra. He could get him in with the Cuomos.

Dana offered Sachs space in the Cassandra office to pursue the hospital workers' union deal. The other employees weren't quite sure what this preppy guy was doing at Cassandra, a creature of Top-Siders. He took over an empty desk. The desks were out in the open, sometimes separated by screens, but everyone could hear everyone. At the other desks: Paul Sevigny, a former broker in his midtwenties, brother of actress Chloë Sevigny. Chloë was a morose-looking, beautiful girl who'd become famous after a date rape scene in a movie called *Kids*. Paul processed transactions, conducted research, and presented it to Dana. At night he lived the life of a starlet's brother: rum drinks and *Where is she? Where is she?* He started a DJ business on the side, and was known for playing bands as old as the Rolling Stones.

Another employee at this time was Mark Pollard, a guy in his midtwenties who'd been trained in accounting and could translate Dana's projected numbers into spreadsheets. *If things go as planned, this number will increase to this number.* Pollard had known Dana since his first New York incursion: Pollard used to answer phones for Glimcher. He remembered the way Dana relentlessly called the Glimchers and their gallery. At that time, Pollard thought to himself, oh this hustler again. But soon all the people at Pace were charmed by Dana.

By 1997, Pollard was happy to have a gig at Cassandra, sitting in the cool offices with all these movie stars dropping by. They smelled of smoke and perfume and clothes that were being worn for the first time. Nevertheless he was a suspicious guy, and he wondered how and when Dana was going to step on him. He says the closer he came to Dana, the more he felt there was something missing, something shady going on: "He was such a climber," Pollard says.

Through Jeffrey Sachs, Dana arranged to attend a democratic fundraiser thrown by Bill and Hillary Clinton. Afterward, if you're lucky, you can have your picture taken with the First Couple. Dana lucked out. In his portrait, Dana stands between Bill and Hillary, looking like he is about to crack up. To me the look on his face says: Isn't this the greatest prank in the world? Rowdy. He doesn't look stiff or boring, rather he looks like the person you hope will arrive soon, before the party dies. The American flag droops on the wall behind him.

Dana took the portrait home to Medford. Cosmo and Alma had it framed. And despite the fact that Cosmo believed Clinton was an idiot and his wife was a bitch, he displayed the photo in the cabinet alongside all the other photographs of Dana's rise.

On October 2, 1997, Russell had been out of prison for two years. Upon his release, he returned to heroin and his heroin social network. This particular night he was doing his normal addict things: meeting up with drug buddies, trying to pull together money, trying to pull together a ride to make a buy.

So it was that he ended up in an uninsured car that didn't belong to him. The story is hazy. "I knew the guy who owned it he didn't want it anymore. I just hadn't transferred the title yet. I was in the process of transferring the title over. But I didn't have any insurance and I got into a fender bender and I got stuck in the mud. So instead of waiting around for the cops I just drove the car out into a field and set it on fire."

I ask him what he means by these terms "fender bender" and "stuck in the mud." And if he was stuck in the mud, how did it get out into a field? But he doesn't explain. He changes the course of the story and I try to follow his logic, but it keeps breaking apart on him.

"I just threw a bunch of matches into the window. But the car didn't explode because I left the windows rolled up. There was no oxygen for the fire. It just burned a hole in the front seat."

Police arrived at the scene of the almost-burning car and arrested Russell. Because of his past record, he was given a three- to five-year sentence in state prison. The crime was "burning of a motor vehicle" and it existed on his rap sheet alongside "possession of heroin and driving with a suspended license."

Russell was committed to MCI-Concord, a medium-security facility on the outskirts of Concord, Massachusetts. To find yourself in the custody of the state amounted to a kind of criminal graduation: You were no longer in county jail. You were a real threat. After state came federal prison, where the famous criminals lived. The ones people made movies about.

Russell heard that Dana was appearing on television, but he rarely watched television in the common room so he never saw him. He didn't want the other prisoners to know about his brother. Too much static. Russell knew not to call Dana at his office or at home because it would be a call from prison and that would reflect badly on Dana. He knew on some level he was a disgrace, or a scandal waiting to happen, and he didn't want to tarnish Dana's shining reputation.

Dana's employees didn't know about his criminal brother. They had heard rumors, but that was all. If it came up at all, Dana downplayed it. "He's doing much better." Being in charge of money, you had to have a clean slate. You had to seem like you came from good stock. Concord Prison was not a name Dana needed to mention in his story, if he could help it.

Alma came to visit Russell in prison, as she always did, but Concord was a long drive and Cosmo's hip couldn't take it, so he usually didn't come. If she cried, Russell said what he always said:

You and Dad have to understand, this is how it is, this is the real world.

She said, Could I have done anything differently?

But what is done is done. This is it. This is your son, Ma.

Sometimes Russell felt like his was the only voice of reality his family had ever known.

* * *

Jay Moloney's drug addict stories started to get the best of him; by fall 1997, the stories could no longer be reconciled with any earthly reality. They were more like a cluster of false alibis and hallucinations. Friends rescued him tied to a bed in a Sunset Boulevard motel; he said he had been carjacked. But why did the carjackers leave the car? the friends asked. Clearly he'd been robbed by drug dealers. Details were starting to fall apart on him. He returned calls to clients at four in the morning. He seemed to know it was four o'clock, he just didn't know which four o'clock it was.

He headed for a posh rehab in Minnesota, a place called Hazelden, where celebrities had been cured. Dana visited him there. According to *Vanity Fair* magazine, "All of his friends had been warned . . . ("No matter what don't send him money"), but Moloney found one who indulged his tale of a murderous drug dealer who was going to kill him if he didn't settle a $6,000 debt. The "friend" flew to Minnesota and handed him $6,000, and Moloney scored the minute he walked out of Hazelden."

This "friend" was Dana. The story of the $6,000 given to the vulnerable drug addict was the first story that really stuck to Dana. Like a stain on his character. A wave of suspicion swelled up around him. Important people blamed him for Jay's subsequent bender, which took him further into the desert than he'd ever been before. People said about Dana: Maybe he is a predator of some kind. Andrew Jarecki—the man who'd made a fortune on Movie Phone and attended the legendary rafting trip—started to believe Dana had seeds of evil in him, that he was not the good person everyone believed him to be.

Dana apologized, and told whoever would listen: "That money belonged to Jay. He seemed really desperate. I couldn't very well as a financial manager keep the money away from him since it belonged to him."

Jarecki was determined to rescue Jay from coke dealers, Dana, and his own dark side. He flew him out to his family's private island. In *Vanity Fair* they described the trip. "Moloney, being Moloney, was wildly popular with the staff. . . . When he wasn't working he wrote in his journal, kayaked, and healed. He read *Darkness Visible,* William Styron's account of his own depression."

In Dana's world, nature kept presenting itself as the antidote that would give you perspective and cure you: the whitewater rafting trip, the sweat lodge. At least one day in the sun. Nevertheless it was harder to say what, exactly, nature was supposed to cure. The feeling of power, of unending money? The noise of urban life? Or the feeling that you had lost control?

In December 1997, *Titanic* was released. "A woman's heart is a deep ocean of secrets," the poster read. The Leo-mania was unprecedented and by the end of its first week in release, *Titanic* had broken all previous box office records. It became for a moment a kind of cinematic religion. Leo was living in Dana's apartment a couple of weeks after *Titanic* hit. He walked outside, headed for the subway tunnel. Girls followed him down inside, crying, they wanted to touch him so badly. From then on, Leo avoided subways.

I remember seeing *Titanic* that holiday season among the hordes, and I remember being part of the American faith in it. I cried, sitting there as the ship upended and people dropped like flies into the freezing water to the music of the doomed string quartet. I cried as the old couple held each other in bed while the sea engulfed them. I cried so hard you would've thought those old people were my grandparents or something.

*   *   *

In *Titanic*'s wake, Dana had so many people calling him, he started to take his phone off the hook. One of the few people he wanted to talk to was Jesse Dylan, Bob's eldest son, a creature of rock royalty but also someone Dana trusted and wanted to talk to for hours at a time. Jesse was an unassuming man with a quietly urgent manner. He hated sleazeballs and parasites, and he thought Dana was a remarkable guy, an innocent guy in a sea of sharks. Often they talked two or three times a day, or if they were in the same city they had lunch and dinner together. They had plans. Finance a production company. A movie studio where the artists have more control of the content. A big company without the corporate BS, where you are not working for anyone but yourself.

On December 26, 1997, Jesse and Dana were sitting around the loft, wondering what they were going to do. Jesse mentioned that his father was performing in Bologna with the pope. Dana said, "We have to go! Let's fly over on the Concorde!"

It was no small thing for Jesse to bring people to meet his father but he trusted Dana, and he wanted to be near him. Jesse had directed music videos and television commercials, he had started his own production company, Straw Dogs Entertainment. Dana was gambling on Jesse. In their talks he alluded to the fact that he was going to make Jesse extremely successful. Maybe so successful no one would care who his father was anymore.

If anyone asked Dana about Jesse, Dana made sure to tell them that Jesse was his own man—he'd made his own money apart from his father. "He is a really successful producer in his own right," he'd say. Nevertheless the myth of the rock-and-roll god attached itself to Jesse; he couldn't escape his royal upbringing.

They boarded the Concorde and they were in Italy before they'd even closed their eyes. They had broken through the sound barrier. When they arrived at the stadium in Bologna they were ushered backstage to the VIP area. Dana remembers it was hectic and crowded, the pope stood off in a corner of the room, surrounded by his minions. Yet at one point Dana remembers meeting eyes with the pope. "We looked at each other for quite a while," he says. "I felt like we had communicated."

Outside, the stadium filled with four hundred thousand mostly young people. The event was a gathering of Catholic youth. Bob was to sing three songs: "Knockin' on Heaven's Door," "A Hard Rain's A-Gonna Fall," and "Forever Young."

According to a Dylan fan site called http://expectingrain .com, "The pope had an extra stage on the far right, he was sitting on his throne surrounded by white clad youth and cardinals in black. He looked extremely tired and grumpy." The pope said, according to the fan's translation, "You asked me: how many roads must a man walk down before you can call him a man. I answer you. Just ONE. One only. It is the road of man. And this is Jesus Christ, who said I am the road."

Later Dana called our house in Seattle and I picked up the phone.

"I met the pope," he said, "You have got to understand, I met the pope!" I laughed and I told him "Oh, Dana, that is so great." Something about Dana made me want to congratulate him; I rooted for him—go, go, go. I was like some kind of cheerleader. It was a protectiveness other women felt toward him, too, especially after Artemis left. Victoria Leacock remembers it. "I wanted to do nice things for him like make him cupcakes," she says.

Both of us now wonder if we were misled by an ingrained feminine response, a sentimental reflex.

* * *

If, from the beginning, Dana's business plan for Cassandra was built around "politically conscious investing" (for example, you will not invest in companies that might destroy the rain forests), over time the guarantee of goodwill took on a certain fuzziness— just as it was hard to remember what the ribbons meant when the celebrities wore them on their lapels at the Oscars. Did it mean AIDS or breast cancer? Did it mean childhood diabetes?

It was in the spirit of charity and thinking-of-the-less-fortunate that Dana organized a trip to Cuba in early 1998. Through the left-wing contacts of the Cuomos, Dana was given permission to put together a "cultural exchange" (one of the only ways large groups of Americans could enter Cuba legally, either by ship or plane). The trip generated a lot of interest: Jon Poneman and Jesse Dylan, DiCaprio and Alanis all signed on. Cuba! Who goes to Cuba! NOBODY. Chris Cuomo agreed, as did Jeffrey Sachs.

Dana shows me a video of his arrival in Cuba, coming by yacht from Miami. Alanis is doing yoga on the deck. Leo is there. Somebody off-camera is steering the thing toward the harbors of Havana. The men say: I cannot believe we are here. CUBA.

The "cultural exchange" was based on a simple idea: If you were rich and powerful, you should go to the poor corners of the world to learn from them. Then you will return to your rar-efied lives with a deeper sense of the world. You will return to the yacht changed.

"Welcome to my country," said a greeter as they entered the Havana airport. Dana kept his camera running as the group was escorted into a holding room and given the introductory speech by a representative of the Cuban government. The room was crowded and hot, people fanned themselves with newspapers. They presented visas and passports. Then it was time for Dana to speak: "We are so happy to be here. We have artists, actors, painters, people from the artistic world and the professional world. We are full of curiosity and grateful for your hospitality!" Everyone promised they would not bring back cigars, and then they laughed.

They had come to Cuba to escape capitalism just as they went out into nature to escape the noise of urban life. Yet the whole world was America, the whole world was in thrall to America's stars. Leonardo was mobbed from the moment they entered the country, and it was difficult to see through the mobs to what the *real* people were doing. According to more than one member of the Cuba trip, the mobs searching for Leo became the central cultural experience. Just like so many American girls, Cuban girls were determined to meet their hero. They shouted his name over and over. They cried as they shouted it.

The group stayed in a hotel where parrots flew through the lobby. One morning a tour guide told the group: "The idea we have is to show you our country, our experiences. They think this is a country of terrorists! We are not a danger to the U.S. We don't want people to change us. We hope to talk about possible changes of the future."

The second-most-famous person on this trip after Leo was Alanis. Her celebrity was attached to a record she'd made called *Jagged Little Pill*, in which she vents a particularly female bitterness—screeds about being dumped and used. By the time of the Cuba trip she was a multimillionaire and one of Dana's biggest investors. She often called Dana sweetie.

For a year and a half since *Jagged Little Pill*, Alanis hadn't been singing. What happened? asked the waiting-for-failure headlines. She told reporters the success had been too much for her. Yet Cuba was her healing journey. There, in that exotic locale, she found her voice again. She sat down at a piano and started singing in an old school house. She wrote about it in her online diary: "I was playing a very modular, stream of consciousness song. When I finished I looked up and there were other people in the room. I was so deeply inspired. I knew it was time to write again."

Dana showed me a film of Alanis's revelatory afternoon. He sets up the viewing telling me how this is the *very moment* when she comes out of her sophomore slump. As it turns out the slump works itself out in front of a group of impoverished Cuban children. The room is full of light, tropic sun, and dust. She is singing raggedly, in fragments. Both she and the piano are out of tune. The kids regard this dissonant spectacle with uncomfortable, fidgeting attention. They are all around seven or eight. Almost nothing or nothing on their feet. I see no girls in the frames.

The kids are not laughing but they are amped. They are having an afternoon to end all afternoons. It is not every day in Cuba or America or anywhere that a million-record-selling pop star just sits down at your school piano.

Ahh ahhhhhh ahhhhh, Alanis sings at the schoolhouse piano. It is loud and she is swishing her hair around.

Alanis finding herself is one of the heroic stories brought back from the Cuban cultural exchange. It is one of the stories Dana told repeatedly: Alanis found her voice again, singing in this old school!

I asked Dana if he thought this might be a little narcissistic: Alanis going searching for herself in another country, using the country as a resting place in which to recover and find her voice. Using the country as a backdrop for your own internal drama, a drama of the privileged: Should I sing or not? He was adamant that he didn't know what I was talking about. Not at all, that's not how it was, he said. It was fantastic. It was important.

By early 1998, we didn't hear much from Bruce Pavitt anymore; it seemed he had completely retreated from the city and disappeared into his beard. Rich had befriended a Sub Pop band called the Blue Rags, who played a beautiful and confused combination of punk and ragtime. They called Rich their record-company guy. They wrote lyrics like: "I feel just like a blind man, I see with nothing but my mind/I was looking for grace/hard times is all I find." They were from Asheville, North Carolina, and at the time I met them, they'd just taken their first plane ride, arriving at the Seattle airport drunk and barely able to carry their guitar cases.

Nevertheless, they had this eminent Southern politeness, even drunk. We brought them back to the house. "Miss," the stand-up bass player asked, "would you have a piece of tape? My shoe's a-talkin'." I looked down and the sole was coming off his wing tips. We taped it together as he thanked me, and complimented me on this big house, bigger than any he had seen in a long, long time.

Later, I woke at 5 A.M. to find them out on the deck, playing their instruments and waking up the neighborhood. "You guys, you guys, you have to come in," I told them, feeling suburban and bossy and sorry for everything.

Dana started to say people were out to get him, they were jealous of him; people wanted his business, his Rolodex, his accent, his hair. As far as he was concerned they wanted to *be* him. He still practiced his winning brand of monochromatic kindness, but paranoia had taken root and it woke him up at night. You could see it if you looked into his eyes for any amount of time.

"Are you taking a picture?" he would say. "You need to ask me if you want to take my picture."

The paparazzi had become more and more aggressive as a new kind of gossip overtook American media, a far more British style of gossip, in which fans wanted to know everything— where the stars were at all times. They wanted to catch them unawares with their mouths full of food. One night the rapper Q-Tip came to blows with a photographer outside Dana's apartment. He was defending Leonardo. There were rumors a gun was drawn. The more famous everyone became, the more they adopted this refrain as they walked out onto the street: "Stay away, stay away." The hand pushing against the lens of the camera, the hostility of the person being caught on film, like Russell's hostility in those home movies where he flipped off Cosmo as he tried to capture the scene.

During this paranoid time, Dana met Steve Stanulis, a Staten Island, New York, narcotics cop. Steve was standing next to him at Moomba bar in the East Village. Dana was there with Leo: Moomba was the kind of place where it was tacky to swarm celebrities, where the celebrities had a fifty-fifty chance of being left alone.

Dana was ordering drinks. Steve and him started to look at each other. Steve was a muscular, intimidating man with blue eyes and carefully arranged hair. He looked like people from Medford or Somerville; like one of Russell's friends. Strong and restless, the kind of guy who could unload a truckload of bricks in fifteen minutes. They started talking. Steve said, "What do you do?" Dana told him he worked for celebrities, that he was with some celebrities tonight.

Steve told Dana how he was a narcotics officer, "but at night I work security," he said.

Dana said, "We need security. Here is my card. We might need you."

Dana hired Steve to guard the parties in his loft. Paparazzi hovered outside Dana's door and tried to make it inside. They disguised themselves as hipsters and followed the crowd as they were buzzed inside. It was Steve's job to hunt these intruders down, flash his badge at them, say, "Are you supposed to be here?" Steve carried a gun and a shield. He tells me: "Once there was a party and a couple of people from Page Six were harassing Leo a little bit and I showed them my shield and was like, 'Hey, don't bother him,' and it worked pretty well. The shield is pretty effective."

Dana told Steve, "I feel like I can be myself with you, like you don't want anything from me."

"He didn't have to put on airs with me," says Steve. They went out to normal restaurants together: steak houses of endless bread and butter, places from which a person emerged reeling and bloated. "One place I used to love was Tennessee Mountain. They give you ribs, meat, and potatoes." For Dana these places were a relief after endless nights at SoHo eateries where food was presented like a work of art: fragile, small portions, pretentious little towers of crab.

Steve became a regular at Dana's parties, even when he wasn't working security. As a friend his role was similar to Artemis's: to remind Dana of who he had been a long time ago, before the stars had descended on him.

Stanulis considered this period in his life to be "a wild ride because one night I would be hanging out with Leo and going to movie premieres. I would get home and have to get up three hours later and then go out into the projects where it smelled like piss, chasing drug dealers." Working narcotics, he spent most of his days busting young black men. Maybe they had cocaine rocks in their pockets or their fists. He followed them down stairwells and said, "Put your hands up and turn around slowly."

In one twenty-four-hour period the ironies came into full bloom. Steve remembers:

> It was three or four in the morning and we had been partying all night. It was at Dana's, there was Leo, Toby, chicks. Everyone was feeling good. My wife is calling me frantically, "When are you coming home?" and I say, "Whenever they let me go."
>
> By the time I got home there was only enough time for two hours of sleep. I am beat tired. I am on patrol in the car, my partner is driving. I am telling him stories about the night before and he can't believe what I am telling him.
>
> We get a call of a man with an ax going into Fort Richmond High School. So we just happened to be right around the block from the high school. So we go around the block, and there is the guy with the ax outside the school. We get out of the car and say, "Drop the ax," and he starts walking toward us. "Drop it, drop it . . ." We ended up talking to him, another cop came, "Drop the ax," and we arrested him.

Sometimes Steve wondered if he thrived on the feeling of at least two lives: waking up in Staten Island in his suburban home, arresting small-time thugs, then riding into the city and partying with the most famous movie stars in the Western world. With Dana, he was off duty. If people were doing drugs in the bathroom, he chose not to pay attention. Steve was an exhibitionist, and he soon confessed to Dana that he moonlighted as a male stripper. WHAT!! Dana said. The male stripper element only made him more exotic among the famous and isolated celebrities. That's him, Dana would say. My friend the cop and the male stripper. "One day I did a strip show for Leo and his friends," says Steve, "all the way down to my G-string."

The gossips started to hear about these wild nights, they became very curious about what was going on in that impenetrable apartment. Roger Friedman was a lumbering, feared columnist from the *New York Observer*. He heard Dana had a cop boyfriend. He took the ferry out to Staten Island and found his way to the gym where Steve worked out. He tracked him down—Friedman, a guy who looked like he hadn't exercised since grade school, wandering among the muscled gym bunnies. "What exactly is going on around here?" he asked Stanulis. "Are you guys boyfriends?" Steve showed him a picture of his wife, and said he couldn't believe he had traveled all the way out here to ask such a question.

Dana bought suits for Steve and jewelry for a new model girlfriend everyone called the Gazelle. He bought presents for the people at home; a champagne fountain, all-expense paid trips to see relatives, to see famous landmarks. He bought Leo a painting by Jean-Michel Basquiat. He took his cousin Gale on a trip to see one of the largest cacti in the world. He bought art books for Rich, heavy and expensive, and mailed them overnight. We felt like we should buy him something, too, but we didn't know what he needed. We didn't know if he was ever in his apartment anymore.

He said he was in control of $300 million. If he took 1 percent off the top, this still meant he was bringing in $3 million a year. All those zeroes, like doorways out.

*   *   *

Every year Dana filled out SEC forms, renewing his license to operate on Wall Street. In his 1998 forms, Dana exaggerated his education. He claimed he'd been educated at Harvard, when actually he'd only attended Harvard night school. According to the *New York Observer*, he started to represent himself as a Harvard graduate to the political high rollers he was meeting, many of whom were Harvard men themselves.

Dana says he never lied about Harvard. He says the filing was a mistake.

Also, according to the SEC, "Giacchetto claimed the firm managed $315 million although their assets were less than $200 million."

According to SEC documents, Dana was "looting" client accounts around this time: emptying money out of one account to hide losses in another. SEC documents claim:

"From at least June 1997 . . . Giacchetto has wrongfully endorsed checks drawn from his clients' Brown accounts . . . and deposited those checks in Cassandra's Main Account at US Trust/Citizens . . . Giacchetto has accomplished these withdrawals by telephoning Brown, which is the custodian for most of Cassandra clients' accounts, and directing Brown employees to issue checks from client accounts. Tape recordings supplied by Brown reveal that Giacchetto has issued instructions to issue checks from client accounts and has directed Brown employees to deliver such checks to Cassandra's offices by Federal Express, rather than send the checks to the clients." Witnesses in the office at the time remember Dana frantically opening FedEx envelopes, before anyone else could see their contents.

Dana denies that this looting occurred, but because he "took the Fifth" and thereby swore himself to a broad, frustrating secrecy, he can't elaborate. He says, "All I can say is that we didn't have a good infrastructure and I regret that."

Dana often called clients to tell them their stocks had gone up (you made $10,000 today!). Often the clients would say: *Let's sell.* He promised to sell if that was what they requested. Yet more and more the sales didn't happen, Dana was too busy booking flights or making sure the birds were fed. *I told you to sell that stock,* a client would say. *I am sorry, I am late on it, I will get right on it.*

Dana calls these "trading errors." People would call and say: *Where is that $10,000 for the stock you sold?*

Oh, it should be there on your statement any day, he'd say. More and more it seemed, though, this is what was happening: He told people their money was parked in one place, when really it was parked in an entirely different neighborhood.

The SEC claims that the deeper Dana went into debt, the more he began to disobey the rule "no commingling funds." His debts by 1998 were considerable: $15,000 in American Express bills (restaurants and plane tickets and hotels), $10,000 a month in rent (at least), a growing staff that would not work for less than $90,000 plus benefits. Catering and limo rides. Suits perpetually dry-cleaned (people still smoked—in even the best bars), ready for any possible power summit that might manifest itself.

And then there was the gift culture. Sometime in 1998 or so he bought a Basquiat painting for Leo, somewhere in the high six figures. If anyone asked how he could afford to do such a thing he would explain: It is an investment that will pay back in spades. Leo was an industry and his loyalty to Dana was, at this point, unquestioned, uninterrupted.

He said he controlled $400 million. *Wait, how much? Where is it?* The questions were coming in like a tide.

It was the right time for someone to come and rescue Cassandra and this is what Jeffrey Sachs and a group of his friends offered in the spring of 1998. Sachs had been in touch with the higher-ups at Chase Manhattan Bank, and he'd told them about this thriving small business called Cassandra. As Sachs presented it to Chase: Cassandra's were huge-money connections Chase would die for. Stars. *Ovitz*. Leo. Soon alliances were being discussed: We have what you need, you have what we need, it is a win-win.

Chase didn't know that Dana's bookkeeping was falling apart. He offered them balanced books, and a Rolodex of rich clients, who kept sending him money. Chase offered Dana a partnership. Cassandra-Chase Partners would be the name of the new business: It would be a $100-million fund targeted toward "entertainment start-ups." Cassandra and Chase would agree on which start-ups to fund. Dana says he was certain they would all come to a consensus.

Even when the Cassandra-Chase deal was on the down low, Dana couldn't help whispering about it. Rich remembers being over at Dana's apartment, reading a fax left out on the drainboard. It was from Chase, reiterating the $100 million figure. "Look at that!" Dana said. "This is one of the biggest banks in the world!" The bank was knocking at his door, asking to be let in. Later, he would depict them as monsters, darker than the monsters in fairy tales.

The Chase partners included Jeffrey Sachs, Sam Holdsworth—who had run *Billboard* magazine and was known for dressing like a cowboy—and Mitchell Blutt, a tan, young banker whose photograph often appeared in the Westchester society pages. The governor's son Chris Cuomo was hired as the Cassandra-Chase in-house lawyer.

Chase teamed up with Dana to underwrite the Standard Hotel. Over $10 million was raised from a few investors, Leo among them. This was the money to pay for the air-condition-ing, the pool chlorine, the constant supply of new towels, the insurance against earthquakes, the liquor licenses, and the maids' uniforms. When the money was "all raised" or promised, Dana and André threw a party in the unfinished hotel.

Russell Shoal, Dana's old bandmate, ran into him in a bar around this time—when the Chase deal was taking shape. The deal to end all deals. Shoal and Dana used to roam around Boston when they were eighteen and nineteen, offering fake IDs to bouncers at punk clubs who tended to turn them away (not without a small fight). It had been so long since he had seen Dana, practically half their lives. Yet the moment he saw his old friend's face in the bar mirror he recognized it. "Dana hadn't changed at all. I was balding and everything but Dana looked exactly the same," he says.

Dana was sitting with Chris Cuomo, a man with the clean and waxy look of a newsmagazine anchorman, which he would go on to become. Dana talked about how great everything was going and how much money he was making. Shoal did what he used to do when they were in school: He rolled his eyes and tried to pierce Dana's ego. "I don't really care, I am into obscure folk music. I don't even know what *Titanic* is." Shoal worked a day job for a psychiatrist and made music at night, collecting records until they filled every corner of his apartment.

After that encounter they talked on the phone a few times. One day on the phone from the psychiatrist's office, Shoal read Dana the textbook definition of narcissism from the *DSM IV*:

- Feels grandiose and self-important (e.g., exaggerates accomplishments, talents, skills, contacts, and personality traits to the point of lying, demands to be recognized as superior without commensurate achievements);

- Is obsessed with fantasies of unlimited success, fame, fearsome power or omnipotence, unequaled brilliance (the cerebral narcissist), bodily beauty or sexual performance (the somatic narcissist), or ideal, everlasting, all-conquering love or passion;
- Firmly convinced that they are unique and, being special, can only be understood by, should only be treated by, or associated with, other special or unique, or high-status people (or institutions);
- Requires excessive admiration, adulation, attention, and affirmation—or, failing that, wishes to be feared and to be notorious (narcissistic supply);
- Feels entitled. Demands automatic and full compliance with their unreasonable expectations for special and priority treatment;
- Is "interpersonally exploitative," i.e., uses others to achieve their own ends;
- Behaves arrogantly and haughtily. Feels superior, omnipotent, omniscient, invincible, immune, "above the law," and omnipresent (magical thinking).

"It sounds like you!" said Shoal.

Dana laughed and said, "You're right!"

In March 1998, Dana flew to Paris with Leo to attend the premiere of *The Man in the Iron Mask* at Paris Town Hall. Other male friends of Leo's came along: a character actor who was too bulky to ever be anyone major, a guy Leo knew from home, from back in the day. They stayed at the Hôtel Ritz Paris, owned by the Al-Fayed family, whose golden son died with Princess Diana in a car crash after leaving this very hotel.

Cosmo showed me Dana's home movie of this stay at the Hôtel Ritz. They all seem like little boys to me. Bored. Waiting for someone to entertain them. Decadent princes, eating chocolate and drinking champagne. They talk of girls from the night before, *Will they be there tonight?* The decor of the Ritz is gaudy, baroque—velvet couches and mirrors everywhere. I half expect someone to come in and powder their feet.

Finally they travel down to the premiere, where the camera loses focus in the crowd. Images emerge: Leo's dad swallowing a lit match. Jeremy Irons trying to stay awake as the French announcer drones. Dana ends this film the way he ends many of his home movies, taping himself in the mirror: *It is 3 A.M. In Paris.* This mirror footage must be a kind of verification that he was really here, that he'd been the one holding the camera all along.

Throughout the spring and summer of 1998, Leo was shooting a movie called *Celebrity* with Woody Allen, in which he played a spoiled celebrity throwing tantrums in a hotel room. He stayed in Dana's apartment during the filming. Allen had recently been caught having an affair with his wife Mia Farrow's twenty-one-year-old foster daughter. *Celebrity* was a movie about how unforgiving the world is when it comes to famous people. It was not well received, and critics wondered about DiCaprio's slump, whether he would really become the bankable star Hollywood believed him to be.

Also in the spring of 1998, Dana and Jesse Dylan started to plot a buyout of a company called Paradise Music and Entertainment. Paradise was an agency that represented jingles and soundtracks; their biggest client was Pokémon and the Pokémon soundtrack. Paradise was on its last legs and needed to be turned around. Jesse and Dana talked about making the company into a studio, a place where Leo could come and make any kind of movie he wanted.

Through Cassandra, Chase invested $6 million in Paradise up front. In 1997, they went public and Paradise became another stock Dana recommended to his clients, although because he was part owner, he was once again in gray ethical territory. Stars put money into it: Leo, Dan Cortese from the Burger King commercials. Both men said all right, and signed the offering materials. Victoria Leacock agreed to put $15,000 into it. Rich put the offering materials in the back of a filing cabinet and forgot about them.

As the investments came in, Dana and Jesse started to hold meetings about who might run the company. Jay Moloney's name kept coming up. They knew he was still in trouble—but he was a natural in this kind of thing, wasn't he? In the context of Paradise, Dana was planning to talk to Leo and Cameron Diaz about merchandising the rights to their images overseas. So the celebrity would sooner or later get paid if someone used their image to bring attention to their products. Dana believed in the idea. These were people who had to wonder about their likenesses appearing on paper cups, cereal boxes, or the faces of wristwatches.

In March 1998, Dana had an Oscar party at the loft. *Titanic* was up for best picture, but Leo had not traveled to Los Angeles to attend the ceremonies. Instead he was there in Dana's living room, shifting around on the couch while a model tried to get him to go into the other room with her. Dana filmed the party with his handheld camera, sometimes passing it around to other people.

In the frame you can see the stars: Michael Stipe and Leo and Kate Moss. They are eating and smoking and watching television. They are watching the pageant of fame. "Dana, you've done it again," someone shouts. People say:

"God, I am glad we are not in Los Angeles."

"Madonna looks like Cruella DeVille."

"We met, didn't we?"

The camera follows two thin girls into the bathroom, where they check themselves. The girls are wide-eyed and plucked. They coo at Dana and call his name. They look like they have been awake for days and are not going to sleep anytime soon.

Lounging on the couch, Leo watches as it is announced that *Titanic* has won best picture. "Yeah, Leo, you bastard!" someone says.

Leo looks tired, as if he is suffering from adulation fatigue.

A magician named David Blaine attended the party; he was an illusionist, and he could make birds and quarters disappear, he could levitate off the sidewalk. There was a rumor he'd levitated into the party. He was the kind of guy who wanted to freeze himself in ice, or hang himself above a crowd for days on end in a plastic box. He was a good addition to the men around Dana, who were flying so much they were defying the laws of gravity, and who were making money disappear only to reappear in the other hand.

Shortly after that party, Dana was named by *Vanity Fair* as a member of the New Establishment.

In June 1998, Russell was denied parole from Concord. He was cited for his combative manner, and the fact that he did not seem repentant about his crimes. Alma told him that when he got out, he could help them at the rental property again, he could live at home. He told her he was sorry, and that he realized these troubles were not her fault, that all of this was about him and drugs. She told him he was so handsome, he was better-looking than any of the stars Dana knew. Maybe Dana could get him a part in the movies?

Alma's fingers were starting to curl inward from arthritis. There was a numbness in her face—the doctors said this was arthritis, too. She thought about the difference between physical pain and emotional pain. She thought about how hard it had been to get the boys to even be born alive, to even see the light of the world. She said to Russell, "This must be my fault because I bore you. Was it something I did? Did I do something wrong?"

In the evenings the neighbors would come over and they would talk until very late. Cosmo might go on one of his rants— maybe he would disappear and then reappear in an outrageous shirt. They all asked about each other's kids. It was inevitable they'd get caught up in the competition. But Alma's and Cosmo's stories about Dana and the accompanying photographs—they could beat anybody's stories.

Photobooks were put together: "There he is with models at a restaurant table." "There he is with Cameron Diaz, doesn't she look happy with him?" "There he is on a Jet Ski off Mike Ovitz's yacht."

In SoHo, Dana's maid Maureen came to clean every day, even weekends. She had immigrated from Barbados and lived in the Bronx. The ride to Dana's was usually twenty-five minutes on the subway. She considered herself well paid at $20 an hour. She was strong and bent over and wore her hair back in a tight bun. She spoke in a heavy Caribbean accent, and she loved Dana and the cockatoos. She attended to the birds and became attached to them. Dana said, "If anything happens to me, I want you to take them."

Birds had been part of Dana's life since he was a kid. There was a goose called Caesar, which followed him to school through the woods, a couple of ducks in the pond, another goose that landed on Alma's back one morning while she was swimming in the pool and tore at her hair. At some point Alma had a parrot, but it flew out the window. She went around the neighborhood advertising it as lost, and someone called and said they had it, but they came over to the house with the wrong bird.

Now that Artemis was gone, girls were birds, too. According to Steve Stanulis, "We were surrounded by hundreds of chicks." They would go to Windows on the World with the chicks and look out over the city. Steve would talk about his exploits as a stripper, and chicks would beg to see his muscles. He says, "my wife wasn't included much, and it made trouble in our marriage." Dana says, "I was having sex with everyone." He won't elaborate, but he says, "It was wild."

In the summer of 1998, Dana had been managing the account of Robert and Cara Ginder for eight years, ever since Boston, when they were charmed by his promises and pamphlets. They didn't have the kind of money his celebrity clients did, but he seemed loyal to them. He sent them gifts: Cassandra martini shakers. They checked their statements. The small investments seemed to be doing well.

They still wanted to leave the city. They figured they could sell their TriBeCa loft and put the money somewhere safe, buy a cheaper place in the country. They weren't poor but they needed a nest egg. They worried about health insurance and their small daughter. When they worried like this they talked to Dana. Dana's rhetoric had always been against worry. They had an old Christmas card he had sent, back when he was still in Boston, in 1992:

I COULD CARE LESS ABOUT THE STOCK MARKET
I COULD CARE LESS ABOUT RETIREMENT
I COULD CARE LESS ABOUT MARKET VOLATILITY
I COULD CARE LESS ABOUT INVESTMENTS
BECAUSE THE CASSANDRA GROUP CARES FOR ME!

The Ginders went to Dana with the money from the sale of their loft, over half a million dollars. They told him about the idea of leaving the city. Dana told them if that is what they wanted, he would make it happen for them. He trotted out the old refrain: "My business is making dreams happen."

They'd never had six figures in the bank before, and it made them uneasy.

Michael Ovitz invited Dana on board his yacht, the *Illusion*. Dana thinks it was the summer of 1998. By now Ovitz's firing from Disney had become an infamous tale; there were articles about him as the most Powerful Crazy Person ever to roam around Hollywood. Mark Pollard, who worked for Cassandra at the time of Dana's Ovitz enchantment, remembers telling Dana: "If you are hanging out with Ovitz you are near evil." This was the story: Ovitz was ruthless. He spied on people. (Later he would be deposed in the trial of infamous Hollywood private investigator Anthony Pellicano, who was known for tapping agents' phone lines and delivering threats to potential client poachers.)

The trip was around the Italian Amalfi coast, a place where the sky was a dark violet, darker than it ever appeared in Hollywood. Dana made a movie of the trip, and in it, he is the enthusiastic receiver of all the evening's beauty.

"Look at this, look at this," he says, in disbelief: a bolt of lightning, a dolphin in the water. His excitement is the same excitement I remember from Yosemite. I notice he is very kind to the yacht's crew—the man untying the boat, the man in the engine room, tending to the steaming pipes.

On the yacht the wait staff brings appetizers on deck, they take drink orders. The men sit in a circle, talking quietly. Dana says, "What a day, amazing!" He takes a tour of the engine room. One of the butlers asks Dana how much his camera cost, and he says he can't remember.

Someone recites the menu, Swordfish and basil mashed potatoes and crème brûlée.

Someone says, We have been eating too much.

The wind picks up over the water and the party is driven inside. Kids play video games on an enormous television. There is talk of buying a new chess set, somebody needs to get a new one because the pieces are missing.

You will come again, one of the kids says to Dana. So it is not really good-bye.

Nikki Finke heard about this yacht trip, and she wanted the scoop. She heard Rick Yorn was there (she was right) and that it was the beginning of AMG, an agency that would poach clients from CAA (as far as I can tell she is right). For years she would ask around about it, trying to get the dirt.

Nikki believed evil dealings were happening on board this yacht. She believed now more than ever that Ovitz was the scum of the earth; and she wanted to write a book about all his secret meetings. New York publishers were waiting for it. They had heard about her. They had heard about her diligent, angry attention. She knew things she shouldn't know. People leaked information to her. Disgraced moguls called her in the middle of the night, trying to tell her the straight story.

PART
SIX

1998–1999

Vicodin is a painkiller prescribed for moderate to severe pain; doctors seldom prescribe it for more than a few weeks because it is an addictive narcotic. It works on the opiate receptors, relaxing the mind and the muscles. Nerves forget pain under its influence. According to the pamphlets passed out by pharmacists who dispense it:

> Hydrocodone is an opioid. . . . It is an orally active narcotic analgesic . . . as a narcotic, hydrocodone relieves pain by binding to opioid receptors in the brain and spinal cord. It may be taken with or without food, but should never be combined with alcohol. . . . Common side effects include dizziness, lightheadedness, nausea, drowsiness, euphoria, vomiting, and constipation.

Despite the warnings about never combining it with alcohol, I can testify that one or two drinks combined with the pill brings the buzz to a sublime level of forgetting, a lightheadedness that is close to amnesia, but not so close that you can't give a cab-driver good directions or find the secret entrance.

Dana was enchanted with Vicodin; it offered a way of being outside the world but not too far outside. When I question him about his escalating Vicodin use in 1998, he is unclear on the details of how he obtained it. But it was continually prescribed to him, and always in his medicine cabinet.

Vicodin has a speeding undercurrent, and it was this side effect that helped Dana stay awake: The drug activated the nerves that lifted his eyelids, allowing him to host the coke-infused partygoers who landed at his apartment long after the normal hour of sleep. Dana barely touched coke; it was too much for him. He never had the sweating, frantic druggie look, like his brother. Maybe he looked a little adrift, like he was wondering if he left something or someone behind. But he never seemed out of control or in need of a fix. The drugs came to him effortlessly, through pharmacies and delivery services. The drugs were a given.

In the fall of 1998, fashion magazines clamored to schedule shoots in the Standard lobby. There is no end to the fantasy of the beautiful woman and the four-star hotel.

In October 1998, Chase Manhattan officially bought a 50 percent share of Cassandra, and the Cassandra Group became Cassandra-Chase. It was absorbed into the bank. According to Nikki Finke and Kevin Gray in *New York* magazine, it was "a venture capital firm backed by $100 million from Chase. The fund's main objective was to ferret out entertainment start-ups and get a first look at the projects conceived by Giacchetto's famous clients. The partners stood to earn 15 to 20 percent of each venture."

The Chase deal brought Dana back into the world of banks and high-rises where he had started at eighteen. For all these years he had avoided the suits—if the suits showed up the party was dead. But these men were definitely suits, even in their forced casual attire. And even though he'd spent years dismissing them, he found he wanted their respect. He wanted to impress them. He organized dinners where Leo met the banking partners.

Between Vicodin and global travel and these new peculiar, distant partners Dana admits he was rattled. He tells me he came to the Chase partners with all kinds of deals, but they'd turn him away. They'd say, *Someone is already doing that. We don't need another hotel.* Dana wondered if they had just partnered with him to steal away his people. To steal his Rolodex: this meticulously built list that was supposed to be evidence of a vast support system.

The Chase deal made it possible for Dana to hire upper-crust people, Ivy League rarities. He would offer low six figures. He was looking around, trying to find someone to reorganize his infrastructure and rescue him from the increasing pressure of unfinished business.

He met Soledad Bastiancich during a meeting at the Royalton Hotel bar, one of his favorite watering holes. He was meeting with a new client, a Bear-Stearns banker. She was the banker's girlfriend. She was a brunette who wore cashmere sweaters and sheer lipstick, a hungry girl who didn't miss anything. She'd graduated from Yale Law School. At this meeting, he was trying to sell the banker on an executive producer credit for a movie that was sure to be an hit among Generation X.

Soledad often had powerful boyfriends, and Dana's friends

would later call her a gold digger. She'd grown up poor in rural Oregon, and she was determined to live the life of the heli- copter set. Sometimes she imagined herself as a celebrity. She'd been the star of her school plays, and she'd never quite forgot- ten the sensation of having an audience. Dana noticed her immediately and hammered her with questions. He believed she was the girl sent by fate to help him clean up the books.

Soledad was a vice president and investment banker at Allen and Allen, making a quarter of a million dollars a year. But Dana started courting her for the position of Cassandra's vice president. "The money he was offering was substantially less," she says. "But I was tempted because it seemed like I could have more freedom."

She had this celebrity dream eating away at her. For this rea- son, Dana seemed important to her. Maybe he could help her get her face on the screen before the years caught up with her.

Dana visited Soledad and her boyfriend in the Hamptons and they talked in vacation-speech, but the terms of her employment were being hashed out through the act of sitting on deck chairs and drinking. Eventually she agreed. Soledad says, "I really loved his pitch, his pitch about really wanting to help the artists. He talked about how many artists really aren't finan- cially sophisticated, in his mind, and he wanted to protect them from people who would harm them because there have been so many investment advisers and people who would do that kind of thing."

On December 22, 1998, Dana called Cosmo and Alma in the middle of the morning. He said, "Pack your bags, I want to send you on your second honeymoon. You are going to Paris in three hours." Here is how the story unfolds in Cosmo's telling:

"We made it to the airport," says Cosmo, "and we told the lady behind the desk that our son was sending us on the Concorde. She said, 'Your son must really love you!' We went into the VIP waiting room in the airport and there were roast beef tips, anything you would want! No tipping allowed. We saw a newscaster from CNN, Peter Arnett, and we said hello to him. He seemed happy to be recognized. There was a German girl, an expensive floozy, wearing gold and silver and diamonds, also a lady who'd bought a seat for her dog, and a guy in a white tuxedo. I remember once we got on the plane there was caviar and shrimp and drinks.

"When the plane takes off it can't land for three hours. There is no speed limit and it's amazing that they don't blow the wings off the goddamn thing. Out the window the earth looked green, on the other side it was all black. You could see Europe and Africa! We couldn't believe how high our son had taken us!"

Dana was worried when he discovered that his parents had told me about the Concorde plane ride. He thought it might look bad, his parents sailing up there in the sky, while he was being accused of these crimes. But he swears it was his money that paid for the trip—it wasn't money that belonged to banks or movie stars or uninitiated punks who had never read a bank statement in their lives.

On December 31, 1998, Dana threw a party that would become his most famous party—the party cited in articles about his rise and articles about his fall. The 1998 New Year's Eve party was legendary because of all the arbitrary variety of celebrities who congregated there: "I went up to the refrigerator, and I saw Janet Jackson standing next to David Copperfield," said one partygoer. "*You just don't see* those two people together in the same room!" Thomas Reardon, our Microsoft millionaire friend from Seattle, was there. He says it was wild, like a casting call of all the young stars: Ben and Matt and Gwyneth and Winona. Bossy daughters of the music producer Quincy Jones—biracial, gorgeous creatures of the spa.

There were certain people you expected to see at these loft parties, the hipsters and the rockers, all of a vaguely similar tribe, people who recognized the same songs. But as Dana moved into this new echelon of celebrity, the sightings were overwhelming and random: magicians and Las Vegas performers, serious character actors, DJs from underground clubs, performance artists, television chefs, politicians, politicians' sons and daughters, tech geek millionaires, trust-fund babies, Wellesley girls.

In early 1999, Rich decided to quit Sub Pop and focus on his own label. He named it Up Records, and partnered with a laconic boy whom all the bands trusted. Fairly soon, without any salary coming in, his savings ran out. He asked Dana if he could break into the Pickens money: turn it from solid to liquid. Dana said certainly, certainly the money is liquid and he sent Rich the checks from the P Cap Fund one by one, $30,000, $40,000. They were Cassandra checks, and on the memo line they said P Cap Fund. The kinds of things you look for, or you do not look for.

For a while, Up Records flourished and bands started clustering around our lives again, although I didn't have as much patience for them. There were dumb and pointless things being written, and sourceless agitated boys, nothing like Kurt. A bratty kid from the suburbs singing meaningless lyrics like "My heart is a bitter buffalo." For me the scene had lost all its charm, it had lost its real bitter heart.

One performer Rich signed seemed real: He was a guy named Doug Martsch who led a band called Built to Spill. He had this acrimonious heat about him—even though he didn't talk much or even argue. Evangelical. I am out here delivering my ten-minute songs. I am speaking in tongues, sort of. He visited our house a few times and something about his personality made me think of those girls who live in trees for three years, just to make sure they are not cut down.

One afternoon on the phone, as they were saying good-bye, Dana called Rich "Rick." "Holy shit," Rich said. "I don't know if he even remembers me anymore." Maybe the names were leaving Dana's mind because there were just too many for him—a kid from a small town. His mind like a computer where the motherboard of memory was shutting down. Everyone was talking about Y2K: the moment when all the information would vanish. As the millennium approached, Dana's memory seemed like it was short-circuiting, too.

Soledad tells me: "Those were illiquid funds Dana paid your husband. He never should have promised you that money." She says it was not long after beginning her job at Cassandra that she started to think something was awry: "Some young actor would call and ask for his account value and I would tell him his account value and he would be like: '*What*? That couldn't be right. I saw Dana at a party and he said it was $75,000, you are saying it is $52,000?' These kinds of discrepancies. I would explain to him the market fluctuates, maybe Dana didn't have the figures in front of him, maybe he didn't quite recall correctly . . ."

Soledad was a straight-A student, a girl of sharpened pencils and immaculate plans. She wanted to be a powerful, respected person and she says, "I wasn't about to let someone like Dana mess that up." She had grown up in a poverty Dana had never known. At one point, her house had been repossessed. Her stepfather was black and her mother was white; they were Oregon hippies, living on the edge of society.

Consequently, as an adult she wanted to know where the money was at all times. She was not the kind of person Dana should've hired; he now wishes he'd never allowed her into his periphery. "I wanted to be organized," she says. "The books were not organized and I kept asking Dana about it. I told him, 'When people call for their statements, they should be able to get them that day.'"

She asked him, "What are these private deals?" Dana told her he would explain it when the time was right. Pickens. Great Southern. P Cap Fund.

She had a litany of clients who believed they'd purchased AT&T bonds. They might excitedly call Cassandra—AT&T guys were intermittently appearing on the financial shows, talking about how they were going to be number one on the Internet.

Yet neither Soledad, nor the clients who had told Dana yes to AT&T, could find evidence of the purchases anywhere.

Soledad says, "A public purchase like that, it should show up right away." Yet all these clients who'd been told their money was invested in AT&T—parked there like a car waiting to be driven—it started to seem the car could not drive, or the parking lot was something that had never existed at all.

By early 1999, the phone was an elusive thing for Dana. Dana protected himself from messages, and avoided retrieving them until he was ready for them. He didn't have a cell phone. He thought it would take him out of the moment. His success was built on a certain interpersonal intensity, and the clamor of a ringing phone would've ruined the vibe.

Rich said, "I have given up on sending him messages. He never answers."

Callers to Cassandra were told: "Still haven't talked to him, it should be any time." Soledad remembers rushing to the phone as he called from Miami and Thailand and Tokyo. She wanted answers about the missing money, but the lines were unreliable, voices sounded as if they were coming from light-years away.

In January 1999, Leo signed on for a movie called *The Beach,* to be filmed on Phi Phi Island, Thailand. The filmmakers were searching for a location that looked like paradise, and they settled on Phi Phi. Crews uprooted indigenous trees and planted palms in their place, to assert the paradise message, the generic mood of Eden. As they built the little rustic huts and the hammocks where Leo would lie with starlets, they were eroding a beach that had been designated a national park. The film crews had removed rare and endangered trees for a volleyball scene. They severed roots that had been holding up the mountainside. When the monsoons came, the beach fell into the sea. Citizens of Phi Phi sued 20th Century Fox for ruining the stability of their island.

For Leo, it was a potential public relations disaster. He'd been a spokesman for environmentalist causes, and by someone like Nikki Finke, for instance, it could be interpreted as the ultimate hypocritical act of a Hollywood dilettante. Dana called the gossip columnists. He said, *Leo is upset! I just got off the phone with him!* He talked to them about how Leo really cared about the rain forests. It wasn't an act at all.

Nikki Finke got wind of this: the story of this money guy calling all the gossips, although he didn't dare call her. He thought she was a maniac. She thought it was absurd: "I mean he isn't the guy's manager! What is he doing calling, trying to spin people about Leo DiCaprio?" She did not like to be spun. Try to spin her one way, and she was likely to spin in the opposite direction.

By February 1999, Cassandra-Chase had taken over Dana's offices and the culture of the place had changed. Dana felt like he was under surveillance. He felt there were secrets being kept. People had ordered walls to be put up, a glassed-in conference room.

Soledad describes moments of storming into the glassed-in conference room where Blutt and Sachs and the others were meeting. She said, "What is going on here?" She claims they said, We know, we are worried too.

Dana heard about a stock called Iridium, a global satellite network. According to the brochures, Iridium's network would provide "voice, paging, 160 character 2 way short text messaging, and internet access services to commercial and individual subscribers anywhere on the surface of the earth. Even the polar caps have Iridium coverage." Iridium promised they would have more satellites circling the earth than any other network. According to *Wired* magazine, "the Motorola-led consortium rocketed 66 satellites into orbit, belting the globe from a height of 485 miles."

Cassandra gave a buy order to Iridium. "Everything I recommended went up," Dana says. But he looks at Iridium as the moment when he lost his powers and was led astray. "I never should've gotten involved with that," he says. "It was one of my first big mistakes. Before that I had a very low failure rate."

Iridium's talk of "anywhere on the surface of the earth" was a marketing language aimed at the global worker, but with Iridium the marketing became irrational, delusional. Iridium phones were expensive; $225 a month and up. It was expensive to keep all those satellites up there, waiting for a signal, waiting for someone to dial the North Pole. The forces behind Iridium wanted some kind of planetary claim, before anyone else claimed it. But they didn't think about the practical realities.

Inevitably, since none of the people Iridium marketed to ever went anywhere near the polar caps, or even to rural America, they bought cheaper phones. Iridium ended up selling its phones to explorers and oil rigs in the North Pole, or soldiers in the Iraq desert. This was not the mass audience they'd envisioned, and they sold the phones for a considerably marked-down price.

As the nineties came to a close and more and more tech billionaires were born, as they were retiring from their jobs and starting half-baked companies going public and promising product, the promises themselves became unhinged from the world. They were promising "content" but they didn't know what they were talking about.

There were dreams of instantaneous messages and images, a camera phone. But the wires, the bandwidth, the cable under the ground could not support them. Systems fell apart and crashed. The server that was supposed to show a live concert instead showed a clipped, slow-moving spectacle, a cubist version where the delay between lips and voice seemed eternal. People wanted to be everywhere at all times, but there were holdups, glitches, ghosts.

* * *

Dana could only promise so many people he was coming back to them and their money was coming back to them. He says, "I was overloaded." His arrivals and departures were often dictated by Leo at this point: When a meeting could be set up with Leo and the Chase partners, when he could go and see Leo in Paris or L.A. and hopefully talk about a merchandising option. But if they didn't talk about it, consider the trip a write-off. To go see Leo was enough; it was a profitable act, it could only get you somewhere. "These were profitable relationships!" Dana says.

Jay Faires, the ex-Mammoth records exec, tells me: "He was always telling me I had made 35 percent gains, he would print this stuff out on statements. But it never really seemed to jive with the markets. That was when the markets were up 20 percent a year. For a while I was like okay, maybe, somehow. But then I started to wonder. He told me I had invested $250,000 in the Standard Hotel on Hollywood Boulevard. And like six months later, it was still before the hotel had opened, I see André somewhere and I told him: 'I am psyched that I am investing.' André said, 'What are you talking about, that deal has been closed forever . . .' I was like . . . uh . . . 'Dana told me I put a quarter million into this deal' and André was like 'No, you didn't.' Dana's answer at the time was like, 'Yeah yeah. You will get in on the deal, don't worry.'"

Dana randomly sent Cosmo and Alma checks, as payback for their early Cassandra investment. Cosmo remembers saying: "Dana! You can't just write these checks! You have to account for them! You have to send tax statements saying what they were for!" But Cosmo needed the money and he trusted Dana so he put the checks in the bank. Rich did, too. He put the money into Up Records. He paid the bands their royalties. He hired a hipster girl with ratty hair who treated him like he was crazy.

* * *

Dana and Jesse Dylan officially hired Jay Moloney to head Paradise, paying him $500,000 a year. Dana said, "It was a great way for this brilliant guy to come back." That was in February 1999. After all these months sailing around the islands of rich men, driving into the desert, meeting dealers or trying to keep himself from calling them, Jay was put to work. He was in charge of brainstorming the merchandising deal around Leo's face. He was in charge of images and jingles.

Dana says Jay had been clean for "at least a year" when he put him in charge of Paradise. But according to *Vanity Fair,* just a month before, Jay had been released from rehab "headed straight for an ATM, bought cocaine, went to a hotel room, climbed into the tub, and slashed his throat and wrists."

Nevertheless, Dana and Jesse wanted him to head Paradise: the President. Dana thought such a title would boost his confidence and rescue him from his self-destructive voices. He would hold meetings—be the boss, be necessary in this important company that nobody could quite define. Sometimes, in the meetings, people would notice the scars on his wrists and neck.

Nikki Finke heard the news and she called her loyal sources: "Who does this Dana guy think he is, hiring a hopeless drug addict to run an entertainment company? I mean, am I *the only sane one around here?*"

The Ginders were starting to fret. Dana hadn't moved their money anywhere; he hadn't invested it, it was simply sitting there in the cash account. They wanted to know the money was safe and proliferating the way Dana had promised. They wanted to know this before they left New York behind for good. Dana's promises were the wind in their sails, pushing them upstate. They felt stalled. They knew enough to understand that the longer the money stayed in the cash account, the less valuable it was in the real world.

They tried to set up appointments with Dana. It took a while; he kept canceling or rescheduling. Finally, sometime around March 1999, they can't quite remember when, they met with him.

They wanted it to work out. They knew stars bought paintings. They'd once run into him in SoHo with Leo, after they'd just dropped a couple of million at a gallery. Stars had enormous houses with blank walls, and the Ginders paintings, Dana said, would be *perfect*.

At the Cassandra-Chase meeting, Bob says, "They put us in this glass room. Dana was sitting at his desk there on the phone forever. And we were just sitting there. He saw us! Ten people working there offering us water, a half hour goes by, an hour, a really long time, we got offered water eight times. He looked very stressed out, he could see we were sitting right there. Finally he comes in and tells us what he is going to do with the money."

He talked to them about a conservative, diverse portfolio. Blue-chip stocks. A good variety. Maybe a little bit of this stock in Paradise Music and Entertainment, which was going places.

He apologized to the Ginders. He said it was just taking a while to set up, but pretty soon they would see the statements about where their money had gone.

Dana showed me a home movie of one of his helicopter rides with Leo, after the Chase deal had been signed.

The ride happened on an afternoon when he'd set up a meeting for Leo out in the Hamptons. The meeting would be with Sachs and Cuomo and others, one of those meetings where you just get to know each other over simply grilled fish.

They board the helicopter; the surface of the water churns. Someone says, Wow, this is a sick copter, someone else says, Pretty deluxe.

They fly over the city and point out the landscape down below, the Statue of Liberty and the World Trade Center. They fly past the Empire State, where the windows are reflecting back gold. The highways unfurl beneath them. A warehouse is on fire. A bright blue public swimming pool swarming with bodies.

Someone complains of nausea. Dramamine has been taken, and they are waiting for it to kick in. *Come on pills, come on, come on.*

They turn the corner toward the Hamptons and the sky changes. There is green down below, nature, the purifier, the place where some of the best deals are made. They land on the beach and are greeted by men in white shorts and white shirts.

You made it.

This ride took place in a time before the flight paths over New York had been restricted. A time when aircraft could hover close to buildings, almost in shouting distance.

I know Dana wants me to be impressed by the movie of the helicopter ride but when I think about Dana at this time I imagine him waking up in his loft surrounded by the detritus of the party, glasses with cigarettes inside them, unfinished plates of food, the birds hungry. No matter what day it was, Maureen would be there soon. She would start in one corner and move out, and the place would be presentable again.

Sometimes Dana hinted at trouble: He told me about being stressed out, about everything being too much. But I didn't see these intimations as warnings. I didn't imagine the story of

Rich's savings might be hidden inside them. I realize now I had a near-delirious sense of luck. I was like the woman just entering the casino with a pocket full of chips and the night in front of her.

In the spring of 1999, Leo started filming *The Beach* in Thailand. In the film Leo is a wandering American tourist, and he believes the promises of a perfect paradise island. Not surprisingly Paradise is pure trouble, and one of the main characters ends up dying a grim death from neglect and gangrene.

Leo invited Dana to join him on the set, and Dana agreed. During the hours Leo was shooting, Dana would travel into Bangkok and find a phone. Sometimes amid the crowds and the noise it was hard to hear and the connection would go out. The wires would go dead. Soledad would say, "Where are you? We have been waiting for you! There are a lot of questions that need to be answered!!"

She told him she didn't understand why he said he controlled $300 million. There was only $100 million here. She said she wasn't sure they could even cover payroll.

One afternoon while Dana was in Thailand, Soledad received a call from a woman asking about some money that was not showing up in her account. This woman was a fashion model, but she was a B-lister, she'd done lots of runways but not many magazines. She'd been squirreling away her runway money, and she read her statements carefully. She read this statement backward and forward, looking for $100,000 that seemed to be missing.

She said to Soledad, "I love Dana and I am sure it is just a mistake. But I am not a rich person and so I am very worried about this money." Soledad and the model bonded over the phone, talking about how they were hardworking women who needed everything in order. Soledad told her, "The files are a bit of a mess here, but I will try to get to the bottom of it." Soledad tried to pacify the woman. She told her, "As soon as I have this figured out, I will call you back."

Soledad searched for the woman's missing money; she searched through trade orders and past statements. Dana had not called for days. She was afraid. In the other offices where she had worked, nothing like this had ever happened. She had come here looking for a release from the confinement of the corporate, professional environment, but now she missed it. Now she was thirty years old and hunting around for this vanished money, thinking: People could go to jail for this. She knew about the SEC and the way it worked; about fraud laws and the Investment Advisers Act. She knew about guilt by association.

Another guy called, a manager for a rock band, the Smashing Pumpkins. They'd made millions selling elliptical songs in which the singer barely brought his voice above a whisper. The manager said there was money missing from his account too, but he wasn't sweet the way the model had been. Soledad remembers him telling her Dana was a criminal: I have seen guys like him. You are a fish swimming upstream. But the Smashing Pumpkins still claimed to love Dana, although their manager tried to convince them to stay away from him.

Soledad says, "I was livid." She went to the Chase partners, and told them, "I am not going down with this guy. We need to get these files cleaned up." The partners agreed. They needed to stop believing what Dana told them. The company was like a car and they couldn't trust him to drive it anymore.

In April 1999, Dana returned from Thailand tanned and rested, claiming to be rehabilitated. He had only been back in the office for a little while when Soledad and the Chase people came up to him and said, "Could you meet us upstairs, in your loft?" They explained that they did not want to talk about it in front of the entire office. They didn't want to frighten people and start rumors.

"We did an intervention," says Soledad, using the same drug language people used around Jay. "I wanted to believe this was not a pattern of abuse."

They took the elevator upstairs and settled into Dana's living room. They told Dana they were going to hire an outside firm to do a "forensic accounting" of Cassandra's books to make sure nothing was wrong. The term sounded like the kind of thing you would say about a dead body. They explained that these accountants would straighten everything out and locate everyone's lost money. It might mean billing people for hotel rooms or helicopter rides they thought were free. It might mean scaling back.

Soledad remembers: "I said, 'You have put us all in a terrible situation. You could go to jail for this.'" Dana reassured her that no one was going to jail. He said, I have done nothing wrong, things are just a little messy. I want to get to the bottom of this as much as you guys do. We will get it cleaned up. Absolutely let's hire the accountants; let's definitely do it!

She told him the accountants were coming up this afternoon, and they needed a large retainer fee.

That's great. Let's do it! he told her.

"We spent hundreds of thousands of dollars on those accountants," he says now. "And I am not sure what they accomplished—it just created more suspicion and fear for everybody."

Soledad says, "I had to be involved in a cleanup, or I had to turn him in."

Like Iridium, Dana started to see the Chase men, Soledad,

all these people as a wrong turn he had taken—if only he hadn't let them in, his rise to power would've continued uninterrupted. These business types came in and they started to peck at him, they started to pull away at the self he had created and ask questions about it.

The gang of forensic accountants combed through the books. They stayed for weeks. They went out and looked for their own lunches and nobody in the office talked to them. Inside Cassandra, morale was not good.

But Soledad felt reassured. If the SEC ever came after Dana, she would be safe, untarnished.

Yet years later, she still feels tarnished by it. I am talking to Soledad in her apartment on Manhattan's Upper East Side. She is married to an extremely wealthy investment banker. It is a penthouse where an elevator opens onto it, and a maid is always in the periphery. The art on the walls is often borrowed by museums. I think it is the kind of place Dana wanted to have, eventually, but he never made it to the elevator set.

Soledad says, "I was at a dinner party and this woman asked, 'How come *you* are not in jail?'"

Soledad says, "I want to get the story straight. I think he is a pathological liar."

During the period of forensic accounting, Dana was advised by Cassandra lawyers to stay out of the media and keep a low profile. Ignoring their advice, he soon went into a state of frantic self-promotion. He hired a publicist, Ken Sunshine, who would eventually become Leo's publicist. A bald guy with a British accent and an unbelievable Rolodex.

Sunshine pitched the story of Dana around town; editors answered his calls. People knew Sunshine's name; they knew the whole you-scratch-my-back setup. Soon Sunshine set the spin going in a better direction. *New York* magazine's editor Maer Roshan planned a story about Dana's possible innocence. In *Interview* magazine he was called a New Mini Maxi Mogul.

"Are you crazy?" Soledad asked Dana. "Why are you doing this? Do you understand what you are going through right now? Do you understand what the lawyers said?"

More and more of Dana's richest clients were putting money into the Pickens Great Southern Water fund. Court papers reveal Cassandra funneled $18 million into this fund over time. Yet Dana claims by spring 1999 that Pickens himself had become elusive, and he claims he didn't know the story of the money. He says, "I should've put investors in touch with Pickens himself, instead of acting as a mediator." On top of this, the failure of Iridium became a scandal in the financial pages. It was reported in *Wired* magazine: "Sales of its pricey handsets and phone service failed to take off." At the end of March 1999 they had only signed up ten thousand customers.

Wired's headline read: The Ford Edsel of the Sky? "Each satellite is only designed to work for five years, after that, Iridium has to shoot up a whole raft of replacement satellites to keep its system running."

For Dana, Pickens was a private stress and Iridium's failure was a kind of public humiliation, the kind of thing that made people wonder aloud if he had lost his touch. People started asking questions like, *Paradise. I mean what kind of name is that?* And, *did you hear his brother has done time in Concord State Pen?*

* * *

There are stories about Dana and the Paradise stock, stories of him buying huge parcels of it with client money without consulting the clients first. Bob Ginder remembers, "We would always have money in one thing or another, but it was spread out over many stocks, Merck, Coca-Cola, things like that. Then one day all of a sudden more than half our money is in Paradise! Like, over 100K! And we hadn't told Dana he could move it!" Ginder called Dana right away and he removed the money, apologized, claimed forgetfulness.

Victoria Leacock has a story about Paradise, too: "He bought me a parcel of it without asking me, a small parcel, but then it zoomed up. So I told him, go ahead and buy more! I had a lot of money in my account, and I decided to be part of the purchase of more Paradise. I went to one of their stockholder meetings. I guess I was thinking I knew what I was doing. So basically half of my account, 110K, was in Paradise."

She did everything she was supposed to do: She went to stockholder meetings, she asked for a stock certificate, she saved all the pieces of paper. One night at a party with Dana a couple of her friends cornered her. They said he seemed like a crazy con man. They said, He has all your money? And he has put it in some company he owns or something? But she didn't register their concern. Dana kept increasing her money. The statements proved it.

The Paradise situation was on the edge of economic law but it was never a case of breaking the law. The law Dana was skirting was this: If enough "insiders" own the stock, they can drive the price of the stock up, and then drive "outsiders" to buy it at inflated rates. At the moment the outsiders have reached a maximum bid, the insiders sell—as friends, they all get out at once. Like friends leaving a party together. Then the bottom drops out of the stock, the outsiders have been sabotaged. One Paradise insider told me, "If I had sold at the wrong time, I could've been sent to jail." On Wall Street the term for it is "pump and dump."

Jay Moloney only headed Paradise for a couple of months, before his demons came back around and tapped him on the shoulder. It is possible that in Jay's case cocaine fueled a latent state of manic depression, and the manic depression fueled the cocaine. A doctor said lithium would cure it, but Jay didn't like the way the lithium made him feel. Just as people had blamed Dana for giving Jay the bender money, they blamed him for giving him this stressful job over this enormous, vague company. Didn't he see that Jay had a chemical imbalance?

When Jay could no longer handle Paradise, Jesse Dylan took it over in April 1999. Seven months later Jay would succeed in killing himself, but people were still going around frantically trying to save him just before his death. They had sent him to islands and rehabs, places in the Midwest, the Northwest, the Southeast, east of everywhere. Places where the will to live was supposed to really take hold. But even his greatest admirers were losing faith.

Dana insists that he always thought Moloney would be all right, that Jay would beat it. Whenever the topic of Jay comes up, an angry grief comes into his voice, a defensiveness and longing. He says he thinks about Jay every day. These drug-consumed men surrounded him, just as they had his whole life. Just as it was in high school, there were the people who went down into the pits and stayed, and the ones who came out. He thought Jay was coming out, that he would rejoin him in the land of the functioning living and see the light as he saw it.

As part of the spring 1999 forensic accounting of Cassandra-Chase, all the old hotel bills and restaurant bills were scrutinized. In Dana's world, stars were accustomed to getting things for free; they called it "swag." Enough makeup for a year at the *Vanity Fair* Oscar party, fruit and cheese baskets, watches, dresses, and jewelry.

Dana entered this world of giveaways already trained to be a generous host: He had heard about his father going broke from his Fourth of July parties. Cosmo always made it clear that the party was worth it. He wanted a life of explosions and feasts. He didn't care how much it cost.

Soledad says, "Dana had been picking up tabs over the years for every time someone famous was in town." When the accountants finished, many of the deficits they found in the Cassandra accounts were about these gifts: whole weekends at hotels that Dana had paid for, restaurants where people ordered dessert, ice wine, and a flaming coffee at the end of the meal.

Soledad says, "When we found a deficit, we tried to pick up reimbursements. We were trying to get every bit of cash we could because we were in the red . . . he had made a number of loans, and we would sweetly ask for the money back. . . . He was not helpful."

The Smashing Pumpkins received a $20,000 bill for a week at the Standard they thought was free. Rich received a $1,300 bill for a night at the Mercer and all the room charges. He sent a fax to Dana with the bill and simply wrote across the top: HEY, MAN, WHAT IS UP? ARE YOU OKAY? People received bills for helicopter rides, limo rides, rides to the airport. They had expected these things to be on the house, but the forensic accountants were saying: *Nothing is on the house.*

"To give someone a week of free rooms if they were going to invest a half million in the hotel? That seemed worth it to me," Dana says, when talking about the culture of gifts.

After all those bills went out, he told Soledad to stop answering the phones. He scaled back her duties and eventually she resigned.

At work the other cops ribbed Steve Stanulis about his night life. Hey, man, jump out of any cakes lately? they would say. Not only did he have stories of stripping, but he had stories of his nights with Dana and his friends. With the pussy posse, he was on the receiving end of the exchange, buying the girls instead of being bought by them.

The entourage hired high-class prostitutes, "the kinds of girls you couldn't tell at all that they were prostitutes," says Steve. These were girls who looked like they had gone to Ivy League schools, who were as pretty as models. Dana is coy on the topic but says, "Yes, there were nights with hookers, a *lot* of hookers."

I say, "How many hookers did you sleep with, twenty-five?"

He says, "No, less. But a lot of hookers." They were girls who were used to drinking Cristal, who were hired by rock stars.

Just as it had in high school, the night would get late and the conversation would turn around to girls. Girls would appear out of the boredom, as if from underground. They would want $2,000 an hour, but they were the kinds of girls who made you realize money was no object. The girls were objects, but the money wasn't.

On May 9, 1999, the *New York Times Magazine* published a profile of Mike Ovitz, written by powerful Hollywood reporter Lynn Hirschberg. The article was about how Ovitz's power might be eroding. He was producing Martin Scorsese's *Gangs of New York.* "Putting *Gangs of New York* out will be a test of Ovitz's power," Hirschberg wrote.

Dana appeared as a minor character in Ovitz's story. He played the part of a crazy young mogul, a loose cannon. An eccentric, someone with big white birds saying things like, "I'm tired of everyone referring to me as a downtown sex-addict party-boy/pretty boy who's friends with Leo." Yet as Hirschberg sat there, he yelled into his phone, "Get me Leo." This became one of the phrases that made him infamous: Get me Leo.

The boys from Sebadoh visited Dana's apartment and witnessed him shouting, "Get me Leo." They would remember it for years as the most irreconcilable and alien moment of their minor rock star lives: *Get me Leo, get me God, get me the richest fucker on the planet. I want him to come over and meet these Boston boys. These boys really have it going on!*

More rumors arose about Dana after the *New York Times Magazine* article: rumors that this guy was unhinged. Rumors that maybe he never should've been allowed to penetrate the inner circle in the first place. The arrogance of it! It didn't go over well. To be living in a world where you think Leo could just appear. People in Hollywood started asking, "Who introduced us to this guy? How did we meet this Dana guy, who said, 'Get me Leo,' in the *New York Times?*" All roads led back to André Balazs. Nikki Finke says, "For a while in Hollywood people were like thanks, André, we have you to thank for bringing this guy in."

Cosmo said to Dana, "Get out while you can."

An old friend said, "Let me come in and help you clean up the books, free of charge."

Dana always had some version of the answer: "Don't be so negative. Everything will be all right."

* * *

In June 1999, Russell was released from Concord prison. He returned to Medford, living in his parents' basement, coming up the stairs for dinner, eating calamari and complimenting his mother. He tried to stay away from Lisa, although he knew she worked at the downtown Kinko's. Cosmo would look at him out of the corner of his eye, disappointed in him. Sometimes they would fight and yell, all about wrongs and accusations— Cosmo would say things like: *You lied about the gun and the drugs, and I think you stole that tape of Dana's trip to Cuba. You were going to try to sell it for drugs.* Footage of celebrities in their private vacation moments were gold to the tabloids, and Cosmo thought Russell might be tempted to cash in. He considered him a boy who never saw a temptation he didn't give in to.

In the kitchen, Russell and Alma continued down the path of their intense, locked-in connection. She'd posted a picture of him on the refrigerator, all buffed and pure and muscular, just out of prison. The longer he was in Medford, the more that muscular prison body wasted away. She would say, "Look at how you looked there. And why are you coloring your hair?"

Russell kept thinking about what Alma said: "You could be in movies." Through a friend in the advertising business, he was given a small part in a commercial for a restaurant called Legal Sea Foods. He showed me the tape. You can barely see him in the corner of a table full of people, everyone acting like they are having a great time eating lobster.

He didn't want heroin anymore, he said he was over it after seven years as an addict, but sometimes coke presented itself to him. He went to a therapist and he was put on Klonopin. One of his first thoughts as the drug took effect and quieted him down was: "All those years, Cosmo needed Klonopin!" He wished he'd known about it back in the day when he'd dosed Cosmo's beer. Sometimes he would bring the bottle of Klonopin to parties, and trade it for coke.

One afternoon I visit Russell at a vacant apartment in Hazlett House, where he sometimes spends the night while working on the property for Cosmo. It is a transitory space: lawn furniture and musty old beanbag chairs. In the refrigerator there are jars of a super-powered drink that is supposed to create muscles overnight. He says, "I am trying to get in shape."

The walls are bare except for one photograph nailed into the living room's south wall. The photo is of a plain-looking girl, sitting on a couch staring into space.

I ask, "Who is that?"

"You don't recognize her? THAT IS JULIA ROBERTS," he says. "She is sitting in Dana's apartment!"

I look closer and I realize it is her, caught unaware, in bad light.

The Sweet Relief Medicine Ball in honor of Dana Giacchetto happened the same month Russell was released from prison, June 1999. The night before the ball, Dana flew his parents to Vegas. Alma had been here so many times, it felt like coming home. Cosmo had barely visited Vegas since the night when Charo asked him onto the stage.

Dana met them at their hotel. In the room, he had a series of gowns laid out for Alma to choose from. He explained that everyone was going to be dressed to the nines. Alma tried them all on and chose a dark strapless number. "Oh," she says, "I looked wonderful, I couldn't believe it!" She wondered about the cost, but Dana told her not to. It was the night before the ball in his honor and who could worry about money?

Dana and Cosmo went out into the malls above the casinos and found a top of the line suit shop. Cosmo tells the story of how the suit didn't fit, and there were only a few hours left before the store closed, but the man took his measurements and fixed it right as he was standing there. Cosmo found it hard to believe that someone could make a suit so perfect, so fast. Afterward, they went for shoes, cuff links, a haircut. He was going to look better than the celebrities.

By the time Cosmo and Alma arrived in Los Angeles they had crossed two deserts in two days. At the Hollywood Athletic Club, they stood alongside Dana as he moved through the crowd toward all the moguls swarming the velvet lobby. Dana said, "These are my parents," and people said things like: "I can't believe I am meeting you!" and "You guys are so cute!"

But the chrysalis of bad gossip had already started to form around Dana. The guests at the ball were celebrating a guy they were already suspicious of. The *Times* magazine article, the story of the forensic accounting, the Jay Moloney relationship, Iridium tanking: All these stories were making their way through the rumor mill. Among themselves, the well-wishers asked, *Is there something wrong at Cassandra?*

Dana had entered a world of sudden manic affections. Cosmo was a great believer in the idea that such affections usually have a dark side. Maybe this belief went all the way back to childhood, when he was sent to his grandmother's to grow up, banished. He sat there with Leo's parents, chattering about the safari, but he was starting to wonder if both of his sons were doomed creatures.

The question was unavoidable. If your father self-destructs, does this mean you will have sons who self-destruct? Is there something in the cells, the way they replicate, form genes? Cosmo knew about the scientific explanations for the way trouble courses through families, and he always had his father in his mind, the bullet in the wall of the house. Still, the children were so happy when they were kids, so alive, screaming at the fireworks. It was hard for him to believe they would grow up out of that rabid enthusiasm and enter the same old darkness.

In the spring of 1999, the Ginders had moved out of SoHo and into the country, the Hudson River Valley. At night they could see stars. During the day, they could walk a few blocks to pick up their daughter from school. This new life relied on the cushion of the money Dana said he would invest.

In June 1999, the Ginders received a call from an SEC investigator.

The investigator asked, "Did you authorize somebody to write a check on your Brown & Co. account?"

"No," Bob Ginder answered.

"Well," the investigator said, "A $100,000 check has been written on your account, and deposited into the Cassandra operating account."

The investigator explained to Ginder that the SEC believed Dana had been looting client accounts to pay Cassandra bills; ordering checks from Brown & Co., made out to clients, and endorsing them with his own signature.

Bob clawed through his mail, trying to find the statement in question. Since the move, their documents were in disarray. Eventually he found the statement in which the money vanished— "$100,000 disappeared, going nowhere," he says. "I could not sleep at all that night," he says. "I felt like the rug had been pulled out from under me. I wondered if I had lost everything."

Ginder called Dana. "He said the money was in some fund and was going over to some other fund. He said that this was a big mistake and people were trying to pin something on him."

The person who had called the Ginders, who was assembling the evidence against Dana, was SEC Senior Trial Counsel Alex Vasilescu, an ambitious thirty-five-year-old working out of the offices at 7 World Trade Center. He was a compact and determined man with an archival mind. He'd grown up in Belmont, Massachusetts, about twenty miles down the freeway from Medford. Dana was like one of the kids from his high school. He recognized him as a Massachusetts boy. But he says he also recognized him as a type: The criminal con man who infiltrates a community, engenders its trust, and then vanishes with its money. Alex says that from the moment he started scrutinizing Dana and Cassandra, "There were red flags that something was amiss."

The SEC had discovered improprieties in Cassandra's bookkeeping dating all the way back to 1997, and Vasilescu says many clients were leaving him by that summer of 1999. (Dana denies more clients than usual were leaving; he says that a financial manager always loses some clients, that is the name of the game.) What Vasilescu saw was a classic version of the "asset-kiting scheme," where one asset is borrowed to cover the emptiness left by the disappearance of another asset. The term "kite" is meant to evoke the way the perpetrator flies the money from one place to another, depending on where it's needed, depending on which way the wind is blowing.

Vasilescu cites Dana's most blatant crimes as "extremely risky private placements"—the Pickens deal, particularly. These private placements shouldn't have been part of the rhetoric of a conservative investor who promised "never to take custody of funds," and "protect clients from the fluctuations of the market." When Vasilescu scrutinized Dana's business he was looking for broken promises. He thought his artist clientele was particularly naive. "These people are not sophisticated in money management; they weren't really carefully reading their Brown accounts," he says.

When he says this I think about the Brown & Co. statements that would float unopened through our kitchen for days, until they disappeared into an overflowing drawer.

"Maybe he was trying to impress some people," says Vasilescu. "Some people he did give 40 percent profits to. But the profits [Giacchetto's clients made] are not real profits. They are profits from taking other people's money. And that is an ill-gotten gain." The term "ill-gotten gain" would become a defining term in Dana's life from here on out. It was a strange term, hard to completely explain, but it followed him like a shadow. It followed Rich and me, too.

Vasilescu had read about Dana in Roger Friedman's *Observer* columns, and he was pretty sure this was a classic con man at work. The con man was a cluster of characteristics, and Dana possessed most of them: the effusive promising, the deals that disappeared like smoke, the money shifting and shifting and never sitting still, as if it was being laundered.

After Vasilescu's call, the Ginders called an attorney—it wasn't a hard case to make, the bank had cashed a check they never should've cashed. The money was released back to them, and they left Cassandra. "It was a strange feeling, someone you trusted so much," says Ginder. Now Ginder believes: "Dana is totally deluded on a grand scale. It is remarkable how disconnected he is from reality."

Coincidentally, for a while in the eighties Alex Vasilescu had dated Victoria Leacock; they'd even lived together for a brief time. Dana would come to see this connection as part of the conspiracy against him. He would say, "Don't you think that is a little too much of a coincidence, that they dated?" He told me, "You should look into it." I told him, "I looked into it, there is nothing there." He told me I was missing a big part of the story.

Leacock says, "I had no idea Alex was investigating Dana. I wish I had. I would've taken my money out."

Vasilescu says: "I wish I could've told Victoria that she was involved with a con man. But of course I could not do that as it was an ongoing investigation."

Yet certain things Alex told Victoria stuck with her. When they were dating he'd always said: *Keep all your papers, never throw anything away, so if you get ripped off by somebody you will be able to prove it.* He described a world where people were hustled out of their life savings. A world of pyramid schemes and operators and snake-oil salesmen.

Remembering Alex's advice, Victoria kept everything she received from Cassandra. She kept every letter Dana ever sent and documented every phone message. She made a chronological file: To Do lists, to be filed, to be followed up. She asked for stock certificates when he told her he'd bought her a stock. She wanted a paper trail. She was determined to document every plot point in the story of her money.

In July 1999, Dana was working on the merchandising of Leo's image: The deal now had a name, it was called Signatures. It was based on a similar deal Dana had heard about where Madonna's image had come under this kind of copyright control. In these deals, whenever the actor's face appears, a royalty is accrued. The East was another frontier for Dana; it was another place where Leo held sway over legions of teenage girls, even if all his romantic language happened in subtitles or awkward dubbed voices. In Japan he was called *Leo-Sama,* a name which in translation meant "royalty" or "king."

Dana says of the Signatures deal, "I really wanted to put it together." He planned trips to Tokyo, hatched plans to meet with Sony.

I started to avoid talking to Dana because his name-dropping had become so intrusive, so frantic. The names dropped like sweat: They weren't signs of power but signs of panic. *Leo, John-John, Bob Dylan.* He would name-drop supermodels and I'd roll my eyes. He'd say, I know she is a model but she isn't stupid! She reads philosophy! Conversations became listless, fragmented, as the names took hold of his imagination. I tried to say to him: The names are transitory. But he didn't believe me. The names were like a roll call of some kind, except the further his troubles escalated, the less the named person ever answered "here."

I asked my Microsoft millionaire friend, Thomas Reardon, if this was normal in a powerful guy like Dana, to drop names like this. Reardon said no. Actually, he did not trust Dana because of all those names. Reardon knew plenty of names himself, he moved among the Forbes 500. He knew the Disney exec with the plane who had taken his money out of Cassandra. Reardon warned: "There is something off about that guy. You are never supposed to drop the names of people who are in on the deal. That just isn't done."

Over time the movie stars complained about the name-dropping. Matt Damon—who was just rising up as the short, trustworthy Ivy League hero who was also somewhat believable as a janitor—told *Premiere* magazine, "I thought that guy was cool, but it seems like he was using my name to get business."

Dana was about to be exiled from both Hollywood and Wall Street. Perhaps he could feel it in the air; in the way his phone calls were not returned, in the way his parties emptied out. *You're leaving already?* He'd known people who'd been blacklisted: a couple of actresses who'd won Oscars, but then Hollywood decided they were psychos. A couple of businessmen who'd been exposed as frauds and photographed doing the perp walk.

He had believed the fickle language of loyalty. People in Hollywood always said things like, "I will do anything for you." "Come to my place any time." "I love you and I will never leave you." But now they were starting to pretend that they didn't recognize his name or didn't know his phone number.

As the trouble came close, he went back to his roots. He contacted friends who'd known him longer than the famous people. He tracked down Russell Shoal, the guy who'd read him the textbook definition of narcissism. Russell was still collecting records and living in the same apartment. Dana called Rich and said, "We should go on a trip! Let's go to Spain or something." He called Bruce Pavitt, proposing a bungee-jumping trip where you would be released in the air above an exotic river: the Amazon, something like that. Pavitt said no.

Dana called Craig Kanarick; Razorfish had become a billion-dollar public company with 1,800 employees in 13 cities. Craig was a multimillionaire by now, and he was gutting a loft in SoHo, painting it two dozen shades of green and red. But he still had a feeling of wounded pride around Dana, and he was glad to be in the position of accepting or rejecting his invitation. He'd felt left out of the big celebrity parties. He'd read about them in Page Six, and wondered, "Couldn't he have called to tell me?" It always irked Craig the way Dana distrusted tech stocks and wouldn't invest in his company. Wasn't he living proof that the tech revolution was real and it was going to last?

Indeed, at this time Dana had started to work tech into his repertoire. Plans were being drawn up for an investment both Paradise and Cassandra-Chase could take part in. As he saw it, both companies would invest $1 million in an online business called Eruptor.com. Via Business Wire:

"Eruptor.com targets males between the ages of 12 and 25 by broadcasting original episodic shows ranging from 2D to 3D animation to live action. . . ." Shows Eruptor was developing included the titles "The Marty Show," "Vidiots," "Foo," "Eruptor College," and "Eruptor Shopping Network." (Eruptor would go on to be the name of a porthole for downloading various entertainments, but Eruptor.com as a pop culture phenomenon never materialized.

Dana and Craig had dinner and reminisced: It was hard for them to believe they had met all those years ago in Boston as roommates, listening to records until sunrise. They talked about their apartment: a squat, essentially, a place they never should have been able to afford. And now look what they were affording. They told each other the Horatio Alger story, and they were the heroes in it. Craig had money to burn and he invested with Dana—he invested big in the Pickens fund, which was now called Great Southern Water.

At the end of the summer of 1999 we went out to New York and saw Dana. Our economic horizons were already shrinking; we were staying in a cheaper hotel than before, a place where you shared a bathroom and you could hear the neighbors coughing. Dana was still saying, "Rich, I am going to make your record label huge, it is genius." But we didn't count on his promises. I had stopped believing in the story of endlessly multiplying money he had been telling us for most of the nineties. I had been asking Rich for the bank statements and the tax returns. I was a meticulous and paranoid bookkeeper, and I paid all the bills early.

Although I had stopped believing Dana's promises, I still loved him and wanted to spend time with him. During that visit we rode the subway out to Coney Island. When the train rose into the light, Dana took another Vicodin and declared the day a victory. He was sentimental. On the boardwalk, he insisted on buying raw clams served in a paper cup. He poured ketchup on them and swallowed them down. He said, "Emily, try them, try them," and they left a planet of salt in my stomach. Dana lay down in the sand in his expensive pants. He talked about how he wanted to stay here forever. He seemed like a conqueror facing defeat, and he needed to rest. He stripped down to his boxers and went out into the ocean where the water was famously polluted. He didn't care. He was outrageous that day and I was happy to be in his company.

It was not long after that Coney Island afternoon when a therapist diagnosed me with "racing thoughts." I was worried about the money, about Dana and Rich and the men with their schemes, about the polluted currents taking them under. The therapist said, "Maybe you need to think about medication."

In August 1999, according to court papers, the Chase partners became concerned enough about Dana and Cassandra that they prepared to end the deal and back out of the Cassandra-Chase partnership. The Chase men called Dana into a meeting. He says it was a "talking-to," about how if he did not clean up his act, the deal was over. Dana was still reciting his mantra:

We just need infrastructure. He seemed to think lost money would always be found, if only he could get everything organized and all the deals squared away, the i's dotted and the t's crossed.

At this point Dana was far away from the lessons of 1987, when he was working at the bank on Black Monday. The boom had lasted so long, almost a decade. In the past, the American economy had crashed in regular five-year cycles. But this was a new economy. "It is unprecedented," they said on *Squawk Box*. "Just wait," said Dana. "All the money in the world is coming here, to these shores."

Dana's optimism and narcissism worked together to create a delusional economic belief: Because there hadn't been a crash for so long, perhaps there would never be another one; perhaps everything would always move up. Lost money didn't matter because more money was on its way. But his life was crashing around him. Later, he would describe the Chase men's "conspiracy" against him in metaphors of a crash:

I was in a very vulnerable place and there was a series of events that happened in a compressed period of time that I couldn't solve. I needed more time. If the roof is leaking and there are a few drips then you put a pan under it. But if there is this huge stick that's hanging out and water's pouring in you need a bucket, but if the fucking ceiling drops in on your head it takes a while to rebuild the roof. And I never got the chance. I was sitting under the crush of plaster nails and rotting wood on the bottom of the floor with a hand up trying to, you know, get out from under it. Meanwhile blood was pouring out of my back.

* * *

In September 1999, Chase said they wanted to separate their accounts from him, and move their business out of the Cassandra offices. Dana was assigned the designation "retired partner." It was as if with the word *retired* they were trying to send him on a permanent vacation, a yacht trip that would never end.

Chase rented an office across the street, started keeping their own books and making their own portfolios for clients. For Dana this was the great indignity; to make him watch out the window as his clients went into the enemy's building. Soon all of the Chase employees were gone, crating everything off, even their paper clips. Dana told the Cassandra employees it was a misunderstanding. But they could tell the company was adrift, and many of them made plans to leave. They started reading the trades, and networking in hotel lobbies.

When Dana told me about Chase moving across the street, I thought about Cosmo and his turf wars. Which side of the street is the victorious side? Which side is the side for winners and which is the side for losers?

For months the SEC had been monitoring Dana's accounts. They were assembling evidence they hoped would put him in jail:

From the court papers:

Transactions illustrate that Cassandra used client funds not for investment purposes, but instead to pay other clients, eliminate overdrafts, and pay expenses:

At the end of September 3, 1999, the Main Account had a debit balance of $116,570. On September 7,1999, checks from the Brown accounts of five Cassandra clients credited the account in the total amount of $1,250,000 and created a credit balance of $410,184. On September 16, 1999, there was a debit balance in the Main Account totaling $215,912, which resulted from distributions to clients other than those clients whose funds were credited to the account on September 7, 1999.

Even as the SEC closed in on him, Dana made media appearances. In the fall of 1999, he appeared on *Squawk Box* again. As he was introduced, they played the obligatory theme song from *That's Entertainment.* By now he was recognized on the show as the Hollywood money guy, and the hosts treated him like a wild old friend.

It was an early-morning show and he looked like he hadn't been to bed.

Later he made an appearance on CNN with Ron Insana, a smart, balding anchorman who would become famous the day of the 9/11 terrorist attacks, when he appeared on television covered in ash. Dana was talking about how the bubble might burst. He turned to Insana with a mischievous look, "If there is a crash, people should buy food and drug stocks," he said. "Because we all do drugs when we're depressed and we all eat food when we're depressed."

As he said this, he looked drugged. It was the first television appearance I watched where I felt uncomfortable for him— where I wondered if he was just asking for his apartment to be raided.

Over the summer, Dana had lost contact with Leo. It's probable that Leo was being warned by his people that he had cast his fate with a bad character. In September, Leo fired Dana as his financial adviser. According to Dana, they both agreed he should leave until the mess was cleaned up. But Dana says they were still friends afterward, and they had lunch that fall. "It was as if nothing had changed," he says. They talked about women and trips and art. Soon Leo's lawyers advised him against seeing Dana under any circumstances, and no matter how many messages Dana left Leo never called back.

That fall Dana went on a date with a woman named Allegra Brosco. "When are you going to go on a date with me?" he used to ask her when he saw her out at the parties. She worked for a filmmaker; she had the same kind of low, throaty voice as Artemis. She told Dana she had a boyfriend, but he persisted. He'd call her at all hours, invite her to a premiere with all the stars.

Allegra told Dana that she didn't care about the stars and didn't like star-fuckers. She was small and feisty and doll-like; her friends were designers who made dresses for her. *Oh, oh,* they would say, *an Allegra dress.* When she talked to you she came on as intense, unwavering, like she was about to launch into a story that could last all night.

Allegra was from a very wealthy family in Providence, Rhode Island. They were old-time lawyers, Brosco and Brosco. When she was in high school, people joked that she was in the mafia. She had that toughness about her, mafia princess.

Allegra says: "The woman who cuts my hair would say, you had better watch out, because Dana keeps asking about you." She was getting tired of her boyfriend. Allegra was part of the Phish crowd, and ecstatic moments tended to happen to her at concerts. She realized Dana was her destiny at a Tori Amos concert:

> I was a bit in the aisle and he was to my left and I looked to my left and in a second I fell in love. . . . He was just stand-ing quietly, listening to the music. All sound around me

stopped. I don't even remember. All I remember is he was wearing this black leather jacket, the collar was up and I have no idea. I don't know if there was a cupid above that hit me with an arrow. Who knows?

Dana and Allegra entered into a romance of epic phrases and gestures, holing up in the apartment for days. "All this stressful stuff was happening in his business," says Allegra, "but we were busy falling in love." They were relieved to find each other. They spoke Italian and made food. They talked about God and the Greeks. For Dana it was a piece of good news he could deliver to Cosmo and Alma: "I have met the woman of my dreams. I feel like taking her all over the world."

She dressed sexy, showing her stomach, but Alma decided she liked her, anyway. She was glad Dana had found a girl who seemed nice. She was still mad at Artemis about those coats she had given her one visit after they'd been drinking and bonding. She wished she had known Artemis was not going to stay around because she would've asked for the coats back. "Those were really special coats," she remembers. "A little fake fur dyed magenta and I wore it dancing. They don't make those anymore."

Unlike Artemis, Allegra liked to fly and escape just as much as Dana did. For their first date they went on a trip to St. John in the Virgin Islands, their second date a trip to Morocco. One afternoon in October 1999, she says, "The phone rang and he's like 'where are you, where have you been, come on we have to go now. It's my birthday and we're going away! Be here in ten minutes.'" She packed her things and met him at the airport.

"He didn't know where he was going and we couldn't get on any flights. So we looked up at the board. It was like one of those American Express commercials where they are like, where do you want to go today?

Dana said, "Okay, pick a place."

Allegra said, "I am not comfortable picking a place on your birthday with your money to where we want to go."

"Okay, how about Paris?" he said.

"I have already been there. Let's pick a place we both haven't been."

They decided on Morocco. They spent two nights there in a hotel Allegra describes as "palatial, insane, over the top. We had two sitting rooms and two balconies and we slept outside on the balconies."

As they sat on their insane balcony, at home the SEC was closing in on Dana, and many of his celebrity clients were preparing to leave in Leo's wake.

Allegra says, "He is firmly grounded in reality. He'll say these things that are so smart and so right on. You are like wow, that's great." He told her about his belief that if you remain hopeful things will come together for you. He talked to her about the fact that he wanted to do good in the world.

When they returned from Morocco, the Chase partners had prepared a legal document officially firing him from Cassandra-Chase Partners. He was no longer a retired partner, he was not part of Cassandra-Chase at all anymore.

On November 13, 1999, Jay Moloney finally succeeded in killing himself. He hung himself from a shower rod in his Holly-wood home; his friend found him there the next morning. He was thirty-five years old.

There are conflicting stories about how much of an outcast Dana was by the time Jay died: Some were convinced that he was a parasite no one wanted to see anymore. Nikki Finke says, "He showed up at the memorial service but wasn't invited to the reception." Dana says this is not true. He says he was invited to everything; he was there, nobody blamed him for anything. Moloney's estate would be one of the first entities to sue him after his arrest.

In December 1999, the accountant for Phish notified Dana that he'd discovered a $3 million discrepancy in their account, and he was preparing to sue. He had an urgent meeting with the band and warned them that they had been robbed. In the story of Dana as a thief—a story Dana still denies—Phish was the extreme loser; their account was mercilessly ransacked. All that money from fans willing to wait in line in mud or sleet. All those muddy five-hour sets, CDs, limited editions, $22.99. And here the money was slipping into Dana's Cassandra account in larger and larger transfers: $100,000, $500,000.

When Dana talks about the money taken out of Phish's account, he talks about the enormity of their fortune: 3 million out of tens of millions. He says they were in on some private deals that went south, and he hadn't accounted for them yet. The Pickens fund, some of the money had been parked there. It was turning out to be a pain-in-the-ass deal.

Dana admitted to "misappropriating client funds" in the case of Phish, and he signed what is called a "Confession of Judgment." According to SEC documents: "The Confessions provided the Phish clients and their manager with enforceable judgments for the total amount of $4.7 million."

Dana says he regrets signing the confession, that it was the result of bad legal advice. "It made me look guilty, when I wasn't," he says.

To repay Phish's vanished money, Dana signed over his art collection. For as long as I knew him, he never stopped grieving over the art collection: the Frank Stella, the George Condo, the little Calder sculpture. These beautiful things that had belonged to him. The Phish lawyers held an auction, and the band was repaid. But Dana thinks many of the items sold for much less than they were actually worth.

One of the Phish wives had known Allegra since college days. She called her to say, If you know what is good for you, you will get away from that guy, he is a slime. Allegra told her she was in love with Dana, and hung up on her. These old friends warning her away from him—it almost made it more romantic. Suddenly she saw the old friends as shallow, and Dana as deeper than before. "There was no question soon after meeting him that I had met my soul mate," she says.

There was a big Phish wedding and they invited Allegra, but not Dana. The Phish abandonment was one more abandonment in an unfolding chain. Dana felt the heat of ostracism, like a shift in the pressure and temperature of his environment.

At one show in the middle of a jam, one of the Phish singers yelled, "Dana, could you please pass the soup?" It was a reference to his upcoming life in prison.

Victoria Leacock wanted to believe in Dana. So far, she'd prospered with him. He called her soon after the Chase partners left and said, "There has been a business disagreement." Then, according to Victoria, he asked her if he could move her money: "He said, look I want to move your Paradise account to Salomon Smith Barney because I am having fights with Chase and they're with Brown & Co. I don't want them to have access to what's going on with Paradise."

Victoria remembers:

I told him okay. He faxed me a document to sign. The document said I gave him permission to transfer my money into this account, and it had the account number on it. I signed it and faxed it back. A week went by, two weeks, a month, I started calling and saying I haven't got anything from Salomon Smith Barney. Employees who answered the phone would say Dana handled that we don't really know and then I would call him and he would say paperwork should come through any time now. I called all through December. I read the account number to someone, Soledad I think, and she said, That's weird, that is a Cassandra account number.

Victoria started to panic. She called Cassandra five or ten times. "Dana was in Niagara Falls or something," she says. "Finally he called me back from there and he said, Oh, actually there was a problem and I had to do something else."

Victoria still believed that she would find out where her money was and retrieve it. "It had never occurred to me that any kind of embezzlement or theft had happened," she says. "But I was concerned that my investment hadn't appeared on any statements. So finally we made a lunch date and I said you have to bring me a letter, I want a piece of paper from you saying that I have that stock and where it is and where it is being put." That day at lunch Dana brought her the piece of paper she wanted: a letter from him on Cassandra stationery. He handed it to her and said, "Are you happy now?" She detected a surge of bitterness in his voice. She remembers, "He was rude to the waiters in the restaurant. I told him, 'You'd better be careful and treat people right, because there is a lot of talk going around about you.' He wouldn't look me in the eye."

I am talking to Victoria in her rent-controlled apartment down near the water in Chelsea. She has lived here for many years. There are pictures of her with Andy Warhol as a teenager framed on the wall. There are CDs of a couple of drag queens she helped produce, Kiki and Herb, *Rent* memorabilia, and piles of *Playbills*. There are magazines showing photographs of her attending high-society charity functions.

When she says Dana "wouldn't look me in the eye," I tell her I know what she means about this tendency he had to look away as the trouble engulfed him. When I saw him around this time, I could never get a direct gaze out of him. He was looking over my shoulder, anxious. I would look where he was looking, but there would never be anybody there. I knew one of the side effects of too much Vicodin is a loud rushing noise in the ears. So I told myself it was probably the Vicodin's fault, the way he seemed to be listening to a voice no one else could hear.

PART
SEVEN

2000

I N DECEMBER 1999, DANA FILED A LAWSUIT FOR LIBEL
against the Chase partners.

In a section targeting partner Jeffrey Sachs, the suit reads:

Sachs, "spread false rumors and innuendo regarding Plaintiff
and the Cassandra Group to numerous persons in the entertainment and financial industries." On information and belief,
among the statements made by Defendant Sachs to a number
of people were a) that "Plaintiff was going to get arrested"; b)
that "the SEC is going to arrest" the Plaintiff; c) that "there
was going to be an SEC investigation of" the Plaintiff; d) that
"there was going to be an FBI investigation of" Plaintiff; and
e) that "there was a scandal at the Cassandra Group." These
statements by Defendant Sachs were, and are, false.

Yet in the coming months, Sachs would be revealed as the
Cassandra in the story. The future he was foretelling was the

one that was soon to come true, even if Dana refused to believe it. The suit was thrown out by the judge. Dana says he was treated unfairly because the judge was affiliated with Mario Cuomo, whose son worked for Chase.

On December 27, Roger Friedman reported in the *New York Observer* that Dana had lied in his SEC filings: He hadn't gone to Harvard Business School at all. Dana referred to Friedman as a "guttersnipe," and said he hadn't meant to write that on the filings, he regretted the mistake. The *Observer* also reported that Dana regularly said he was investing Spielberg's money, but Spielberg had never been a client. ("I never said that," Dana claims.) ("He said that constantly," claims Nikki Finke.) At the end of his story, Friedman asked: "Who is Dana Giacchetto?"

The question clamored in the air and Dana could not sleep. He'd turn on the kitchen light in the middle of the night, mix a powerful drink and take a pill. He will not tell me exactly what the name of the pill was—I guess he wants to protect it. But he says it was the kind of pill that made you slow down and feel relaxed, an opiate. When he woke up in a panic, Allegra didn't even want to know the story: She said, Don't tell me. She remembers thinking, "This poor guy."

When Dana tells the story of himself at this time, he renders himself as a victim. He says he knew he needed to go to rehab, but no one would help him get there. He says, "I asked for help and no one helped me. They just wanted to take over my business." As the evidence against him mounted, he portrayed himself to friends and attorneys as a vulnerable and dissolving man, instead of the conqueror he had claimed to be for so long.

* * *

In December 1999, the SEC descended on Cassandra; a cluster of officers, arriving unannounced to inspect the files. This was called a "special exam," and it was one step away from being raided. While firms like Dana's regularly underwent audits by the SEC, the special exam was a process in which the officers could look at anything. Implicitly, they were already looking for wrongdoing. You were theoretically innocent but being treated as guilty.

Alex Vasilescu says, "As an investment adviser registered with the SEC, you have to maintain books and records and ledgers. You can't just not keep track of stuff. And at any moment those records need to be made available to us. So we can inspect and examine and see what is going on." In Dana's case, the special examiners were there for a month, asking for files.

"They don't tell you anything; they are just there," Dana says. He refers to the time they were there as a terrible time. He resented the way the SEC acted like he had done something wrong.

The news of the SEC poring over the Cassandra files soon leaked out and a quiet panic ensued among the celebrity clients. The stars were being warned by their lawyers that they should stay away from Dana. All the famous clients left, one by one, each day a call from a new representative severing ties, never the star themselves.

There they went: Ben and Matt and Winona, Fiona and Helena and Cammie, Courteney and Christie and Ed. The *Los Angeles Times* reported on a "mass exodus of celebrity clients" at The Cassandra Group.

Nikki Finke had landed a contract job with *New York* magazine; her boss was a flamboyant publishing world star named Maer

Roshan. Maer knew everyone who knew anyone who knew everyone. He had been to Dana's parties; he hugged Allegra whenever he saw her. Maer had been hearing about Dana's troubles; André had called him and told a story of the Chase men as invaders, turning Dana in to the Feds, ruining this great kid's life over matters of bookkeeping.

When Maer called Nikki Finke a couple of weeks before Christmas, Nikki says, "He wanted the story to be about how there are lots of rumors floating around about Dana, but none of them have been proven yet." Nikki was already convinced Dana was a crook. But she needed to meet her contract.

Something she'd heard about Dana:

"This guy has drugs written all over him. Coke. Something."

Nikki told Maer she was on her way to Mexico. She asked him if the story could wait. Maer believed it couldn't wait. Dana was news of the moment, and it was important to weigh in. The whole pressure campaign made Nikki angry: being forced to think about this guy who she was convinced was a fake, when all she wanted to do was sit on the beach. Yet her life had become so embroiled with the Hollywood power list, it was if they followed her wherever she went. Scandal-mongering had become a form of drudgery.

Down in Mexico, as she tried to finish the story and get it out of her hair so she could lose her worries in the sun, messages started coming to her: "All of a sudden I get this message that the story has been held," Nikki says. "It was Christmas Day. I ran up a $2,000 phone bill calling *New York* magazine, trying to figure out what was going on. I was breaking my ass! Maer realized when the news about the Feds came around that we couldn't do a puff piece on this guy," Nikki says. "Suddenly that changes everything. Why was the government going to all this trouble if he was clean? And why were all his clients so spooked? We are talking about terrified people."

All over Hollywood, publicists were doing damage control, trying to revise the story of their clients' involvement with Dana. Superagents and junior superagents were saying, "Oh, I never knew him, I never introduced him to anyone."

Nikki says reporting on Dana during that month, as his reputation eroded, was like writing a story when the ground was disappearing beneath her feet. "We heard Leo had cut off relations with him," she said. "All of a sudden people were like I never told people to invest with him. Oh, I had a tiny amount of money with him . . ." But she believed she heard traces of deceit in their claims of innocence.

On New Year's Eve, 1999, Dana had his traditional party at the loft. Even though the year was epic, 1999 was the worst party Dana had ever thrown. It was half empty, and the guests were hometown friends, B-list stars, hangers-on, the waitress from down the block. Alanis was there with her blissed-out promises. "I will never leave you Dana." Russell came up from Medford. Steve Stanulis came out from Staten Island. But that was pretty much all there was to it, and there were no reports on the party in the gossip columns.

Craig Kanarick attended the 1999 party, and he remembers that it felt like some kind of ironic homecoming. "All these years I hadn't been invited to his parties, and now I was finally invited and the party was over." The era of celebrities walking through the door as if they were home had come to a close. Craig had missed the moment of the parties like a person missing a train.

Computers stayed on as the year turned; the great American Y2K disaster did not arrive as it had been anticipated, hyped, and sold. Dana woke up after his party and knew it had been a pretty sorry affair. Outside, on the street, walking out for breakfast, there were lines forming for New Year's Day brunch; there were flyers on the telephone poles: IMPROVE YOUR CREDIT; CONSOLIDATE DEBT; the underworld blowing up from the subway vents. Dana almost never said things were looking grim, but lately, the great wall of his self-confidence was starting to crack.

By January 2000, the SEC and the U.S. Attorney's office had access to all Dana's transactions, and they were monitoring him closely. In the past, he had been called One to Watch by the entertainment magazines, but this was a different kind of surveillance.

"We asked for all this accounting, all these past records," says Vasilescu, "and he showed up with this little red folder." The SEC asked him whether any clients had sued him, or come after him for lost money. He said, no, no. Everything had been great.

He never told them about Phish, the paintings. It was as if he thought the story was a sordid tale he didn't feel like discussing, something better off left in the past. He didn't seem to understand that the Confession was part of the public record. Soon the SEC found out about it. "He lied to us," says Alex Vasilescu. "He lied to us consistently and repeatedly."

Through his actions Dana was creating a narrative of recklessness. In legal terminology, "Recklessness is 'highly unreasonable conduct which is an extreme departure from the standards of ordinary care.'" They saw Dana drafting money from client accounts to "eliminate recurring overdrafts and debits in the main account." They saw money disappearing into "nonexistent bond purchases."

When I asked Dana about these offenses he admitted that yes, he had commingled funds, he had written notes assuring clients that transactions had occurred when they hadn't really occurred. He was going to make the transactions, he just hadn't gotten around to them yet. He admitted he should never have taken custody of anyone's money. Yet he believes that whether the money was in his hands or in the bank vault, it was there and it was multiplying. Just leave it alone. It will be fine. It is when you try to track it all down that everyone gets upset.

Why are you so upset? This was a persistent question in his repertoire around this time. A way of trying to quiet everyone down, like Russell putting Valium in Cosmo's beer. One day I called him, upset, certain we were going to be bankrupted by Rich's Cassandra investments. Dana said, "You have your house, don't you?" It was a strange question, cold and mercenary. But there was an undeniable truth about it.

As the SEC investigation accelerated, the officers asked for much more than the red folder. They wanted everything— every tax return and phone message. Dana became convinced he was being framed. He believed there were legions of people who were jealous of him, people who wanted to *be* him. He believed "Everyone who reads the *New York Times* knows who I am."

In one of his conspiracy theories, the Chase partners enter the office and they have come to destroy it. They are like the stranger entering town in a western. They act like they want to help Dana, but really they want to steal his power. One of Dana's celebrity friends (who will not allow me to print his name) says, "Think of *Macbeth*. Have you read *Macbeth*? You should read it, because what happened at Cassandra is like that."

* * *

Dana's cousin Donna was having trouble keeping her emotions in check. At the salon where she worked, she sometimes had to run into the bathroom and cry. She was in the middle of a divorce and winter was coming. Two kids. She thought about childhood, sitting between Russell and Dana on the piano bench. She remembered falling off the bench, and Alma pouring iodine on the cut. She missed Dana, and wished he'd never left Medford. He could always make her happy, make her feel alive and protected. If she told Dana about the divorce she knew he'd say something like: It is okay to leave because the world is waiting for you.

But that winter, whenever she called him, he sounded like he was succumbing to something, like there was some pressure crushing him. "Everything all right?" she'd ask. He'd say, "Just some business stress." The more the trouble gathered around Dana, the more Donna started to see childhood as idyllic—the days when they went on the roller coaster ten times in a row. The days before trouble found the Giacchetto boys. It was not sad back then, she thought, the way it was now in adulthood. Back then the only trouble was a few cuts that needed to be soaked in iodine.

In February 2000, Brown & Co. tapes recorded this transaction, later described in SEC documents:

> Giacchetto gave instructions to a Brown employee to issue a check in the amount of $75,000 from the account of Gabe Doppelt ("Doppelt"). Giacchetto can be heard explaining to the Brown employee that "she," Doppelt, would be picking

up the check from Cassandra's offices. In fact, Doppelt never authorized the issuance of that check and she did not learn of the withdrawal until on or about March 9, 2000, after she read her February 2000 statement from Brown and confronted Giacchetto.

The confrontations were happening all around him. Sherry Vigdor, a longtime client, found $200,000 missing from her account. Good Machine, the movie company Allegra had worked for, came to the conclusion that Dana had raided their retirement account. Bruce Pavitt had invested $250,000 in the Standard Hotel, but only $200,000 had surfaced. He sued Dana for "grossly negligent and reckless conduct."

Victoria Leacock had her piece of paper, the letter on Cassandra letterhead in which Dana swore the money was there. But the money hadn't surfaced in any of her account statements. It was lost in the sea of Dana's bad debts. She was almost 40, and she was starting to realize she had a peripatetic history. Her life didn't really translate onto paper, it didn't make sense. She received her Social Security statements, and her income fluctuated wildly—many years, no money was made. She'd been the producer of infamous drag shows; she had an underground reputation. But it did not translate to the aboveground world, to the Social Security Administration.

The only thing that translated aboveground was money, and Dana had all her money. She thought of that money as the thing that would allow her to grow old without worry. But Dana had it and wouldn't give it back. She wrote down a chronology of Dana's behavior: the days he had made promises, the days he had given her certain vital pieces of paper. She made a list called IMPORTANT NOTES.

The list included numbers for:

LAWYER WHO WANTS TO PERSUE [SIC] CLASS ACTION
ANOTHER LAWYER RE: CLASS ACTION
SECURITIES AND EXCHANGE COMMISSION

If she was feeling powerless, she could dial these numbers and leave messages. A good day was a day when there was an answer: *"We are looking into it."* A bad day was when there were no answers, when she felt like one more member of the crowd of creditors, the spurned. Was it possible she was a chronically unlucky woman? Dana had given her two martini glasses. As her $100,000 eluded her, she started calling them "the $50,000 glasses."

In March 2000, a team of FBI and SEC officers raided Dana's loft. While the SEC had been searching his offices, they'd never entered his home. But because of his resistance they'd requested a warrant. They believed that he was hiding vital materials. They wanted to pin something on him soon, before he found a way to escape. They were in the process of freezing all his accounts.

They arrived very early in the morning, and Dana and Allegra were asleep. She remembers the shock of their arrival; the buzzer pulling them out of sleep, like cold water to the face. She stumbled to the door. She wasn't wearing very much. It took a while for her to realize all these officers were eyeballing her. "A nightmare," she says.

They didn't make a big mess, like they do on television. But they swarmed into the place, focused on the shelves and drawers, directed, like machines. In the closet, Vasilescu says, they found the records they'd been asking for the day Dana brought that small red folder: past accountings that showed the company was running at an enormous loss. That it had never been in control of $400 million, as Dana said. It had always been treading water, laundering the same $100 million over and over so it looked like $400 million.

Dana called Rich and whispered, "Ricardo, you wouldn't believe it FBI, FBI, FBI." He said he couldn't explain it all now but he would explain it later. Rich looked pale when he hung up the phone. He said, "I sure hope we got out of that mess in time."

Vanity Fair reported: "Giacchetto is the subject of inquiries by the Securities and Exchange Commission as well as investigations by the U.S. Attorneys in New York and Los Angeles, and the FBI. Authorities are attempting to ascertain whether or not Cassandra was involved in an elaborate Ponzi scheme."

In the wake of the raid, Dana felt like he needed to take a trip: this time, Tokyo. He was frantic to get some new deals going. He says, "I had been talking to Sony about the Signatures deal, and I flew out to Tokyo to complete the transaction." He stayed at the Park Hyatt, where the lobbies were a velvet purple and waitresses dressed like geishas. He was taking Vicodin all the time—floating through the plush hallways on the drug's painless currents.

The Park Hyatt was an enormous hotel where many Americans congregated. One night in the bar he ran into Craig Kanarick. *Here you are again.* The global businessmen who kept running across each other. The next morning Dana and Craig had a meeting and talked about a film production company, about distribution deals, about deals down into the future. Craig had no idea of the trouble Dana was in. He knew the parties had emptied out, but he didn't know Dana had been raided, warned, pursued.

Dana was feeling productive, wearing his suits and scheduling meetings. Yet it soon became apparent that he was moving around inside the end of something. He says, "I never even got to meet with Sony!" On April 1, 2000, he called Cassandra asking for the rundown, and he was given a message: There was a warrant out for his arrest.

Dana says, "My reaction was: You've got to be kidding me! I had no indication. I found it very bizarre. I had the SEC in my offices but I had no indication I was going to be arrested. I knew I was having big problems, but I thought they were just going to go through my files."

Andy Levander was Dana's attorney at this time. Levander had been hired by Dana at the beginning of his SEC troubles. He was an efficient man who wore round glasses and tweed coats. He knew his way around criminal and corporate law. He spoke in a clipped manner—the type of lawyer who believes the fewer words, the better.

Calling Dana in Tokyo, Levander informed his client, "You have to self-surrender immediately at Kennedy. They won't arrest you in Japan, but they will arrest you when you get to New York." Dana said, "This is very bizarre."

He flew the twenty-six hours from Tokyo to New York, drinking vodka and swallowing Vicodin. Despite these efforts at self-medication, the fear would not go away, it would not be numbed. *I am getting arrested.* He couldn't fathom it. They had frozen all of his credit cards and bank accounts. It was the kind of thing that happened to Russell, not to him.

The police were waiting for Dana when he came off the plane. Handcuffed, they led him from the airport toward their car. Outside the automatic doors, the media were ready for him. Dana put on a hat to hide himself—a strange floppy lady's hat, about which Cosmo said, "That was really dumb, that hat."

Pictures flashed across the entertainment news. Bob and Cara Ginder were in the country, and they saw it. Cousin Donna saw it in Stoneham. "There he was in handcuffs being walked in front of the cameras. He looked so lost. I am thinking, Oh, my God, I can't even help him. I couldn't talk to him. And I couldn't see him." The phone started ringing in Medford, but this time the friends and relatives were not crowing about how handsome he looked.

He was taken to a holding cell in the U.S. courthouse. He spent the night there, and he remembers "coming down from Vicodin, all these weird dreams of Technicolor little people."

All the time Dana had been in the air, Cosmo and Alma were pulling their papers together. They were going to bail him out; they had to. They couldn't imagine him there in the dark among the prisoners. Maybe Russell, but not Dana. They needed to come to the scene of the accident and rescue him, pull him out of the ditch. They put their house up for collateral, handing the deed over to the judge.

Andy Levander proposed to the judge that Dana surrender his passport to the court, thereby showing them that he was not a flight risk. The judge agreed to this, plus $500,000 bail. Dana brought in the passport, a nostalgic book of stamps, an artifact of his jet-set life. He signed an agreement that he would not travel beyond the eastern and southern districts of New York.

Victoria Leacock read about Dana's arrest in the *Post*. She had tried to convince herself that the letter he'd handed her that day at lunch really meant something, with the letterhead and the signature. Certainly it was some kind of binding document? Maybe not. She was starting to realize it might be just one more piece of paper blowing around.

She bolted upright one night with a premonition: Dana has hidden all the money in Thailand, and he is going to flee the country. The next morning she made a batch of cupcakes and packed them up in tasteful paper. She took a taxi to Dana's apartment and rang the buzzer. She said, "Dana, it's Victoria. I have a present for you, I have heard what a hard time you're having." He let her upstairs, and they hugged and kissed each other; he said, "*Cupcakes,* how great."

This girlish gift was like a Trojan horse, a way of penetrating the walls of his apartment. Spying on him under the cover of her sweet act. She was so sure he was leaving the country, she was certain there would be suitcases everywhere. "But everything looked normal," she says, "so I felt a little better."

At two-thirty in the afternoon on April 4, 2000, Jules Crittenden paid a visit to the Giacchetto home. He was a columnist for the *Boston Herald,* and he wanted to get Dana's parents on record. He remembers: "The front door was opened, the storm door closed." Russell came out, yelled at him, "Get lost." Russell had a pad and paper, and was writing down the license plate numbers of Crittenden's car. Crittenden remembers, "He said, 'If you come back I'll shoot you. You're on private property. I have written down your info and I am going to find out who you are and come after you.'"

Cosmo and Alma were in New York, dealing with Dana's lawyers and their fees. Russell thought he was guarding the fort, but, as was his tendency, he went a little too far. Crittenden pressed charges that appeared on Russell's rap sheet: Threatening to Kill. For a few weeks afterward, Crittenden was watchful around his house, in a suburb neighboring Medford. He had written about mobsters and crooks but he was afraid of Russell. He wouldn't have been surprised to find him circling his property, trying every window until he found a way in.

A prisoner out on bail is in the realm of the last chance: one more chance before you are incarcerated. One more chance at taking responsibility for your movements and actions. The judge asked Dana: Do you understand these rules as I have described them to you? Dana said, Yes, Your Honor. He said he knew his parents' house could be lost if he did not follow the letter of the law. But two weeks after his release, he started down another course of delusional and reckless action.

On the morning of April 10, 2000, Dana sifted through his pile of frozen credit cards, until he found one the Feds had neglected to deactivate. With this card, he bought a plane ticket to Las Vegas. He says, "I was going to try to meet with Cirque du Soleil about doing some consulting work. They had opened at the Bellagio! And they were really big!"

For the trip he packed: a pile of one-way plane tickets, which he'd accumulated over the years; $3,500 in cash, collected from that same credit card; and an expired passport, upon which he wrote in a new expiration date with a ballpoint pen. Also, at the airport, he bought two one-way tickets to Rome on that same credit card. The idea was: one for him, one for Allegra.

After crossing every sea he could cross and becoming a regular on the Concorde, Dana resisted the limits of his bail. He had always moved as if flight was in his nature. For this reason, he was an ideal global citizen. He was also a classic flight risk.

Allegra called Alma and Cosmo with news of the Vegas trip. The call came in on Alma's cell phone as they were driving around Medford. Cosmo yelled in the receiver: What the hell. Is he crazy? We are going to lose the house!! His voice shook the car.

Dana had checked into the Desert Inn, an old Vegas classic waiting to be imploded. The phone started ringing. Cosmo and Andy Levander, everyone yelling. "Where the fuck are you? Are you crazy?"

Dana said, "I am in Las Vegas. I left a message on the machine. Why are you so upset! Calm down, why is everybody so upset?"

Levander said, "You can't just leave a message on the machine!" He explained that there was a bureaucracy to go through, there were papers to sign, a prisoner on probation had to wait until they had the official stamp of approval.

Your parents might lose their house, Levander said.

That is not going to happen, Dana replied.

Dana booked the next flight to Newark. When they'd arrested him the first time, coming back from Tokyo, the police allowed him to disembark with his things before cuffing him, as if sparing him the public humiliation. This time, they came inside the plane and cuffed him and dragged him out. "It was horrendous," Dana says. The passengers gasped and stared. He was such a high flight risk, the Feds thought he might try one of those doors that leads out onto the runway.

The next morning, he appeared on the cover of *Newsday*, walking into the courthouse after a night in jail, tearful. GROUNDED said the headline. SCAMMER TO THE STARS BIDS TO TAKE FLIGHT, BUT LANDS IN JAIL, declared the *New York Post*. Under the headline BAIL REVOKED FOR INVESTMENT ADVISOR TO THE STARS, the *New York Times'* John Sullivan wrote:

Mr. Levander constructed the best defense he could. Mr. Levander said Mr. Giacchetto was holding airline tickets because he traveled constantly as an investment adviser. He said the tickets were a reflection of Mr. Giacchetto's former lifestyle, and were bought before his arrest.

Mr. Levander said that Mr. Giacchetto had bought the ticket to Rome, but intended to obtain the court's permission before traveling. He said his client wanted to propose marriage to his girlfriend, and "thought Rome would be a great place."

Finally, Mr Levander said, Mr. Giacchetto carried the expired passport because he did not have a valid driver's license and needed a photo identification. The prosecutor objected to this explanation, saying it did not pass the "straight face test."

Soon thereafter, Levander recused himself from Dana's case. He explained to me, "Since I'd promised the judge he would not use a passport, his use of an expired passport put me in a position of conflict of interest, so I had to remove myself."

Dana didn't see it this way. He saw it in terms of abandonment, the way he would begin to see many things. He said, "Andy Levander left me for dead."

Dana tried to make me understand the logic of this ill-fated journey: "I didn't have any ID, I needed to just write a note on my passport, saying what the real expiration date of my real passport was. I was fucked up on drugs, I couldn't be lucid. I was so infuriated that they were suggesting I was fleeing!"

He says, "There was another side to the paper of the rules, and I didn't read it. [He is talking about the rules of his probation.] We had it posted on the fridge but I was so freaked out and I didn't really understand it."

*   *   *

The morning of April 13, Victoria Leacock looked at the *News-day* GROUNDED headline, and the truth about her money sunk in and made her breathless. *That money is gone,* she said to herself, over and over like a mantra. She looked at the tumblers from Cassandra. The thing about them both costing $50,000: It was no longer a joke.

In Seattle, a friend sent me the *Newsday* cover and I put it in the cabinet, next to the bowl Dana had bought at that restaurant the night before our wedding. Cosmo and Alma would place the tabloid clippings about him in their cabinet, too, and there would be dozens of them: SCAMMER TO THE STARS, THE FALLEN FINANCIER. When I visited Medford, I was jarred by this display at first—the way they'd placed the stories of his success alongside the stories of his disgrace. Then I started to think there was something honest about it, or something brave. Like a confrontation: Yes, this happened. We aren't going to deny it.

A week after the GROUNDED cover, Dana appeared in court; he pled not guilty, and the judge set an end-of-summer sentencing date. Dana was transferred to MDC Brooklyn, a slightly less violent facility than MCC New York.

Few white-collar criminals ever darken the door of the facilities where Dana spent his first eight months of prison. But then again, he was the first in a wave of late nineties white-collar criminals, and perhaps the rules had not yet been determined.

In the courtroom, as Dana proclaimed his innocence, Cosmo cried, his whiskers growing out. Dana cried in his orange jumpsuit. Roger Friedman was there, taking notes for his *Observer* column. Victoria Leacock was there, since she needed to see the whole thing for herself to believe it had really happened. The room was full of curiosity seekers and press people, but no celebrities. No celebrity in their right mind would've been seen there.

The court had mercy on Cosmo and Alma and they did not take the house. "The clerk handed me the deed," Cosmo says, "He looked at me and said: You take this back, you are nice people." All the way back to Medford and all night for many nights, Cosmo ran down the story in his mind. He started to see a conspiracy against Italians in the way the court had treated Dana. He thought about that whole "Don" comment in the program from the Sweet Relief Medicine Ball—as if they were making Dana out to be some kind of Italian mobster.

The news of his arrest rippled through Medford and Stoneham. Donna was moving into her new place after leaving her husband. She was there among the boxes trying to put a good face on it, and then she turned on the television. There was the plastic lady on *Entertainment Tonight,* talking about Dana like he was evil. Donna thought of Dana as innocent and naive, pure somehow. "Russell, he was streetwise and you knew he could hold his own in prison. Dana, I wasn't so sure."

For the first time in his life, Russell was not the black sheep. Or he was a black sheep, but not the blackest sheep. Dana was in federal prison, a world Russell had only heard about but never penetrated. Realizing this, Russell almost felt lucky to be himself. It was not a feeling he experienced very often.

Russell had been out of prison for almost a year when Dana went in. He was again working at a retirement home patching holes in the walls, flirting with the nurses, starting his own painting business. He was staying away from Lisa and heroin but he'd started using coke—"zips," he called the little white lines, inhaled off tabletops, dashboards, and fingertips. Russell told me he needed zips because they gave him energy for sex. He said sex on coke was so much better than any other way.

The same girls who visited Russell in prison would drive him around Medford, now that his license was suspended for eternity. Russell tried to structure his days so he could have a meal with his parents and make sure they were all right. He worried about them. He figured they'd seen enough. The Klonopin helped him hold his tongue with Cosmo, and he tried in small ways to be good.

Russell started a website to raise money for Dana's legal fund. He enlisted the Web-design services of a guy who was rumored to be really good at this sort of thing. On the site, Russell posted a letter, proclaiming Dana's innocence, using language from Dana's own letter about, "I am truly sorry for the pain I've caused." He provided a link where you could send a check to 39 Winford Way and buy Cosmo's book at a discounted price.

Dana found out about the website and told Russell it was tacky: He should shut it down. "People might take it the wrong way," Dana said.

Allegra had been evicted from the loft. Maureen had taken Angel to her apartment in Brooklyn and cousin Gale had taken Caesar to Long Beach. Officers collected Dana's belongings and a list was constructed. It included:

1 Il Bisonte black leather attaché
2 Internet access CDs
10 Music CDs (various artists)
1 Sennheiser British Airways headphones
1 Blue leather Concorde document case

Arresting officers found his bank account contained about $10,000.

The sole remains of Dana's empire were his suits and his shoes. Together with Cosmo, Allegra made a plan to rescue Dana's tycoon clothes—those Pradas and Calvin Kleins that would likely end up moldering in police evidence if she didn't do something. So she and Cosmo bought suit boxes, and Cosmo rented a truck to drive into the city. They moved through Dana's closets unbelieving—how much, how much. Silk and cashmere. Handmade Italian shoes. Cosmo wondered: When had Dana found the time out of work to buy all this shit?

In Cosmo's Medford garage, Dana's suits were packed in mothballs, plastic, padded hangers, the works. The order of the house was: *Don't let anything happen to damage these things.* The suits lived among the fireworks, waiting for Dana to return.

Dana spent the next six months in MDC Brooklyn, an institution flanked by the sprawling Green-Wood Cemetery on one side and Gowanus Bay, at the end of the subway line. MDC Brooklyn is part of the Federal Bureau of Prisons; it is an intimidating, thirteen-story brick structure that covers two city blocks, and it houses male and female inmates. Of the 2,000 or so inmates, more than half are in for drug offenses: selling or using. It is located in a desolate area of fast-food restaurants, adult video palaces, boarded-up windows, broken sidewalks that are a hazard to navigate so pedestrians tend to walk along the edges of the street.

The prison is the meaning of the neighborhood. The prison's visiting hours dictate the neighborhood's population: when visits are happening, the streets are crowded with people, mostly women and children, released from buses and arriving to see their men. In the off hours or late at night the streets are empty, although all along the sidewalks there are signs of the prison visitors: hair ribbons, little shoes, massive paper cups.

Entering MDC Brooklyn, signs warn visitors that they will be thrown out if they are seen "demonstrating actions that might otherwise endanger institution safety, security, or good order." The fear dictating the architecture of the place is a fear of escape. Cars can't idle outside the prison yards; they could be getaway cars. The cell windows are so thin no ordinary man could find a way to slip through them.

MDC was an unusual place for a white-collar criminal to land: It was generally the destination of the poorest offenders, and it had a reputation for violence. Dana says he saw a man get his ear cut off. He says he was afraid all the time. He is pretty certain there were terrorists in there with him.

He was only a few miles from SoHo but it was like he had been swallowed by the architecture of another world.

Sometimes word would get out: "Hey, did you fuck those pretty movie stars? What were they like?"

To pass the time, he wrote letters. He wrote to Rich and me. One letter spoke about how he had been exercising ("I'm no Jack LaLanne") and reading novels. He said he hoped he had not hurt us. In conclusion, he wrote, "My heart is still pure. The swirl of misinformation and half truths is drifting away from me."

I read the letter first, then I brought it down to the basement where Rich sat in his workshop dreaming of how you might form the border around your state so you could be a country unto yourself. He was falling down into himself. He was starting to look afraid. He made a T-shirt parodying that hippie slogan: Visualize World Peace. It said, Visualize World Fear. He wore it around our neighborhood, and the old couple next door stopped talking to us.

Rich also had a sense of doom about the music business. He knew about these new things called MP3s, files you could download for free and you would never need to buy a record or a CD: The music would become public, floating out there for anyone to hear. Rich says, "I would never tell a kid not to pirate music just like I never busted kids when they shoplifted at Yard Birds."

Property Is Theft! This was one of his favorite phrases, even as our property value increased and our liquid money ran out.

Steve Stanulis visited Dana at MDC Brooklyn. For him it was easy to get visitors' clearance because he had his badge. He could bring Dana care packages no one else could, he could stay as long as he wanted. By this time Steve's wife had broken up with him. She no longer trusted him, after all the Dana business. Although he didn't see the movie stars anymore, his time among them had convinced him maybe he could be an actor, too. He told Dana he was trying out for soap opera parts. Dana wished him luck from the other side of the glass.

Allegra came to know the waiting area of MDC Brooklyn; she knew the drill of putting all her possessions into a locker before being led in to visit. Allegra felt a kinship with the other women visitors, even though all of them were black or Hispanic, and poor. Here she was, a rich Mount Holyoke girl who looked like she'd been crying for three weeks. They were kind to her, and mothered her as they all waited to be called. "I will always remember it," she says. "They helped me get through it. We were friends and we saw each other more than I saw anyone else." The women told her things were going to be all right, and that she should try to be strong.

The visitors' rules were strict:

Inmates and visitors cannot use the same restrooms.
Once the visitor leaves they can't come back.
Maximum four hours a month visitors outside immediate
family.

This immediate family rule was the one Dana and Allegra felt victimized by. They seemed so immediate to each other. So all-consuming. Isn't that what immediate meant?

Allegra came to believe that Dana had been betrayed and neglected by his lawyers. She set out to find a lawyer who believed in him, who could help him get out of this mess and come home. She wanted the most powerful lawyer she could find. She reasoned that they would scrape together money, or the lawyer would take it because it was a high-profile case. This was after the O. J. trial, after lawyers had become blow-dried celebrities, guys with their own PR firms and websites.

She tried F. Lee Bailey but he was booked. Second on her list: Ron Fischetti, a New York trial attorney who was "supposed to be the best." Fischetti was famous for defending a New York City police officer in an assault case that had been called a hate crime. Abner Louima, a Haitian immigrant, had been beaten and sodomized by a group of white cops. Charles Schwarz was one of the officers who was arrested for the crime, but Fischetti won his innocence arguing that Schwarz had only watched the beating—he hadn't participated.

Fischetti had also worked as a mob attorney. He had the demeanor of a wise guy. Like Cosmo, his hair was gray and unruly and he could threaten to sue you into oblivion with a smile on his face. His office was a shrine to his accomplishments: drawings from the Schwarz trial, the day when his name was on the front page of the New York Times. A picture of him being handed an award.

Allegra took the subway to midtown and met with him in his office. She gravitated to him. He felt like family to her. He agreed to take the case, even though the money was frozen and intermittent. It seemed like a case that was important, that could get him somewhere.

When he first visited Dana at MDC Brooklyn, Fischetti believed his client was in a manic state.

"It was very difficult to communicate with him. He made all kinds of claims that he was absolutely innocent, that the money was there, that the Pickens bonds were going to be paid, that there was a lot of money in AT&T bonds, and things like that. It took us weeks to try to unravel the financial mess. It was impossible. The SEC had records, the FBI had records, he didn't have any of the records. We couldn't decipher them one way or another, he had very little money to pay us, so we couldn't hire forensic accountants. But it became obvious to us after a couple of weeks that the money was gone, it wasn't there. And that he had commingled the accounts. And it became necessary to convince Dana that he had to plead guilty, which he didn't want to do. And that was a major hurdle. To take responsibility for his actions. Because, to his own mind, he wasn't a thief."

When Dana finally came down from the ledge and admitted his guilt, Fischetti scheduled a sentencing hearing. He told Dana he would fight to get him shipped to a nice, minimum-security prison where he'd be treated right. Where he wouldn't be treated like a common criminal. Maybe the place the Watergate guys went, which was supposed to be very nice.

Fischetti had convinced Dana that he was guilty, that what he'd done was wrong, that he would never be able to convince the powers that be to let him back out onto the other side of the law. "All the drugs were finally out of his system," Fischetti says. But if the reality of his actions had set in, his sense of guilt was inconstant, like a radio signal to the mind that only comes in at certain times. "I only pled guilty to one count of fraud," Dana tells me. "I never said I did anything else wrong."

A few days before the sentencing hearing, Dana sent the judge a poem. It ran over seven pages, and it read in part:

> *Blink blink winged*
> *With the resolve of benediction*
> *As I approach this singular*
> *Reality.*
>
> *Blink Blink winged*
> *With knowing for an instant*
> *How it all went*
> *Wrong.*
>
> *Oh, the good I can do*
> *Oh, those healed and*
> *Children I smile at,*
> *Filling and forever I*
> *Look at God and Love . . .*
>
> *Your Honor, I bare my neck.*
> *Please continue to believe in repair.*

The hearing took place in August 2000, down by the water in the financial district. This was the same neighborhood where he'd reported for work when he was twenty-one years old, riding up to the 103rd floor of the World Trade Center. Now he was thirty-eight and cuffed, being led inside to hear his sentence. When he was young, he thought he could see countless powerful versions of himself. This was not one of them.

Fischetti argued before the judge. He presented Dana as a victim—someone who needed to be treated to a more civil kind of containment:

"For ten months Dana Giacchetto has not seen the sky. There is no outdoor facility at the MDC. . . . You are there all day with some pretty—some dangerous characters, as Your Honor knows, and you just live with your open thoughts and with your own mind."

He talked about all Dana had lost. He included in his catalogue "a Calder sculpture worth over a million dollars."

After Fischetti spoke, it was Dana's turn. He talked about how sorry he was for his actions, how he had "lost his moral compass."

"But I looked around when I was falling apart, begged everyone, please will someone please help me, and they all wanted to run because it was too messy and they couldn't figure it out and the world's biggest bank was involved and everyone else was involved and every time I tried they said, shut up, we don't believe you. . . . Yes, I did exaggerate, yes, I did lie, I animated, I lived a world of fantasy. I am guilty of all those things."

Fischetti had collected twenty-two letters from friends and family, testifying to Dana's strength of character. These are handwritten letters from aunts in Medford, from a surgeon in Los Angeles on fancy stationery, from former female roommates working for newspapers and fashion magazines, from Maureen in a looping script, from Luigi the neighbor who taught him about Wall Street, from his dentist when he was a kid. The letters all say things like *He is a good person.* And, *We beg for your mercy.* Allegra wrote: "He is the quintessential Libra who lost his balance." Rich wrote a letter that declared: "My intuition is that a few months out of the 'fast lane' might help to bring back the clarity and sense of purpose that I have admired in him so much." There were no letters from famous people.

Dana wrote his own letter in defense of himself. It was a strange document, dense with five-dollar words:

> *Writing an essay to save a life. The confluence of thirty-eight years of existence have become inculcated, compressed into some immutable, contemplative orbit. Given this, isn't any attempt at a self-directed palliative the ultimate adventure in futility?*

Dana was sent to Allenwood Federal Penitentiary to serve out a three-year sentence. He believed it was too long a sentence, that he'd been dealt a bad hand. He believed the judge should've let him out into society—he'd learned his lessons, and he could be productive again.

After the sentencing, Allegra wrote a letter to friends, trying to raise money to pay Fischetti. The letter said, "Whatever you can donate would be much appreciated, I know you know this has been difficult for all of us." Craig Kanarick received the letter and he thought it was a joke. He'd just realized he might've lost a million dollars in the Pickens water. When Allegra called, he told her, "Forget it. I have lost enough money with this guy." She appealed to his sense of history, his sense of home. He said, "Forget it. Seriously."

PART
EIGHT

2000-2003

ALLENWOOD IS LOCATED IN MONTGOMERY, PENNSYL-vania, close to Amish country. The town is barely a town, more a sparsely populated stretch of highway: a few stores and gas stations, rolling hills, farms out at the end of long driveways. It is a country of meadows, virtually treeless. This is why it is an ideal location for a minimum security prison. The green wide-openness of it makes escape almost unimaginable; a prisoner would have to run out into the open in their bright clothes. All prisoners wear electronic ankle bracelets that send signals back to the prison the moment they cross the threshold.

The prisoners at Allenwood are all men. They are bankers convicted of fraud, doctors convicted of insurance skimming, famous politicians who took back-door deals, mafia bosses, or their underlings.

Although Allenwood was supposed to be a better place, a place where he could relax and reflect on his crimes, Dana says he was more afraid of the other prisoners here than he was at

MDC Brooklyn. "They would act like they were your friends," he says. "But really they wanted to get something on you. Make a plea bargain." Many of his fellow prisoners were people who, like Dana, had been the toast of charity balls, embraced by society. They hadn't recovered from treating their entire life as an important meeting.

"I had to learn to be predator, not prey," he says, but he won't elaborate.

I saw Bruce Pavitt in Seattle and he seemed skinny and compromised. He had the same bravado: talking about what would work and what would not work in the marketplace. But to me he didn't have the same authority. He just seemed like a wanderer, not a discoverer. All these young men who thought they knew Dana, who thought they were getting in on the ground floor of something, they were getting older and realizing that they should've held on to all their pieces of paper, they should've filed their taxes on time, they should never have taken that DMT because it had rattled their judgment and memory.

The entrepreneurs who thought they knew the future were becoming part of the past. They had charmed their way through the nineties but the charm wore off. Craig Kanarick had become a billionaire with Razorfish, but the tide was turning on him. In February 2000, he and his partner were interviewed by *60 Minutes* reporter Bob Simon. The interview was recounted in *Wired* magazine in an article called "Brattitude Adjustment."

According to *Wired*:

Simon praised Razorfish as "one of the most successful companies on the Web," but then his tone abruptly changed.

"Successful at what?" he asked. . . . "Tell me what you do," Simon insisted, "In English." . . .

"Well," Kanarick said, "we radically transform businesses to invent and reinvent them."

Kanarick was speaking to Simon in a kind of vague nineties tech speak that was not quite translating anymore. In November 2000, Razorfish stock tanked. (Eventually Razorfish stock would rise again, under new owners and a new, generic model.) Kanarick and his partners had talked up a digital dream of superfast delivery; they promised a revolutionary, radical reenvisioning of something, but the words seemed like empty sales tools, and people wanted to know what exactly they were buying. "Revolutionary" and "radical" were words used in lipstick commercials, words that didn't really mean much anymore.

On January 27, 2001, the *New York Times* published an article about Dana, a sort of postscript:

[Mr. Giacchetto] was not making nearly enough money to pay for it all, officials said. To tide himself over, Mr. Giacchetto hit upon a scheme about as sophisticated as stealing Social Security checks out of mailboxes and cashing them.

Victoria was featured in the article, and she posed for a photograph—wearing penny loafers sitting on concrete stairs, looking sad. Her friend called and said, "You were posing like a victim." Victoria said, "I am one. I am not posing. I am a victim, that is what I am."

Near the end of the article, Alex Vasilescu was quoted. He

said, "Unraveling the effects of Mr. Giacchetto's financial mis-
adventures could take years."

In our case, it would be almost a year before we would discover that Dana had lost Rich's savings, too, that there was no
accounting for the Pickens money he'd paid back. As far as the
SEC was concerned, Dana paid Rich back with ill-gotten gains.
It would be another two years of lawyers and court appointments before Rich would realize what he'd lost. But we read the
article without thinking we were part of Vasilescu's prediction,
without thinking we were still embroiled in Dana's "financial
misadventure."

"We got out," Rich said. "We really did." But it turns out
everyone was claiming the same thing. Magician David Blaine
said it to the *New York Daily News,* "I got out early and I
made really good money." We were all talking like escape
artists.

Victoria tried not to think or talk about the money too much.
She told herself "You have been ripped off, get over it." But she
described the way it shook her sense of self. "When you are
embezzled or robbed it psychologically undermines your confidence. It does a lot of damage to one's own psyche. There is
something about someone being in your bank account that is
really invasive and mysterious."

She wanted a child. The desire had built up in her as she
approached forty and for her pregnancy had now become high-
risk. It started to seem all the men were like Vasilescu—someone
to break up with or be dumped by. Someone who is not quite
right. Yet she had always wanted to take care of a child and put
it to bed.

She considered getting in vitro, artificial insemination, picking a sperm donor. Maybe she'd pick one of her gay friends, and make a true Bohemian child, the kind her father would understand. Yet as she researched this she realized all the procedures cost $12,000 and up. She could never get ahead. She looked at the $50,000 glasses in the cupboard. On some level, the glasses were the baby that would not come. The Dana money became the loss of a certain possibility. The possibility of calling the doctor and saying: Okay, I am ready for the procedure.

Sometimes the subject of Dana came up for her at cocktail parties. If people spoke about him as a victim, as a lost boy, she would say, "He is a pathological liar and a criminal. How can you have any sympathy for him?"

She ran into Soledad on the street. She thought maybe Soledad knew something about the missing money, that all of those Cassandra employees must have known something, must've been in on it somehow. She heard rumors about Dana going to Thailand and hiding money. In this scenario he is released from jail and lives an island life. Drinks out of coconut shells. The child she wants recedes from her life so Dana can live in the style to which he is accustomed.

In Allenwood, to pass the time, Dana read *Artforum* and Dave Eggers. He volunteered to play organ for the church choir down the street, and he advised inmates in accounting. He had his own space, what the white-collar prisoners called "cubicles," but he did not put up photographs. He wrote letters to clients asking for mercy.

He wrote about how he had suffered. He wrote about searching his conscience. He had decided he needed to heal everyone and find "normalcy." He asked old clients to forgive him and said he was only trying to help all along and he was never trying to hurt anyone. He appealed to the memory of their art-filled SoHo friendship.

To the Ginders he wrote:

> *Bob, I remember seeing one of your installation pieces in your loft tiny pieces of poetry, severed, cut up—sealed in glass tubes or pipes, permanently transfigured and left alone from the art of the whole. I feel like one of those lost lines of poetry, and I hope one day you'll break open that cylinder and rejoin me in a poem that brings life back in balance.*

When Cara and Bob read the letter, they thought they detected a great emptiness in his apology. Nowhere in his letter did they see their experience reflected, their months of insomnia and doubt. "He was always making himself into the victim," Cara says. They searched the paragraphs, but they didn't find the repentant language they felt they deserved.

On September 11, 2001, Dana heard about the World Trade Center bombings and he watched the news in the common room. That night he put his ear to his radio and dreamed about himself as a twenty-one-year-old working on the 103rd floor in Tower Number Two. In the dream, the ceiling caved in on him.

Although Allenwood was driven by routine, and although order was kept by creating an illusion of timelessness, still history rippled through its corridors. Dana says most of the Arab prisoners disappeared after 9/11. One day they were there in the cafeteria, and then they were gone. None of the other prisoners knew where they had been taken.

*   *   *

The morning of 9/11, Alex Vasilescu had set out from his West Village apartment to walk to work. It was a clear morning and the walk would only take about twenty minutes. Halfway there he heard the impact, and felt a violent shift in the air. Then the sirens began. He returned to his apartment to wait out the news.

The SEC offices were located at 7 World Trade Center, one of the buildings adjacent to Tower Number One. On September 14, this building collapsed, a delayed result of the impact, of the shifts in the earth due to the power of the explosions.

Eventually the SEC would move into a building on the border of Ground Zero, and when I interview Alex in 2004, his offices look out over the crater. By now the colossal empty space has become a tourist attraction, and hawkers sell pictures of the Trade Towers: "9/11, Never Forget," in glittery letters on the frame.

Alex tells me that when the SEC offices collapsed, most of the papers from Dana's trial went with them. After I am finished interviewing him I cannot shake the image: The whole case against Dana as part of the rubble of history, part of the tidal wave of decimated paper, tiny pieces of plastic and metal from computers and discs and ergonomic chairs and file cabinets, all this office material, all these previously important papers, all these messages saying things like ASAP, or Call Immediately, all of it reverting to dust.

On September 29, 2001, Rich and I visited Dana at Allenwood. We had flown East for my best friend's wedding in Massachusetts. Air travel was all about fear: People were talking about anthrax in airplane sugar packets. Our flights came in and out of Logan Airport, where the terrorists had originated. Men in plain black, unmarked uniforms carried Uzis in the airport. We said, "This must be like Israel." The planes we were riding were mostly empty. The stewardesses said things over the speakers like: "We hope things will get back to normal soon."

In this petrified environment, we drove out to Allenwood in a rental car. As we worked our way up into the country, all the houses had their flags at half-staff. We carried an edition of *USA Today*; on the front page were brightly colored graphs and lists about anthrax poisoning: "First you may feel flu-like symptoms. This may progress into difficulty breathing, shock, or death." When one of us coughed we'd glance warily at each other, wondering if that cough was a sign of the poison settling in, the poison in those airport sugar packets.

We made our way to the Comfort Inn outside of Montgomery, Pennsylvania. When we arrived we met Allegra at the hotel bar and drank powerful gimlets as CNN played at full volume, all about the attacks. Anchor people stood in front of the smoking crater, behind them the workers came in and out, retrieving whatever could be retrieved.

Allegra told us her story of that day. She was in TriBeCa, in her apartment. People wandered up her street covered with ash, carrying dead cell phones, looking for land lines. There was a working phone line in Allegra's apartment, and word got out on the street. Soon her living room was full of ash-covered people making quick phone calls, saying *I am all right, I am all right.* Allegra and her roommate gave the ash-covered people water and crackers. Then the people made their way uptown, out of the dust.

The next morning, Rich and Allegra and I drove the five miles out to Allenwood. It had taken weeks for Rich and I to get on the visitors' list. We had filled out forms:

Persons entering upon the premises are subject to routine searches of their person, property (including vehicles), and packages. The Warden, upon a reasonable suspicion, that a person may be introducing a contraband substance, or demonstrating actions that might otherwise endanger institution safety and security, or the good order, may request the person, as prerequisite to entry, to submit to a visual search, pat search, urine surveillance test, breathalyzer test, or other comparable test. A visitor has the option to refuse any of the searches or tests, with the result that the visitor will not be allowed entry into the institution.

The waiting room was all white light, hard plastic chairs, rows facing each other but too far away for knees to touch. It took him a while to appear, and we were instructed not to embrace. There are rules about touching the prisoner: If you come too close, you could be trying to slip him something.

We had not laid eyes on Dana since his arrest. His head was down, and his face was red. He wore a beige uniform with his number on it, and his eyeglasses were coming apart on him. In the beginning of the visit, he couldn't really look at us, but little by little he came back and acted like his old self.

It was a five-hour visit fueled by snacks from the vending machines: microwaved hamburgers, bagel dogs. Dana and Allegra had recipes they wanted to try out on us: the burger with a piece of cheese from the turkey-cheese sandwich, the turkey from the sandwich inside the bagel-dog bread, the bagel dog on its own, as an hors d'oeuvre. We sat out on the deck, and deer came up and ate potato chips from our hands. We commented on the beauty of the sunset, the same way we had on the trip with Artemis in Yosemite eight years before.

In the past I'd never spent time with Dana without the taste of alcohol on our lips. Yet I came away thinking he was the same person he had been on the outside. He was not broken. His ego still burnt brightly. During the visit Dana said, "Maybe you should write a book about me." I said, "That would be great, let's write letters about it."

Rich and Dana talked about what had happened. Dana tried to explain the conspiracy—the same conspiracy that had appeared in his libel case, the one the judge had thrown out. The more Dana talked about the conspiracy, the more the veins stood out in his neck. Rich said, "Okay, okay," in a quiet voice, like he was trying to get Dana to come down from a bad trip. I could tell Rich was disappointed in the way Dana talked about his crimes. It seemed Dana believed all his crimes were committed by someone else.

Dana told stories about seeing famous people in prison: a young filmmaker whose dad was a drug dealer, a movie star who was making a film about a prisoner, and was loitering around studying the prisoners. Even now after the belief in fame had exacted such dire consequences, after I had come to believe to a certain degree that the celebrities destroyed Dana, celebrity made its way into the conversation; it still held us in its thrall.

Dana said to Rich, "Don't worry, you got out of the mess fine, I am pretty sure you are fine."

"Good," Rich said. "Glad to hear it."

On the way back, Rich reassured me: "I took my money out in 1998. Surely, if Dana had blown apart in a 'period of three months' as he told us, then the period before was clean? That the money he said we had, we really had?" But even as he reassured me, he told me he didn't trust Dana anymore after seeing him in prison. He said, "He is not repentant, he doesn't think he did anything wrong." I tried to spin it the other way. I said,

"He screwed up, we loved him, we will always love him, right?" I reminded him of the time Dana pulled the paint chip out of his eye.

Cousin Donna couldn't afford to visit Allenwood, but she wrote him letters. She reported on her daughters, their grades, how quickly they were growing into women. She wrote that Russell seemed to be doing better, he'd been clean and clear of the police for quite a while now. He was helping Cosmo and Alma with their rental properties.

Donna tried to be cheerful in these letters but Dana's arrest felt like an enormous blow to her, like the end of something. Maybe the end of an ideal. Because there at the salon in Stoneham, trying to see her future, she had always thought of Dana as some kind of hope figure. She had imbued him with her own dreams of getting out. But now his life was in ruins, and it seemed he would've been better off if he'd never left in the first place.

While Dana was in prison, the bankruptcy lawyers sued Cosmo and Alma for ill-gotten gains. There were checks in the ledger adding up to hundreds of thousands of dollars, with no explanation. For Cosmo, it was Dana paying back the family loans from all those years ago. For the SEC, it was Dana skimming off people's money, giving gifts to friends and family members.

Cosmo thought the prosecutors were vindictive, that they were going too far. They were just trying to get money to pay themselves and buy themselves lunch. (Indeed, most of the settlement money ended up paying the lawyers, and very little of it went to creditors.) The lawyers sent Cosmo registered letters, but Cosmo threw them away. They called him and Cosmo yelled into the receiver, "I AM AN OLD MAN and you are not getting a dime from me, I'll die first." Then he hung up.

Dana's infamy had attached itself to Cosmo and Alma like a bird at their backs. Everyone in Medford knew about Dana's crimes. They were written up in the local papers. People read the *Herald* and they heard the scandal about Russell threatening Crittenden, chasing this popular columnist out into the street. Cosmo was glad when they mentioned his book in these articles; at least it meant the reporter had done some legwork. Sometimes he went down to the Medford library, to see if *When the Act Accuses Him* had been checked out.

When their friends came over they asked fragile questions like, "Do you need anything?" That was the question that had always belonged to Alma. Yet between the boys in jail and the lawyers calling, she was not sure she could meet anyone's needs. She went off on a negative streak: "I bore these boys," she said. "I must have done something wrong."

Her friends had always called her streetwise, tough. But they started to wonder how much bad news one small woman could take.

Cosmo asked, "Am I like King Lear or something? These sons turning on me?"

One afternoon Alma and Allegra went out and visited Dana at Allenwood. Allegra could not believe how fast Alma drove, "like Mario Andretti," she said. Cosmo stayed home. Alma says, "It just upset him too much; he couldn't take it." He needed surgery on his hip, and the car ride aggravated the pain. (The doctor had given him Vicodin but he hated it and flushed it down the toilet.) So while Alma and Allegra drove away to see Dana in the flesh, he puttered around the house among the photographs. He made himself lunch. He watched the movie of the wedding. He wondered if bad luck comes in threes or if it just keeps coming.

* * *

The lawyers served notice to Rich, too, a few months after Cosmo. Rich's name was there in the papers, with amounts posted beside it, but the lawyers could not figure out who he was. They thought he was a friend Dana was stealing money for. They knew these Sub Pop men had made out with a lot of dough. They wanted to look into it. They sent Rich a registered letter telling him it was possible he had been the recipient of ill-gotten gains. Rich talked to the man on the phone. He was down in the basement so I wouldn't hear—he didn't want me to know what was happening. He knew how spooked I was about money. He told the man he had tried to keep track of the money, as far as he knew the money was there.

Rich built a file on the Dana case, he tried to remember to think about it, but he also put it out of his mind. He said, "I am not going to let worry about money run my life." After quitting Sub Pop and buying the house, he was having a kind of second adolescence: putting on rock shows at a collective performance space run by teenagers, tattooed kids who said they were Communists and wanted a revolution. He made experimental art films where he attached a camera to his bicycle and rode up and down the streets around our house. We talked about the fact that we did not need many things. That we believed in public school if we ever had a kid. He said, "If the money runs out, I will auction off my Sub Pop first editions." He believed in these records like they were famous paintings or something, sure to be sold for huge amounts at auction.

The auditors were asking Rich for $120,000 in ill-gotten gains. This was the Pickens money, which Dana had paid back to Rich, with interest, when Rich started Up Records. I said, it is your money anyway, just get it fixed. But the stress built up around us. We were intermittently trying to get pregnant and as I waited for the baby to appear I would feel angry about this false reassurance we had, driving away from our visit with Dana at Allenwood. I would think: "What a lie that was." I felt conned, burned. If I was feeling particularly shrewish, I would accuse Rich of lulling me into a false sense of security.

I was a high-risk pregnancy at this point. The doctors said, "If you want to do it, you'd better do it soon. All kinds of problems can happen for women over thirty-five."

The lawsuit fostered a claustrophobic, mean feeling in me, a desire to hide, or stay in bed all day. A depression kicked in, stronger than any I had known. Maybe it was related to what my dad meant about the bills breaking his back. I went on anti-anxiety medication.

Rich hired a lawyer to talk to the bankruptcy trustee in a language he understood. I said, "Maybe you should just talk to him, without a lawyer, lawyers cost $400 an hour." But he told me I was naive. So he hired a guy in New York, a guy whose bills came on fancy paper that must've cost a dollar a sheet. Every time the lawyer called, you could hear the money vanishing minute by minute in his voice. I was making around $20 an hour teaching writing students, and as the minutes ticked by I would think: There went a day, there went another day.

Even the dead were asked to pay back ill-gotten gains. On June 14, 2002, court papers were filed in a settlement with the Jay Moloney estate. The estate had been sued for $795,000 plus accrued interest, and they settled for $500,000.

Details of the Cassandra settlements, which gossip columnists later reprinted, were published by www.thesmokinggun.com:

Courteney Cox, $500,000
Tobey Maguire, $325,000
Winona Ryder, $500,000
André Balazs, $82,532
Jesse Dylan, $109,480

The paybacks were a scandal, but not a scandal that really had legs. VH1 aired a show about Dana's victims called *Celebrity Suckers,* but otherwise he was soon forgotten. In Hollywood, there was an amnesia around him. The interval of Dana's dominance was like a bad trip everyone would just like to forget. When I called celebrity assistants, trying to get their celebrities to talk to me about him, there would inevitably be an awkward silence, and then a rush to get me off the phone.

Dana entered a drug rehabilitation program in prison, and as a result time was cut off his sentence. Speeches were made about how drugs can lead you down the wrong path. In these sessions Dana realized exactly what kind of addict he had been: the kind of person who could sail around his life slightly high for days. The kind of person always looking for a stabilizer: something to pick him up or relax him, something to get him to sleep. Always needing some drug in his blood to get him through the day so the night could happen.

In Allenwood, he would see people released and he would congratulate them. Sometimes small parties were thrown for departing inmates. As his release date approached, he started mentally preparing for his second act. Although he knew the Fitzgerald quote "There are no second acts in American lives," the second act kept presenting itself to him, it kept becoming more and more detailed in his imagination.

He was certain his life story could fetch millions and millions of dollars. He and Allegra started to talk about a food line, high-end canned goods to be sold at gourmet food stores. Or maybe he would be a consultant to Hollywood, telling them who might be in possession of the celebrity gene.

On January 28, 2003, Dana was released from Allenwood to a halfway house in the Crescent Heights neighborhood of the South Bronx. According to the rules of his release, Dana had to check in with the halfway house three times a day, and be there at 6 P.M. or a warrant would be put out for his arrest. He was randomly tested for drugs and alcohol, and he had to submit a detailed itinerary of his days out in the city, with phone numbers. The halfway house might call: "Is Dana Giacchetto there?" If he wasn't where he said he was going to be, a warrant would be put out for his arrest.

A halfway house is a place where the residents are not quite prisoners but not quite free, they are somewhere in between. They still have not earned the trust of the authorities, but they are being given a chance to show they are on the straight and narrow. The sooner halfway house residents get a job—a real job on a payroll—the sooner they are released on their own recognizance. *Their own recognizance* is a term meant to denote that inmates recognize what they are, they know what they have done wrong.

Dana called me from the South Bronx. He said, "It is a terrible nightmare and I need to get out of here." His voice was breathless, panicky. He said, "Thank God you answered the phone." He'd tried to call twenty times, but I hadn't picked up because the caller ID said Unavailable. I said, "I am so glad you are out!" I wanted to know the details of the halfway house, but he said, "You don't want to know."

Dana needed to find a job. He called up old friends in the city: He said, "Filing, copying, anything. I need a desk and a phone number and a paycheck. I need a paycheck from a real bank." Many of the people did not take his calls. He was trying to make contact with his old life. But it had been three years and people had moved on, their numbers had changed. Dana was an anomaly; a creature of the nineties, emerging into a new world.

For two weeks he cold-called his old friends, using the halfway house pay phone until the residents started to grumble, "Anything yet, anything yet?" Finally, Dana was hired at *Jane* magazine as an editorial assistant. It was a women's magazine targeted to fifteen- to twenty-three-year-olds. Article topics included: How to look skinny when you feel fat, and Who is the coolest boy in Hollywood?

Dana had met Jane on that long-ago rafting trip, and he was close friends with *Jane*'s entertainment editor, Jauretsi Saizarbitoria. She was a Cuban girl who had worked in André's hotels; exotic, with nails painted three different colors. She used to come to Dana's parties and raise the volume. She had a real job now, and she was worried about Dana. She had the same mothery thing for him I did. She told me, "I knew he needed to get out of there, and I pulled all the strings I could."

Dana was hired to help out around the *Jane* offices in midtown, and also to write an article about his life in the penitentiary. He would ride the elevators up to the magazine and he would try to forget about the halfway house. The contrast was almost untenable: nights in the house where he could hear rats in the wall, and days in the *Jane* offices where the girls passed around cocktail recipes. Sometimes at lunch he would walk out into the noise of the city. Since he had disappeared, cell phones had taken over urban life. There were people whose phones were so small, they seemed to be yelling into thin air.

Technology had left Dana behind and he rushed to catch up. When I talked to him on the phone during his first weeks out, he seemed overwhelmed. He was afraid of these things called computer viruses; he asked me if I knew anything about them. He was afraid to send e-mail because of all these viruses. But it didn't take long for him to become modern once again, the modern person he'd always claimed to be. Soon he was listening to Allegra's iPod on the subway, and he had sent around a notice to friends with an electronic business card. He used his *Jane* computer to conduct Internet searches of his name. Sometimes, his name would come up over two hundred times. He learned how to search for both his name and his image.

He had faith that once everything was resolved the celebrities would come back and he would be allowed back into the fold. The actor Willem Dafoe invited him to a play put on by the Wooster Group. Probation gave him permission to attend. He was taken backstage, like a guest of honor. He called me, ecstatic. He said how lovely it was, how Willem hugged him and welcomed him back to the world.

In the May 2003 issue of *Jane*, Dana's article was published. It was headlined: FROM MY CELEB-FILLED PENTHOUSE TO THE BIG HOUSE. Dana wrote it in what he called a "stream of consciousness" style. In a section subtitled: "How to Jerk-Off in Jail," he wrote:

> Sometimes when I close my eyes, I imagine I'm back in my huge warehouse loft, and instead of being in the company of inmates, I'm surrounded by the incredible artistic spirits who always used to give me so much energy. Flash back to New Year's Eve, 1998. I remember Q-Tip spinning Prince's "1999" while I watched through a drug-induced haze. Hundreds of friends and clients were partying in the orgiastic

glow, and we all reveled in knowing that we were together in the penthouse of SoHo's Singer Building—what felt like the center of the earth. . . .

Incidentally, here's a little jailhouse trick I learned that will allow you to create a hermetically sealed universe in which to facilitate your deepest masturbatory fantasies. Select a stall with a working door, tear one approximately three-foot sheet from your roll of Communist-era-Russia toilet paper (you get one roll per week!), lick or spit on (I prefer the latter because I'm not fond of licking tree dirt) the paper until it's wet enough to stick, apply to the vertical slits at each side of the toilet door. This will simultaneously block out the eerie glow from the lights and prevent other inmates from peeking in and "blowing up your spot."

With this cool maneuver complete, you can now jerk off crazily to your heart's content in relative privacy.

Jane placed the article in the back of the magazine, back by the advertisements for permanent hair removal and permanently white teeth. For the editors, it was not clear how Dana's detailed jailhouse advice would translate to fifteen-year-old girls.

In July 2003, Dana was released from the halfway house, free to live with Allegra in her SoHo apartment. It was a smaller apartment than Dana was accustomed to, but still there were mirrors everywhere. Probation called at odd hours of the day and night, making sure he was there. Sometimes they arrived unannounced for random drug tests. He thought they were targeting him. He wanted to be trusted but trust was nowhere near him.

Dana didn't drink much anymore, and he went to church

every Sunday, thanking God for giving him another chance. Yet he was in some ways the same person he had always been: living in SoHo, wearing designer suits retrieved out of his father's garage. In this way, he had not been rehabilitated from his former self because he still wanted to be the Dana Giacchetto he had been before. He saw his incarceration as an interruption in a narrative he still believed in. He said, "I will rise again. Everyone will know when Dana Giacchetto is back."

In August 2003, Russell was arrested in a grocery store parking lot in Medford. As Russell tells the story, he was in the parking lot meeting a drug dealer, and the guy wanted $200, but Russell only had $150. He knew the security guard at the grocery store, and he knew his drug dealer liked shrimp. He proposed to the dealer: "Let me walk in there and get you $50 worth of shrimp, and we'll call it even."

Russell walked in and lifted five bags of shrimp out of the freezer. He breezed out the door, waving at his friend, the security guard. They exchanged signals like: Let's just allow this to happen.

Russell sat in his car, waiting for the drug dealer to reappear. In the backseat, the shrimp thawed and reeked. Russell was about to nod off when cops knocked on his window. They said, "Son, get out of the car. We suspect you have stolen property in there."

As Russell took inventory of what he had on him that might be illegal, he was relieved. The shrimp, the shrimp were all he had. There were so many other afternoons when they could've found heroin or OxyContin or a bag of pure coke, but today it was shrimp. Russell was busted for stolen property. When he tells the story, he laughs like there is no tomorrow.

He was put on probation and every week he would check in with his officer at the Somerville Police Department, coming through the double doors, the erratic fluorescent light, and the hot waiting room. Russell's probation officer liked him, he thought he might be a good kid someday. When Russell walked into the Somerville PD, he could walk right downstairs, hang out with the cops down there. The guy who worked as the office manager, Frank Frameuni, had known Cosmo way back on Warren Street. He said, "Cosmo was a great fighter, crazy." Whenever he saw Russell, he would offer him a cup of coffee; he would say, "Come in here and sit down."

Frameuni had theories about Dana. He thought Dana had hidden money in other countries. He whispered this theory to me one afternoon when I was visiting the Somerville Police Department with Russell, and Russell had disappeared for a moment. The rooms had yellow tile floors and gray desks, and on each desk files were stacked up, infractions. There was the hum of soda machines, and snow threatened outside. Frameuni spoke slowly and clearly, like he wanted his story taken down for the record. He said, "You know I heard Dana has $20 million overseas. You could retire on that and not have a bad life."

Russell returned, and said, "What is he saying to you?" But there was a smile on his face.

For all intents and purposes Dana was poor, the U.S. Attorney's office was checking his accounts daily, garnishing his wages. But he still paid his respects to the world of the rich from which he had fallen. In October 2003, the Concorde was retired, and that day Dana wore his Concorde cuff links and made a ceremonial day out of it. The passing of something great. The plane that made it possible to be in two places at once.

In Seattle, most of the Internet dreaming was finished. All over town there were houses where the construction had stopped because the money had run out. You could drive by and see the beams around the unfinished living rooms, the holes where the doors were supposed to be, doorways into some life that had not quite transpired. Downtown, a four-star hotel was built for the global traveler but no one came to it. The global population had run out. They were a dream the city had been having, these phantom people. But they had stopped traveling. They had stopped moving so swiftly and effortlessly. They were afraid.

Thomas Reardon with his multiple millions and framed patents and awards for charitable works. Worth his racing technical mind that Bill Gates had zeroed in on and cultivated the way you cultivate a rare iris—well he ended up in the psych ward. He checked himself in when he was sure his suicide was imminent. He had been waking up in his million-dollar bedroom. The bathroom tiles had been shipped in from some village across the world. Each morning he found himself wondering, *Am I going to do it today?* He had been collecting guns and pills. Like all truly suicidal people, his own death had become an event in his mind, a day to end all days. The fateful day that was on its way.

The doctors at the psych ward said, It is a good thing you came in. They gave him medications to bring him down. They told him he should think about what he wanted. For himself.

Yourself, they said. Before everything else. Myself? he said. He didn't really know what they were talking about.

By the time Reardon ended up in the psych ward, we had not heard about our ill-gotten gains for a long time, years or months. I think we were hoping the Cassandra bankruptcy trustees had forgotten about us—our money was so small it had disappeared into the flotsam of the lawyer's office. I diligently paid the bills and constructed a system, but there was this shadow of worry over the system. We should've faced the worry, I suppose, but I did not feel like facing it, it didn't make any sense to me. We could lose $200,000. We might have to sell our house. We waited for this law we did not understand to take control of our economic lives.

Rich started to retreat and live off the money that was left. He said, "I am trying to figure out what to do." I told him, "You should put the money in savings and get a normal job." But he was stubborn, an entrepreneur. I tried to sound authoritative but my heart wasn't in it. I figured it was his business, his money. He had never been to college, as I had; he'd never been given the time to sit around dreaming. Maybe he should be allowed. He had his projects: a sculpture made out of insulation, a band called the Shrugs, a homemade radio that could receive pirate signals.

I knew there were people out there who were feeling ruined. I heard about Fred Schneider, the lead singer from the B-52's. Some of his songs were part of American pop history, but really he had barely enough money to pay the lawyers back. I heard painter George Condo was treading water, trying to hold on to his houses.

It was January 2004, and it had been a long time since we'd heard from the lawyers. I took a pregnancy test and it came out positive. The two lines appeared, I went to the doctor, and the appointments began. "She will be here soon," the ultrasound technician said. "You had better get ready for her. You should get all your ducks in a row."

I was about five months pregnant when I went to visit Allegra at their apartment in SoHo. By this time they had moved into a bigger place with a mirror all across the back wall. The rent was $4,000 a month, paid for by Allegra's family. There was a quote from Mother Teresa on the refrigerator: "If we cannot live for others, life is not worth living." Dana hired Maureen again, although now she only came once a week instead of every day.

Allegra and I sat there in the spotless apartment among the big art books and some new, forgettable songs on an iPod Shuffle hooked up to the stereo. Dana was at work. She told me her theory, the theory that there weren't any victims.

"Who are the victims?" she said.

"What do you mean?"

"I mean the bankruptcy hasn't named anyone who really lost money. There really weren't any victims. The victims were paid and everyone made a ton of money."

This was similar to Dana's logic when one day he said to me: I bought you a house. But I couldn't quite reckon with this. (1) Was it my house or my husband's house? (2) Would someone else have sold Sub Pop if Dana hadn't? (yes); and (3) Didn't Kurt Cobain buy the house? (I think so.) These were my arguments, anyway, although I never made them and am only making them here.

Well, the house was there, and it sheltered me at night, so in Allegra and Dana's logic I wasn't a victim. After that meeting with Allegra, I turned over her statement in my mind for a few days. The people made money, so is it all right if the money disappears? Maybe she was saying: We should all be thankful for the money, the way you are thankful for a nice party. Just because the party is over, and the hangover is worse than you thought, that does not mean you should blame the host.

The day the contractions came was the same day the lawyer called with news of a settlement proposal from the bankruptcy trustees. It was a cold winter day of horizontal rain. "Okay," Rich said, after getting off the phone, a look of fear and exhilaration on his face. "We can settle for $40,000. You could give me the money your grandmother left you. I think we should do it. It will mean an end to all this. We can get a mortgage for $400 a month. We can rent out the downstairs apartment. We'll be fine."

The baby was pushing her way out. Blinding pain every ten minutes or so. I said, "Could we talk about this later? I think it might almost be time."

"Well," Rich confessed, ashamed somehow, suddenly realizing the absurd legal game he was playing. "The lawyers said it is now or never. We accept the deal today or no deal."

"Okay, okay," I said, *"Fuck this,"* I said. "I don't want to worry about this shit!"

He said, "It is a game to the lawyers. They don't care about us. But part of the game is we messenger the money tomorrow."

"Okay, whatever," I said, doubling over in bed.

He disappeared to put the paperwork together—to sell the stocks, to do whatever it is you do when you send $40,000 to someone. I lay in bed, ready to call him if the contractions got any worse.

Maybe my daughter sensed it was not a good day to be born, because the contractions stopped. It had been a false labor, and she waited another day and a half before she arrived.

That first night as the baby slept we banished the financial worry from the room, and ate the steak dinner the hospital made to congratulate mothers and fathers. I was high on Percocet and feeling intensely optimistic.

We filled out the mortgage papers and sent the check. With lawyer bills and Rich's travel we ended up losing about $80,000. In the aftermath of the settlement we were broke but we drained the bank account and searched for jobs that would pay us better. We felt lucky by now that it was only $80,000 we had lost, and we mostly felt lucky that it was over.

Steve Stanulis remained close friends with Dana all through prison and after his release. After retiring from the police force he'd started running a traveling male strip show called Savage Men, "like Chippendales, but a little raunchier," he explained. He was no longer a stripper due to his bad knee. Instead he was backstage, directing, getting the guys in order for their numbers. Dana always told him he should be an actor, and he hired an agent who sent out head shots and called him with occasional auditions. Sometimes he would get bit parts in soap operas. In *As the World Turns,* he was cast as an Italian mobster—one of a gang terrorizing the people of Oakdale.

By 2004, Steve Stanulis was not part of the rich elite anymore; his nights did not have that charmed, never-ending quality. The time of the movie stars seemed long ago and he tried not to brag about it.

I attended one of the Savage Men performances, in a club called Bananas, right off the boardwalk in Atlantic City. It was Mother's Day weekend, and the place was full of wild, intoxicated women. Some of them were drinking out of cups shaped like penises. Shirtless men led me to my seat; they told me about how later I could order a massage, and it could be a very dirty massage, if I wanted. Ten dollars for a crotch massage, one dollar for a hug.

The men came out dressed as soldiers, firemen, a lifeguard, a cop. Their résumés were shouted by the announcer: This guy was in *Playgirl.* This guy is a real fireman, not a fake one. There was a lot of talk about getting lucky tonight, about getting the guy to meet you later, afterward. Women put money into their G-strings and laughed hysterically: *I can't believe we're doing this.*

After the strip show I walked out into Atlantic City. Beneath enormous chandeliers, perched on gold-plated chairs, people gambled away their last paychecks in the bright and hypnotic slot machines. The language of the casino was the same language Dana had used on us: You are the lucky one, you are special, this is the bet that is going to set you free.

Dana's contract ran out at *Jane,* and he needed to find another job. Ron Fischetti agreed to hire him as a paralegal in his midtown office. Part of the deal was: When Dana was back in touch with the celebrities, maybe he would bring Fischetti some celebrity clients.

I visited Dana in his apartment right after he'd landed the job with Fischetti. I asked him what he was making and what the job was about. He said, "I am making $100,000 a year and it could lead anywhere, to all kinds of partnerships, connections; you know I am not just a servant for him or something." Later I talked to Fischetti and he said, "I am paying him $600 a week, and it is a short-term job."

That afternoon Dana was waiting for a call from Courtney Love. After a brief reign as a powerful celebrity, her life was in shambles, and she needed someone to help her sort through it. She had called Dana and said, according to him: *Come on, we would be perfect together. We are both outcasts and we need to come up out of the ashes.*

He roams around the apartment, nervous. He is dressed in designer clothes, and there is a spot of dirt on his shoe that is bothering him. He is getting pristine again, he is trying to get back to where he started, he is trying to get the story going in the direction he believes in, where he is the hero and not the villain.

Once again, he is talking about a celebrity as if the celebrity is not really a person, but some kind of manifestation. Can you believe it, *Courtney Love?* he whispers. It is the same way he used to whisper "John-John." It is not just a story to him. It is some kind of proof: He needs me to know these things. He needs me to know that the famous woman was next to him. He was in her bedroom in TriBeCa. Stars could be heard in their apartments downstairs and upstairs from her. He was there with her and she was crying and he stayed for quite a while.

EPILOGUE

Dana SPENT FIVE YEARS ON PROBATION, CHECKING IN with his officer, submitting to random drug tests and occasional searches of his apartment. Prisoners on probation are not allowed to keep in touch with their officers via cell phone; they must be where they say they are going to be, speaking from a land line. So he was tethered to certain locations in the event that probation called: Fischetti's office, his apartment. He needed to get permission to venture out into the city.

Ron Fischetti employed Dana variously as a gofer and delivery boy, as a reader of contracts and documents. He said to me, "I have never done this with one of my clients before, but Dana really has something. He is really smart." He wanted Dana to bring him celebrity clients. For a while Courtney Love worked with Fischetti, until Fischetti recused himself from her case after she filled up his answering machine with long, rambling messages. She was the only celebrity that Dana reeled in.

All the time Dana was working for Fischetti, he was planning a business with Allegra. It was called The TASTE Group, Inc., and Dana thought it could be the very thing to make him rich and powerful once again. They'd come up with Taste during their long prison visits, as the hours unreeled and they tried to avoid hopeless topics. "When I get out we will start a business together." Dana declared, "I want to work with something real, like food, not something unreal, like money." They settled on the idea of a line of gourmet canned goods—the kind of thing you might find at Dean & Deluca, the upscale grocery store that was across the street from Dana's old apartment in SoHo. Taste would be top-of-the-line stuff. Fresh Maine lobster, Italian tomatoes. Exotic. Real Italian nougat. A trendy designer to create the label. Yes, yes, they agreed, there in the visiting area as the vending machines hummed. Yes, yes, there is a market for this.

Allegra approached her family about investing, and they agreed.

Dana started drawing logos and designs for Taste. He drew them in his prison cubicle; he drew them on the subway to work for *Jane*; he drew them on pads in Fischetti's offices. He wanted the logos to emanate class. He and Allegra scoured supermarket shelves for beautiful cans. I visited their apartment and the cans were all lined up: the classic Goya cans, an exotic can of tomatoes from Italy: on the label, a drawing of a buxom woman who looked as if she had been picking tomatoes all day.

In the end he chose a sleek, simple look, almost like astronaut food.

Dana cold-called canned goods factories, trying to figure out how the business worked. He liked the fact that there was no return on canned goods: that when a grocery store bought them, they had to keep them, even if they didn't sell and grew dusty on the shelves.

Just as he had with Cassandra, he constructed a series of promises. Part of the Taste investor pitch reads:

THE OPPORTUNITY

It has become clear to the entrepreneurs at The Company that the food industry is in a state of tremendous flux, replete with opportunities for start-ups that bring to the market innovative and dynamic new brands. . . . Aging brands are losing the market share of savvy consumers who are more than willing to change brand loyalty when a healthier, chic, better tasting, and higher quality product is introduced into the marketplace. . . . The Company believes there is considerable demand for a new product line. . . . The Taste group intends on becoming the nation's premier hip food company . . .

On the website, there was a picture of the cans on a sleek shelf:

Introducing our Sturdy Metallic Display Unit for
Premium Retailers

Designed Exclusively for Taste
by Serge Becker and Thomas Sandbilcher

ALL NATURAL LUXURY

Distributors of the finest canned foods in the world

Taste Metal Display

68" x 17" x 15"

NOW AVAILABLE

Individual foods are described:

EPILOGUE

Premium Italian Roasted Peppers
Product of Italy
Unbelievably delicious, these roasted red, orange,
and yellow Italian peppers are packed in their own juices
and make every sandwich a gourmet meal.

Premium Wild Chinook Salmon
Premium quality hand-filleted Chinook salmon from
the Pacific Ocean. Never farm-raised, this fine salmon is
the best we've ever tasted. Delicious and loaded with
omega-3s this salmon will forever change your opinion
of the possibilities of salmon from a can.

Premium Whole Maine Lobster
A New England favorite now comes hassle-free to your
table. Premium Maine whole chunk lobster meat is the
ideal choice for lobster rolls, salads, and stews . . .
Requires no refrigeration.

The prices were high: twenty-dollar cans of crab and lobster.
There were glitches: One can I received quoted "calories for
fat" instead of "calories from fat." But Dana worked night and
day to smooth out the enterprise.

THE TASTE GROUP, INC.
Distributors of the finest all natural canned foods
in the world.

Dana and Allegra went to food shows, to boat shows, selling the cans to yacht owners. No refrigeration! You can be out
there on the yacht for a long time, and never worry about running out of provisions.

EPILOGUE

Probation allowed these business trips as long as Dana was everywhere he said he would be at all times, as long as he did not drift. In his former life he had always drifted a little bit; he had always been at least a half hour late. But this was a different world. He flew coach. He stayed in ordinary hotels, with intensely chlorinated pools and corny saxophone music in the lobbies, not the exotic preserves of André Balazs. Sometimes people stared at him on the street, as if they knew him from somewhere.

On a trip to L.A. to attend a convention called the Fancy Food Show, he says, "I thought about calling Ovitz but I decided not to." He went to visit his cockatoo Caesar at Gale's house in Manhattan Beach. He went to the set of a movie Jesse Dylan was directing—an ill-fated comedy about soccer-playing kids and their crazy coach. On the set, the trailers were set up in narrow aisles; production assistants trotted around anxiously, whispering into walkie-talkies. There was a fake soccer field with extras pretending to be parents. Kid actors, who were going to be screaming and hysterical once the cameras started rolling, sulked in the lunch tent.

Dana told me, "Barbara Walters called. I think she wants a big interview." I said, "I heard she had pretty much retired from interviewing, except those top-ten-people shows."

He told me, "Oprah is on the line."

"Really, it's her?"

"Well, maybe one of her producers."

He went in for laser eye surgery, so he wouldn't need his glasses anymore. For so long, his glasses had been part of his look—it was disorienting for those who knew him. For so long he had been staring over the rims, like he is on the jacket of this book. He said, "Now my vision is perfect."

When I started writing this book, I had not looked too far

into his story and I think on some level I still believed in his naïveté and innocence. All I knew of his story, really, was the rush of my belief in him. By the time I finished, this rush had subsided, and he could tell by the kinds of questions I was asking.

The court cases seem like they could go on indefinitely, although often in bankruptcy cases like this a judge will end the proceedings, since all money ends up going to legal fees. As of this writing, Cosmo and Alma are waiting it out, determined to go to trial. Russell is also named in the court papers, for loans totaling up to $13,000.

In August 2005, Dana and Allegra gave birth to a baby boy, Giacomo. Alma and Cosmo were ecstatic, traveling to New York to see him. When I heard the news, I remembered the way Alma had said to me, "I don't think we will ever have any grandchildren."

We were sitting in their dining room. She had been showing me a series of plastic animals she had collected, perfect for kids to play with. She explains that between Dana and Russell and their troubles, and the way she and Cosmo feel tired every morning, like their bones aren't meant for work anymore, much less carrying children around, she is starting to give up on the grandparent thing. The whole thing where you put a stork flag on the lawn. Arthritis has climbed into her face. She says, "I just think grandkids are unlikely." I say, "Russell wants to get married and have kids! He told me last night." She rolls her eyes and looks at me. Her look says, *You don't know the half of it.*

ACKNOWLEDGMENTS

Thank you to the Giacchetto family for all time and all stories. Meeting all of you changed my life.

Giacchetto brothers: If there is a mold, you both broke it, and then went back and rebroke it.

For support and love:

Josephine Astoria, Josephine Spaulding, Rich Jensen, Ivy Meeropol, Julia White, Holly Cundiff, Dug Monahan, AJ Jimenez, Trisha and Roberta, Steve Erickson, Claire Dederer and Bruce Barcott, the Whites. The POETRY boys with their mean and nice jokes. Emily Warn.

I thank Nan Graham, Brant Rumble, and Scribner for their amazing support. Susan Moldow. Kim Witherspoon, my lucid and sane agent. Anna deVries. The army of copy editors.

For people who gave their stories or their expertise, named and unnamed, thanks very much. For the phone tag, the hot conversations in coffee shops, parks, wherever. I would especially like to note these names:

Michael Meeropol, Jed Perl, Nikki Finke, Alex Vasilescu, Brian Booth, Victoria Leacock, Soledad, Craig Kanarick, Russell Shoal, Robert Polito, the Ginders, Jim McSweeney.

ACKNOWLEDGMENTS

Artemis: I have a photograph of you and you need to see it. It's from the wedding.

Reardon: Stay with us, we need you.

Thanks to the lawyers who helped me vet all this.

This would have been *impossible* without Bill Clegg, who loves books even when they are not books yet, when they are feral cats pissing in every corner. Bill, we would've all been taken down by the dogs without you.